Construction
& Computers

*Made possible through
a grant from
The Fremont Area
Foundation*

Construction & Computers

William and Patti Feldman

Publishers of Construction & Computer Newsletter™

McGraw-Hill

New York   San Francisco   Washington, D.C.
Auckland   Bogotá   Caracas   Lisbon   London   Madrid   Mexico City
Milan   Montreal   New Delhi   San Juan   Singapore   Sydney   Tokyo   Toronto

McGraw-Hill

A Division of The **McGraw·Hill** *Companies*

Library of Congress Cataloging-in-Publication Data
Feldman, William and Patti
   Construction & computers / by William Feldman & Patti Feldman.
    p. cm.
   Includes index.
   ISBN 0-07-021494-8 (pbk.)
   1. Building—Superintendence—Data processing. I. Feldman,
William. II. Title.
TH438.F43   1996
690'.025—dc20   96-17142
                                        CIP

McGraw-Hill books are available at special quantity discounts to use as premiums and sales promotions, or for use in corporate training programs. For more information, please write to the Director of Special Sales, McGraw-Hill, 11 West 19th Street, New York, NY 10011. Or contact your local bookstore.

Acquisitions editor: April D. Nolan
Editorial team: Robert E. Ostrander, Executive Editor
          Kellie Hagan, Book Editor
Production team: Katherine G. Brown, Director
          Lisa M. Mellott, Coding
          Donna K. Harlacher, Desktop Operator
          Linda L. King, Proofreader
          Lorie L. White, Proofreader
          Jodi L. Tyler, Indexer
Design team: Jaclyn J. Boone, Designer   AN2
          Katherine Lukaszewicz, Associate Designer   0214948

To our daughter, Rebecca, and our son, Zachary.

Contents

Contents

Introduction

We started using computers for business in the mid-1980s, both to speed up paperwork in William's general construction business and to streamline the word processing in Patti's freelance writing. After a few years, William switched entirely from hard hats to hard drives and went from being a contractor who used computers to a former contractor and full-time journalist who, with Patti, now writes about computers for business use. In preparing the manuscript for this book, we've melded Bill's 20 years of immersion in the construction business with Patti's almost as many years as a writer to bring an understanding of the computer needs of contractors to the written page.

While perusing the shelves of even the larger bookstores, we found plenty of technical books on hardware and operating systems, and lots of titles covering the use of broad-based business and productivity computer programs, but not many titles devoted to informing contractors, specifically, on what's available for them or which of the broad-based programs would be suitable for use by contractors. In *Construction & Computers*, we've tried to fill the gap by focusing on the essentials of what contractors and remodelers need to go electronic. We start with hardware and then move into software, covering the basics of both, and then tackle CAD, specifying software, estimating, project management, accounting, template software, contact management, and marketing. Our aim and our hope is to help those who want to automate their construction business establish a clear path to success.

1

Making your move towards computerization

E QUIPPING your office electronically for success is one of the best forward moves a contractor or remodeler can make. Your computer can be the most versatile tool you buy for your construction business. For processing information in all areas of your work fast and accurately, computers can save time and money and increase productivity for all construction companies, large and small.

You don't have to decide beforehand exactly what you want to do with a computer. Whether you resolve to computerize all aspects of your office at once or whether you're more comfortable with the idea of easing your way into using a computer in one business category at a time as you become more computer-savvy, one thing is clear: the most important decision is to start.

Computers as indispensable tools

For contractors, the introduction of information processing by computer is arguably as significant as the advent of electric tools. For workers in the field, muscle power and mechanical advantage did the job before the twentieth century, but many thriving construction firms now choose to rely totally on power drills and saws when building or renovating structures.

No doubt about it; computers are increasingly viewed within the industry as indispensable, must-have tools. Some contractors furnish their operations with the minimum of a desktop PC, a printer, and a couple of programs to handle a few chores. Others put together a judicious mix of desktops, notebooks, peripheral hardware, and a broad array of software programs, right from the start, ready for tackling almost every aspect of a construction business. They're the ones who are gaining the most from technology and from their investment.

Computers confer the means to get more work done, accurately, in less time. Less than a generation ago, small- and medium-sized contractors used electric typewriters to produce proposals, contracts, and business letters. They also used adding machines and hand-held calculators to eliminate arithmetic mistakes in estimates and billing, verify material costs on vendor statements, calculate payroll, price out the costs of change orders, and reconcile their books. These machines were considered standard office equipment that everyone used as a matter of course. All the functions handled by those devices, however, can be accomplished on a computer more efficiently. And that's just the beginning.

The first desktop personal computers, or PCs (as distinguished from multiuser mainframes), were introduced by IBM in 1981. The moniker

PC is used today in reference to IBM personal computers, IBM-compatibles, Macintoshes, Apples, and other desktop computers. Ten or even five years ago, PCs were still the exception in many contractor offices, but by the beginning of the 1990s things had changed.

It's a different world now. Electronic equipment is pervasive on desktops, drafting tables, and—for today's progressive contractors—in totes and on the job. If you're still traveling through your business day eighties-style, think productivity and hop aboard the shuttle to the future of contracting.

Computer prowess in every nook and cranny of the business

Construction & Computers is designed as a primary resource for information on how to best make your construction or remodeling company more competitive and take advantage of the myriad opportunities that computerization affords to further the goals of your business. Some of the chapters address construction-specific applications, and others describe broad-based software and how to use various packages in the construction business. This book is intended to be a kind of tutorial guide to get you started.

Computer prowess can increase your business visibility, enhance your company presence, and help you win jobs and run them more effectively than in precomputerized days. This is possible by employing a judicious selection of industry-specific, general business, and productivity programs. *Construction & Computers* will provide an overview of what you can do with general and industry-specific packages. Most chapters cover one or two categories of software applications useful in a particular aspect of running a construction business. The programs described in detail in each chapter are usually representative of the strongest entries in each category or field of interest.

Today's computers and programs are easier than ever to learn, largely because of the increasing prevalence of the Windows operating system and the programs that work under it. Most programs discussed in the book are Windows-based, though some are current DOS packages that aren't available in a Windows format.

The first step to real success in implementing computer hardware and software to the fullest in your business is buying the most robust, versatile, multimedia computer you can afford, finding the software best matched to your business style and needs, and using them together on a daily basis. Each new generation of computer hardware is more powerful than the previous, permitting greater functionality for less money. A generation is somewhere between 18 months and two years, and is closer to half a year for notebook computers. Once you pass the initial learning curve with a computer and with most programs, you'll find the combination indispensable to enhanced productivity and a better bottom line, regardless of your company size.

As a home remodeling contractor or remodeler or as a builder, you might not have a multidepartmental organization, but by using hi-tech industry-specific (vertical market) and general business (horizontal market) software, you can act as if you do.

By using computer power, you can run your business with time- and effort-saving accounting, estimating, spreadsheet, scheduling, and job-costing programs. And with the word-processing, desktop publishing, and multimedia communication possibilities afforded by computers, you can also learn a variety of resourceful ways to create and convey the image of a highly successful, prosperous, well-staffed operation. Image might not be everything, but it's often a hefty component.

The appearance afforded by computers of a flourishing business will also help inspire confidence in prospective clients so they feel comfortable when selecting your company over the competition. They can feel they're going with a winner in more ways than one. From how your estimates, proposals, and other presentations look to how your office receives and fields phone calls and faxes, the capabilities of a high-performance multimedia computer can make it one of the most cost-efficient "employees" you ever put on the payroll.

If you're like most contractors, you usually start your workday before 8 A.M. and don't slow down until the day is done, which could be well into the evening. The very nature of the industry dictates that you often have to be out of the office a good part of the day, checking on jobs, meeting with clients or prospective clients, dealing with subcontractors, visiting supply houses, and perhaps collecting money from clients who are afraid to use the mail to send a check. Contractors and remodelers wear many hats and serve many functions.

Making a habit of it

Computers can help you plan and monitor your day, prepare drawings, estimate jobs and write proposals, specify materials, balance your books, plan for material deliveries, produce invoices, document problems on the job, and schedule appointments. They can also allow you to lay out the progression of the job schedule and market your company services.

The aim of this book is to help you use a computer and various kinds of software to increase individual employee and overall company efficiency, help you win more jobs, tighten schedules, minimize cost overruns, and—overall—pump up company profits. Reliance on a well-loaded, smoothly operating computer can minimize risks encountered in just about *every* stage of running a construction business, from *estimating* through job performance, and it can indeed be the bedrock of a successful, thriving construction business. *Construction & Computers* is focused on helping you maximize the potential benefits of this most potent, late-in-the-century business tool.

Hardware and software basics

BEFORE you start computerizing the operation of your construction business, you have to decide on the level of sophistication you want in your system. You need to have a computer, your computer needs to have an operating system to control the computer's operation, and you need a variety of applications. This chapter will help you get started.

Multimedia hardware makes the most sense

If you're furnishing your office for the first time with a computer, or if you're looking to upgrade from older equipment, think multimedia. A multimedia computer is the way to go; it's the new standard in personal computers. Multimedia combines sound, graphics, video, and animation capabilities. Multimedia machines have CD-ROM drives and sound facilities preinstalled to play back the sights and sounds of various programs and provide audio and visual capabilities to your computing.

CD-ROM is an acronym for compact disc, read-only memory. CD-ROMs can store prodigious amounts of text, audio, and video data (up to from 600 to 650 megabytes of information)—the equivalent of what can be held on over 100 floppy disks—all in one easily accessible place. For numerous reasons—space efficiency, versatility, liveliness, and ease of referencing—CD-ROMs are increasingly the medium of choice for many updated and new programs and suites. Without multimedia capabilities, you're liable to be left in the dust by all the new technologies coming down the pike for contractors and remodelers as well as the general public.

The cost of sophisticated systems that contain what used to be considered high-end features has never been lower. Multimedia computers are more fully equipped with high-performance capability than standard-issue business computers that are used primarily for individual applications like word processing or spreadsheets. In addition to being able to play CD-ROMs, multimedia computers designed for the home- and small-office market usually come equipped with fax/modem boards to handle faxing, e-mail, phone calls, and voice mail, all of which allow even a small contractor or remodeler to function and sound like a big business, regardless of the actual size of the staff.

Competition for the home and small business multimedia market is fierce, with retail and discount outlets and mail-order companies bidding for your attention and buying dollar with all sorts of packaged specials. Do your preparatory homework carefully and evaluate what you get more or less of in each deal. The Windows 95 operating system is currently the standard; it's preinstalled on most new multimedia computers.

Minimum hardware requirements

Consider right off the bat bypassing 486 machines. Think of buying a Pentium chip instead. Look for at least a 100-MHz Pentium machine or higher, preferably 150 or 166 MHz, with 16 megabytes (16MB) of random access memory (RAM), at least 1.2 gigabyte (GB) of hard disk space to handle the growing size of graphics and multimedia files as well as applications and Windows 95, and two megabytes of video RAM. These units come configured with amplified stereo speakers (either attached to the monitor or designed for desktop placement), a 16-bit (minimum) sound card, a sophisticated built-in telephone answering system, an internal 28.8-Kbps (kilobits per second) fax/modem board, and at least a quad-speed CD-ROM drive. Quad speed is currently the standard for all new home and small business PCs, but six-speed drives and high-performance eight-speed drives are becoming more and more prevalent, as are multi-CD changers.

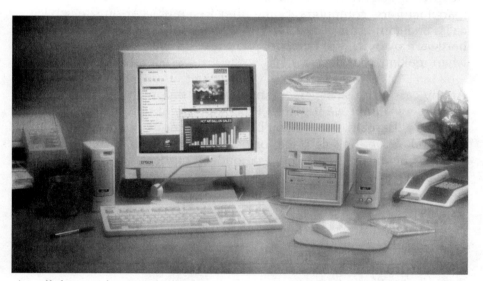

A well-designed tower desktop computer has the floppy drive and the CD drive at lower than eye level, convenient for disk identification. Epson America

With all that sitting on your desk, you'll be ready for just about anything in the near future. With computers, unfortunately, you can't think in terms of a much longer time period. A new generation of computer comes out about every 18 months to two years. There's a fine line between balancing your budget and fulfilling current and anticipated needs. Buy as powerful and as well-equipped a set-up as you can afford to take advantage of increasingly powerful software. When new, more powerful machines come out and replace older computers, within a short period of time buyers pay no more for the more powerful machines that they would have, months before, for the less potent ones. It's a continuous merry-go-round of change; ever more competent hardware leads to more flexible, better endowed software, and vice versa. The consumer is the winner every time.

Read the ads carefully

Generally, one or more components in an advertised special is a low-end component or is on its way to being outdated by a more powerful replacement. (The monitors and the hard drives included in most packaged deals are usually from the low end of the manufacturer's offerings.)

Read the numbers (RAM, MB, CD-ROM speed, monitor size, and resolution) carefully and buy at least the minimum specifications you're looking for. If necessary, err on the safe side and buy *over* rather than *under* because soon enough you'll likely wish you had more anyway.

Keep your eye on the warranties that come with particular manufacturers' computers. Some offer free multiyear on-site service calls, and some companies offer free technical support for the hardware over an 800 number. Add these considerations into the mix when making your decision.

At any case, let a salesperson know you're shopping around. Perhaps the price will improve if you let it be known you're willing to negotiate. Bargain. Maybe you'll save some money on the package, over and above the sale price, or perhaps you can pick up a program or two that wasn't included in that outlet's particular prebundled software.

Prebundled software

Multimedia units come prebundled with various CD-ROM packages of business productivity and family entertainment titles and programs that run the fax and telephone answering features. The ads usually tout that the software is worth up to a thousand dollars or more, but the numbers are based on how much you'd spend if you bought each program separately. Most likely you wouldn't buy even half the titles. But there are so many bundled together that you're paying hardly anything for each individual title. Furthermore, you won't be able to find a multimedia machine sold without software bundled into the package.

Concern yourself with the overall mix of programs so you get a majority that have value to you. (If you work from your home, the computer can serve the dual function of both business and family computer.) If you have no need of the children's or general-interest programs, you can easily delete them from your hard drive to save space.

Sometimes, several of the programs that come bundled are either scaled-down versions of well-known applications or just not very powerful programs. If it's a scaled-down version, you might be offered the opportunity to upgrade to the full version at a special reduced price. If you don't feel you need the more powerful program, then the multimedia bundle was valuable in providing you with what you do need.

Back-up program disks act as a safety net

Some computers that come with preinstalled software don't offer the programs on diskette as well. If you had a computer failure at any time, then you'd run the risk of losing all that software unless you backed up your hard drive at the outset.

Other computers—and this is preferable—come with the preloaded programs also on diskette, which, if you suffered a computer failure, could then be reloaded to the original factory configurations on the hard drive. You would, however, be loading only the original programs and not your data, so it's wise to periodically back up your files anyway.

Evaluating the speed of your hard drive

The speed of a CD-ROM's hard drive (quad, six, or eight speed) refers to the rate of data transfer or the movement of information from one location to another, for example from the disk drive to random access memory. The rate is the amount of data that the computer can read each second, expressed in kilobytes (K). A single-speed drive (already a veritable dinosaur) can read only 150 kilobytes per second. A double-speed drive can read 300K per second. Typically, the quad drives offer transfer rates in the range of 600 kilobytes per second.

The other variable to consider when comparing CD-ROM drives is the access time. The access time, measured in milliseconds, is the time it takes to retrieve the data from the CD disk, typically 100–200 milliseconds. You want a unit with low access time.

Software on CD-ROMs is on its way to becoming the preferred way to deliver programs because of the quantity of information they can hold and disseminate. Not only do users get the program on disk, but they also get the full manual on disk. The CD version of a floppy disk program might also include ancillary reading and graphics on the main and branch topics covered by the software.

Communications devices

A fax/modem is a communications device that either is incorporated into your computer or plugs into one of the ports (sockets) on the back of the case. It takes documents straight from your computer and sends them out over phone lines or, alternatively, receives them for immediate viewing or printing. A stand-alone fax machine limits you to receiving paper documents and sending printed documents you already have in hand.

The inherent advantages of a built-in fax/modem include the very important time-saving concept of not having to print out a document created or stored in your computer first before you fax, saving that extra step. Also, because you're eliminating the scanning process, the faxes at the receiving end are of a higher quality than those coming from stand-alone fax machines. (When you scan a document into a stand-alone fax machine, some of the resolution is inevitably lost in the process.)

What fax software can do

Faxing software provides basic message (fax) communication between or among computers. Theoretically, anything that's text or graphics can be sent out from or received into your computer.

If, for example, you receive a progress schedule and want to send it to a client, architect, and various subcontractors from your computer, you could send the same document, individually addressed, to all selected parties. You can save incoming faxes to a file and print out a clear, sharp copy on plain paper. Then, with the addition of optical character recognition (OCR) software, you can convert the fax image—whether it's an updated contract, change order, revised drawing, or faxed-in catalog cut—to a text file, edit it, combine it with another file, and send it out.

Faxed-in documents are treated as graphic images. If you need to alter the text or use it in some other way, you have to send it through OCR software to change the document to text.

Some of the features to look for in integrated fax software include automatic logging of fax activity and the ability to share one phone line for fax, modem, voice, and answering machine. The fax should operate in the background, with no interruption of ongoing computer use when a fax comes in or goes out. Another built-in bonus for cramped-for-space contractors is that, because it's inside your computer, the whole fax system takes up no additional desk space.

Keep in mind that many of the fax/communications software packages that come with multimedia computers aren't as feature-rich as stand-alone dedicated programs.

WinFax Pro for Windows 95

WinFax Pro for Windows 95 (Delrina, 800-239-2254) is a powerful faxing package that, along with all the basic features, offers usability enhancements like faster transmission (which saves on telephone time), the ability to fax high-quality grayscale images (including photos), and automatic hardcopy transmissions so users can track faxes and have records for billing and other purposes. The program also includes optical character recognition software to convert faxes to text-based documents. It's especially good for contractors on the go, as an auto-forwarding feature lets you automatically forward faxes and e-mail messages to a preselected number.

Upgrading existing computers to multimedia

If you already own a 486 computer that didn't come with multimedia capabilities, you can usually upgrade it by buying a multimedia upgrade kit. This isn't the preferred way to get multimedia power, however; you're better off buying a new multimedia machine, especially considering the purchase is a deductible expense.

Furthermore, there's no guarantee the kit method will work smoothly with your existing machine. If you have an older computer, keep it for less demanding tasks or as a backup. There's very little resale value in an old computer. Anything more than five years old is likely to be a bulky white elephant (actually, taupe-colored) on the market. The time spent installing new components into an older computer and configuring them to work (if at all) can better be served running your company.

Scanners

Optical scanners are another category of electronic equipment that, until recently, seemed far beyond the realm of most small contractors. Like other entries in the small-business market that were formerly reserved to high-tech, high-end solutions, recent models are affordable and user-friendly.

Scanners transfer text or graphics from external hardcopy sources to the computer for direct use in your applications or for faxing to another computer or fax machine. It's the last component you need to turn your computer setup into a full-function faxing system.

Epson Flatbed Scanner ES 1000C. Epson America

Full-page flatbed scanners sit on your desk and work like a copier. The paper doesn't move; the scan head moves across the paper. A sheet-fed scanner generally has a smaller footprint (takes up less desk space) since the source paper feeds through the machine. With a hand-held scanner, you pass the scan head directly over the material or page. If the primary material is wider than the swipe of the scanner, accompanying software stitches together the scans from up to four passes. This process requires a steady and slow hand.

The way prices are dropping for flat-bed scanners (available as desktop models) and sheet-fed scanners (available either as desktop or portable models), contractors shouldn't bother with hand-held scanners but rather should go for the models that do a page (preferably up to 8.5 × 14 inches) in one fell swoop. You can get sheet-fed scanners very inexpensively. Flat-bed scanners are somewhat costlier, but the payback is in potentially very high resolution.

Optical character recognition software

If you're scanning in material for direct faxing and you have a fax/modem in your computer, the image you've scanned can go right out without any intervention. Anything scanned into your computer is initially treated as a graphic, or digital signal that must be manipulated by software. If you're scanning in text material that you want to work on, you have to use OCR software, such as TextBridge OCR for Windows (Xerox Imaging Systems, 800-248-6550) or OmniPage (Caere Corporation, 800-224-0660), that usually comes with the scanner.

The OCR software recognizes the shapes of printed characters—the patterns of light and dark—and translates them into formatted text files that can then be manipulated. The software can convert a graphic representation of text into a word processed file, database, spreadsheet, and other text formats.

Always read over your scanned-in text and run a spell check. Optical character recognition software at this stage of the game is not perfect and mistakes do occasionally slip through.

Software to work with scanned-in images

Graphics—photos or other illustrations—require graphics software in order to become available for manipulation. This is known as image-editing software and includes applications such as Adobe PhotoShop (Adobe Systems Inc., 800-521-1976) and CorelDraw (Corel Corporation, 800-772-6735). These packages allow you to blend several images, adjust the color of an image, lighten and darken the graphics, and perform a host of other editing tricks on your work.

You can also create a library of scanned-in images to use for your presentations. Because graphics files take up large amounts of disk space, you might want to save the image sets to disks and choose from your library when needed.

On many types of jobs, you can use scanned-in graphics for product submissions to an architect or client, and add them to contractor documents so they actually become part of the documents. This assures that the other parties know exactly what you're proposing or submitting. You can scan in spec'd photos and catalog cuts to be used in preparing bid and contract documents, transfer the image of hand-sketched floor plans and elevations, or scan in tile faces or wallpaper samples to facilitate computer-aided design with those materials.

If you're often on the go with a portable or a notebook computer, a light-duty, small-footprint, full-page, sheet-fed scanner will allow you to scan in, on the spot, a document that contains your signature, such as a change order or invoice. The sheet-fed scanner has the added advantage of being able to do double-duty as a light-use copier.

Monitors:
What you see is what you get

Monitors (also called video display terminals) aren't normally part of the package when you buy a computer. It's a separate purchase, so you can usually pick what you want. The life cycle of monitors is longer than that for computers. You might be able to keep a good-quality monitor through a couple of generations of computers, so don't skimp on features that you want when buying.

Bigger is better

Within a small range—from 14 to 17 inches—bigger is better, especially if you're going to be working with graphics or computer-aided drawing (CAD). A 21-inch monitor, still quite pricey and far less common in offices, is ideal for CAD.

Samsung 17-inch Syncmaster 6Ne Monitor. Samsung Electronics America, Inc.

A larger screen offers additional work space (and less scrolling) for spreadsheet, database, and both multitasking (the ability to work on multiple programs simultaneously on one screen) and multiwindow applications; it also provides more impressive and effective viewing if you're doing any kind of on-screen presentation. Working on a larger monitor is also less physically tiring and minimizes the possibility of eyestrain because the type and details can be made quite a bit larger.

All things being equal—resolution, refresh rate, dot pitch—trading a few extra dollars for the extra square inches of viewing space is very worthwhile. The average 17-inch screen offers about a 28% greater viewing area than the average 15-inch monitor.

Make sure to buy a color monitor. Unless you plan to stick totally to basic word processing, spreadsheet, and database applications—and you'd really be limiting yourself if you did—a monochrome monitor is useless. Likewise, grayscale (showing black, white, and gray tones) is monotonous and very limiting. By all means opt for color.

CAD benefits from clarity

What you're looking for in a good monitor is a clear picture. The higher the resolution, the clearer the screen image. A 640 × 480 resolution generates 640 pixels—short for *picture element* (the smallest element of light a screen can display)—across the screen and 480 pixels down the screen, and is standard and fine for most applications. A 1024 × 768 or 1280 × 1024 resolution, however, is that much better for sharp, clean images with CAD applications. Beyond numbers, try to evaluate the monitors in person, side by side, if possible.

Higher refresh rates and noninterlaced monitors

You also want a healthy vertical refresh rate; something along the lines of 75 hertz (75 times per second) is okay. This is the number of times per second the screen is redrawn, or displayed. The higher the refresh rate, the less likely you are to experience a flicker on the screen.

To minimize eyestrain, you also want a sharp, smooth image, rather than a grainy one. The relative sharpness of the image is measured in dot pitch, which is the vertical distance between like-hued color dots. You're looking for a low dot pitch. Don't get a monitor with a higher dot pitch than .28 mm for 14- or 15-inch monitors, or .31 mm for 17- to 21-inch monitors.

Also, make sure you buy a noninterlaced monitor rather than a cheaper interlaced monitor. Interlaced monitors require two passes of an electron beam sweeping across the picture tube surface to form an image. (Most standard TVs work this way.) This process can result in an annoying flicker, particularly if you're sitting close to the screen and looking at a static image. (When watching TV you're usually at a much greater distance from the image, which is most often moving, and so don't notice it.) Noninterlaced, or progressive scan, monitors manage the maneuver in one flickerless sweep.

Don't skimp where it shows

As a rule, the more details your screen needs to show, the clearer the picture should be. A bigger screen lets you have more application windows open that you can see, which is a benefit if you want to switch among applications or if you're taking advantage of multitasking. There's also less scrolling when viewing a full page of text, a spreadsheet, a drawing, or other graphic. The difference between a disappointingly fuzzy screen image and a near flawless image can be just a few hundred dollars, so it pays to shop around.

Most good large-size monitors include six controls for both adjusting the height, width, size, contrast, and brightness of the picture and presetting various resolutions. The most common resolutions are VGA 640 × 480, Super VGA 800 × 600, and Super VGA 1024 × 768. The higher the resolution, the more material is shown on the screen and the smaller the image. Being able to change the monitor resolution is particularly handy if you work on different types of applications, including CAD programs.

Speaker placement

If you buy a monitor that includes attached speakers, then it might be easier in terms of installation and desk configuration to buy a unit from the same manufacturer as the computer. Also, speakers attached to the monitor free up desk space. The downside of buying a monitor with attached speakers is that you're confined to the quality of those speakers, which are usually smaller than normal.

Hewlett Packard Pavilion 7000 series. Hewlett Packard

Integrated phone systems

Many contractors rarely have clients come to their offices. A great deal of business is conducted on the telephone. Phone presence—how a company fields calls—can heavily influence how that company is perceived by the public. A lot more than "Hello" is said when a business phone is answered. In this age of proliferating automated phone services, callers expect to be routed. You, too, can not only offer that but also reap the benefits of an organized, efficient phone system.

Enhanced phone presence

With a voice mail system that works within a multimedia computer, a small company can create the same phone presence as a larger, more plentifully staffed company. A facilitated computer can answer the phone, direct callers to prerecorded information, and store and forward phone messages and faxes. Callers can even leave private messages in specific mailboxes, up to the limit of the particular mailbox system.

Ideally, a multimedia computer should be equipped with a phone system with such features as a 10-number speed dial, last number redial, hold (perhaps with music), mute, flash buttons, call monitoring for screening incoming calls, and several voice mailboxes for individualized message retrieval. The system should also be able to automatically discern between incoming faxes and phone calls and store them appropriately, for later retrieval either in the office or remotely via a touchtone phone or a fax machine. If you have a cellular phone and a laptop with built-in fax capability, you can transfer everything that comes into your office to the job site. That would surely save on legwork.

A computer that contains a speaker phone (by way of a desk microphone) provides hands-free conferencing capabilities and allows you to enter information on the keyboard while talking. You can also switch to conventional conversation by picking up your regular phone handset.

Add-on phone boards

Those who already own a computer without built-in phone/fax/ modem capabilities, but who want a level of functionality equal to that offered by multimedia computers, can purchase an add-in phone board such as Phone Blaster (Creative Technology, 800-998-5227). This after-market product is well-suited for installation into existing 486 or Pentium desktop computers that aren't factory-configured with a fax/modem and accompanying software.

The device comes with two speakers and a microphone that enables the computer to function as a speaker phone and bundled software that offers a full-featured call-management system. The phone system allows you to send and receive phone calls, faxes, and data files and store, forward, and broadcast voice and fax messages. It can hold up to 9,000 passcode-protected mailboxes.

You can also retrieve faxes and messages remotely from outside your office. If you carry a pager, Phone Blaster will find you and forward the message. The card comes with a 16-bit Sound Blaster sound card, interface for a four-speed CD-ROM drive, and music on hold.

Modems

A modem is a device that enables two or more computers to communicate, i.e., transfer and receive information, over telephone lines. Computer data is digital, but current telephone lines are mostly analog, so a modem (modulator/demodulator) must convert digital information (computer data) from the sending computer to analog information (sound) and then back to digital data at the receiving computer.

Interfacing software

Modems require communications software installed in your PC in order to work. The software is the interface between the modem and the computer. In most PCs, the modem is internal. You plug the phone line into the modem through the back of the computer and the other end into a standard phone jack.

Online services and the Internet

In addition to enabling you to send or receive data from architects, subcontractors, supply houses, and others, modems are an inexpensive, convenient conduit to the world of information right from your desk chair. Popular online services like America Online, CompuServe, Prodigy, and Microsoft Network offer gateways to the world-wide network of millions of computer users linked through smaller computer networks and collectively called *the Internet*. Many software vendors, themselves hooked onto an online service, provide free upgrades or fixes over a modem. It's just a matter of calling up through your computer and downloading the files.

You can gain access to the Internet (often referred to in the popular vernacular as "the information superhighway") for browsing or downloading files either through an online service you've signed up with or an independent dial-up service (IDS), which is often available through either an 800 or local number.

Different online services also offer their own selection of downloadable databases; newsgroups; hobby, career, and other special-interest groups; forums; bulletin boards; shopping; advice columns on marketing, finance, hardware and software tips, accounting and tax tips; and other goodies—all available 24 hours a day. Check into the various offerings before you sign on.

E-mail for instant communication

For many users, the most valuable aspect of signing on with an online service or gaining access to the Internet is the ability to use e-mail—electronic mail—to transport messages to and receive messages from other computer users, interoffice or internationally. The recipients need not be sitting in front of their computer when you send a message. When they log on, the message will be waiting in their electronic "mailbox."

You can use your own mailing lists to e-mail the same message to many people, which is very handy if you want to send reminders of job meetings or copies of changes in project work schedules as soon as you know about them.

The faster your modem transfers data, the less time you spend clocking phone charges and connect time. The major online services now support the 28.8-Kbps (28,800 bits per second) modem standard, also called V.34, so look for that when you shop. Independent dial-up services, on the other hand, usually have a flat per-month rate, regardless of modem speed. That's all you pay (unless your connection is by way of an 800 number, in which case you'll also have to pay long-distance phone charges).

You might want to elect to use a particular online service either by its menu mix or by its cost. If your main interest is access to the Internet, either consider an independent dial-up service (with a flat monthly rate) or evaluate how many minutes per month you'll be on. The monthly rate that most commercial services offer might be a bargain if you're using the Internet a lot, but keep in mind that you'll be charged extra for anything beyond the allotted amount of time per month (10 hours, for example), and the charges can be quite steep. Plus you often have to pay long-distance phone charges, unless there's a local access or reduced-rate 800 number. If you're only an occasional browser, see if you can pay as you go.

The World Wide Web

The World Wide Web (WWW) is an access tool that's basically a graphical interface for the Internet. "Hot buttons" link one site to others, branching out like a spider's web, a graphical nonlinear information system called *hypertext*. Hypertext lets you follow associative links among documents in a nonsequential manner, sort of like stream of consciousness—as long as there are available links on the screen to click on. Clicking on the word or phrase that represents the link brings up a new page with associated information. That page itself might have links to other pages, and so forth. Essentially, you can move from document to documents at multiple sites in a nonlinear fashion as your interests dictate. Programs like Netscape are available for helping you explore sites on the Web.

Shareware: Try before you buy

Modems also offer a relatively risk-free way to try certain programs as shareware. Shareware is software, usually less fancy and sometimes less powerful than commercial programs, that developers allow potential buyers to view before paying the price. If, after sampling a program, an individual decides he or she likes it and wants to use it, the developer requests a fee for a licence to use the program and for a manual. The premise works on an honor system. Many specialty, business, and other worthwhile programs created by independent developers are marketed as shareware.

DSVD transmission

Digital simultaneous voice and data (DSVD) transmission is another upcoming online feature. It allows users to transfer voice and data simultaneously over a single modem connection. Like a movie just slightly out of synch with the sound track, the voice transmission ever so slightly lags behind the picture. This technology hasn't yet filtered down to everyday multimedia machines, but it is a feature to keep an eye on.

Keyboards

The traditional manner of communicating with a personal computer is through a keyboard and a mouse. The keyboards and mice that come with most computers are basic entry-level products that are prime candidates for replacement by upgrading.

The standard computer keyboard has historically had 101 keys, adding to the basic layout of a typewriter keyboard a set of standardized computer keys and numeric keyboard on the far right and the function keys F1 through F12 across the top. Most computer users now think of this configuration when hearing the word *keyboard*. A standard typewriter keyboard, in fact, would look undersized and incomplete to most eyes nowadays.

Enhanced 104-key keyboard

With the release of Microsoft Windows 95 late last summer, Microsoft provided the means for using a keyboard with 104 keys. Most computers still come with standard (usually low-end) 101-key keyboards, through which you can access Windows 95 features by using a series of predefined keystrokes. But given the number of applications written for Windows, you might want to start with or upgrade to a 104-key keyboard. The three additional keys are used to perform common Windows tasks in one step, like minimizing and opening windows, finding documents, and performing other system functions.

Microsoft's Natural Keyboard (Microsoft Corporation, 800-727-3351) is one of several 104-key entries. It was designed with ergonomics (the fitting of the workplace to workers and their natural body movements), as well as enhanced productivity, in mind. The raised, curved convolutions might seem awkward at first, but once you get the hang of positioning your wrists and fingers on the keyboard, you'll most likely find the hand positioning less stressful than on a conventional keyboard.

Microsoft's Natural Keyboard. Microsoft

The curvaceous keyboard has a sloped, split keypad with 104 keys, including two Windows-specific keys and an application key. The keyboard has a forward tilt so it slopes gently toward the user. A built-in wrist leveler/palm rest accommodates various body sizes and workstation heights, and the keyboard helps keep users' wrists straight while typing. The concept is something like a tilt steering wheel: users adjust the slope of the keyboard for optimum comfort. The 104-key keyboard comes with its own software that provides several time-saving keyboard options and nine additional hot keys for quicker, easier Windows-based computing. These include shortcuts to the Control Panel or Print Manager.

CompuPhone 2000

CompuPhone 2000 (Integrated Technology USA, 800-393-8889) is a handy package for contractors who run small offices, answer the phone themselves, and would benefit from being able to do two things at once—in this case speaking on the phone and typing notes or other data into the computer. This is a straightforward replacement computer keyboard coupled with a phone headset and software. Wearing the lightweight headset instead of balancing the handset of a phone between your ear and raised shoulder allows you to easily type and hold a phone conversation at the same time.

Directly out of the box, the unit functions as an unadorned (single-line) telephone. (It isn't a telephone answering system.) With the additional software, you can build a telephone directory into your database and log calls by date, length of call, and phone number. The software, designed to work on either Windows or DOS platforms, can also pull numbers from most software equipped for modem dialing, such as contact managers and personal information managers. Instead of dialing through a modem, the "virtual modem" software will dial the call for you. The software isn't limited to built-in fax/modem use.

CompuPhone 2000. Integrated Technology, USA

The integrated unit includes full phone features such as redial, mute, volume adjustments, and—if you have the services from your phone company—call waiting and call forwarding.

You use the numeric keyboard as the phone pad. Extra keys have been unobtrusively added to the keyboard, and a few keys altered in position, in order to accommodate activating the phone and the numeric keyboard to either keyboard or phone functions.

Pointing devices

Pointing devices are the means by which you control the on-screen pointer. Traditionally, it's a mouse of some sort, but it can also be a trackball or a graphics tablet.

Mice

You can choose from a multitude of mice with different configurations and capabilities. Most come with software that increases their functionality and many of them offer, if not all, then at least most of the following features. You can replace double clicks with single clicks and assign a specific task to a two-button click. You can personalize the on-screen pointer by establishing preferential settings for speed and color, as well as the shape of the pointer. You can also readjust the distance required to move the mouse on the pad to cross the screen, and have the pointer disappear from the screen when you start typing, to reappear only when you move your mouse.

Screen wrap is another handy pointer-related feature. When the pointer is moved off the screen along one edge, it will appear on the opposite edge of the screen. Thus you need very little mouse movement to move the pointer from the top to the bottom or from left to right sides of the screen. Another convenience is the snap-to

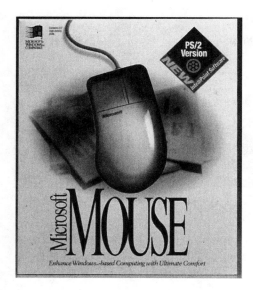

The Microsoft Mouse. Microsoft

feature, which automatically places the pointer on the default button in any screen that calls for a decision on the user's part.

The Microsoft mouse (Microsoft Corporation, 800-727-3351) isn't your garden-variety mouse. Its included IntelliPoint software provides all the functions discussed in this section, plus it's remarkably comfortable to use.

Trackballs

A trackball performs the same functions as a mouse. Basically an upside-down mouse, it moves in the opposite fashion. While the whole mouse is moved to achieve results, with a trackball just the ball rotates in its seat. A trackball is particularly well-suited for finely detailed work because it's easier to maintain adept control with your fingers. Just as with mice, trackballs come in various sizes and the overall bodies come in myriad shapes. And since a trackball moves within its own housing, you don't have to clutter your desk with a mouse pad.

You can position the function buttons on the unit either on the sides or on the top. With some trackballs, however, you have to extend your fingers to click the accompanying keys, which can put stress on the fingers.

Logitech TrackMan Vista

The Logitech TrackMan Vista (Logitech, 800-231-7717 outside California, 800-552-8885 within California) is an example of a well-thought-out trackball design. The two strategically placed mouse buttons on the side of the ball enable users to cup their fingers to operate the ball and the keys, circumventing potential finger stress problems.

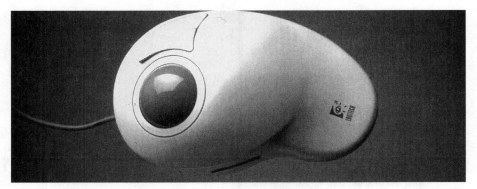

Logitech Trackman Vista. Logitech

The unit also comes with software that enables you to assign functions to the two keys. For instance, you can assign a single click and a double click to each button.

Voice recognition

If you buy the right software and hardware, talking to your computer and getting a response isn't science fiction or a pipe dream but a reality. Contractors who shy away from computers because they hate keyboards and mice—or who suffer from repetitive strain injuries—should take a close look at what's currently available in the rapidly growing arena of speech recognition software. Not just for the niche market anymore, the concept of voice recognition technology has filtered down from specialty markets where it was positioned five years ago to the commercial market, and has hit at least the fringes of the mainstream.

There are two major types of speech recognition software that contractors can use on standard desktops: personal free-form speech dictation systems, which take dictation much as a secretary would, and continuous speech systems, which are less text-intensive and primarily accept verbal commands. These are used primarily for form-filling and entering data in spreadsheets.

Speech dictation

Speech dictation systems allow users to talk into a microphone connected to their computers, and convert spoken words to on-screen text. Continuous speech systems will convert the words on screen and also read back on-screen data aloud, which is an excellent verification method for contractors to cross-check numbers in estimates or spreadsheets.

Dictation systems essentially offer you hands-free computer input. Once they're activated, i.e., the microphone is turned on, they respond to the spoken word and transform spoken words and numbers into text entry, as well as accepting oral navigational commands as a means to that end.

This category of software can certainly be a potent productivity tool for automatically translating speech into text. Contractors and remodelers can dictate contracts, change orders, letters, bills, and other long and short forms with minimal or no hand contact with the keyboard. Because you don't have to look at the screen directly, it's much easier to write data review notes and other paper-based data while composing your thoughts.

After you're accomplished in using a dictation system, you should be able to convert up to 70 correct words or more per minute, if you can think that fast. This type of system typically accepts not only free-form text dictation, but also lets you save time with macros, programmed shortcuts that carry out a sequence of steps with one command. You can set up macros that, when the trigger word is spoken, will automatically transcribe all the text associated with them almost instantly.

It's also possible to use voice commands to tell the computer to perform common computer functions such as saving a document or sending it to the printer. You can handle text formatting, for example, by saying such phrases as "new paragraph, size 14 (or 12 or 10) type, bold, italics, etc." before the actual text dictation for that section.

Voice recognition packages that take dictation are user-specific and must be trained to recognize a particular speaker's voice and inflections, which requires about an hour of repeating sample script words into the microphone. When speaking, you must articulate distinctly, with pauses between each word or punctuation mark. The program will either understand the word or request you to repeat it until understood. With repeated use, the accuracy of the program increases. You can also add words to the dictionary. Reaching peak efficiency, therefore, takes good diction and a lot of practice.

Though dictation-capable voice recognition programs work with one user at a time, they can generally hold the recognition capability of multiple users, so others in your office can use it when you aren't.

You can tailor the software for fast input of repetitive information. By using customized dictation macros, you can recall and enter recorded phrases or boilerplate paragraphs simply by uttering the trigger word or words. This saves time. You could enter clients' addresses, for example, by just saying something along the line of "letter to Thomson," and specify the standard follow-up sales pitch letter with just a couple of key words.

Generally, the software packages are designed with built-in context sensitivity, to handle homonyms—words such as too, two and to, right or write, or our and hour. In addition, the programs are developed to be able to distinguish between possible ambiguities, such as the word *period* and the verbalized punctuation instruction for a period.

Voice dictation software

The PowerSecretary, Power Edition (Articulate Systems (800-443-7077) has a 120,000-word built-in vocabulary, broken into an active dictionary of up to 60,000 words and a back-up dictionary stored in the hard drive. If a spoken word isn't in the active dictionary, the software will search the back-up dictionary for the word. If the word is found, it's automatically installed as part of the active vocabulary, replacing the least frequently used word in the active dictionary. If the word isn't found, you can add it by voice repetition. In this way, you can add terms specific to the construction field.

Other voice recognition software packages that work similarly include Voice for Windows (Kurzweil Applied Intelligence, 800-380-1234), with either a 30,000- or 60,000-word dictionary capacity; and IBM VoiceType Dictation for Windows (800-TALK-2-ME), with a 20,000-word installed general-language vocabulary and the ability to add 2,000 more words. Featuring functions that exploit the Windows environment, the IBM software also lets contractors use voice commands to fill alphabetical and numerical information into data fields on spreadsheets and estimating forms.

Voice recognition software isn't yet 100% infallible, so it's prudent to always proofread your words. You can correct errors by either voice or keyboard.

Continuous speech programs

Continuous speech programs designed for voice command, navigation, and data entry take direction but not dictation. Listen For Windows (Verbex Voice Systems, 800-275-8729) allows users to utter mouse and keyboard commands for Windows or Windows 95 and for more than 45 Windows applications, including Microsoft Office and spreadsheets. You're not expected to remember everything you have to tell the program; a list of context-relevant commands is always available on screen. (If you're an old pro at speaking your intentions to your PC, then you can choose to hide the commands.)

With this type of program, not only can you eliminate tedious keying in of numbers for form-filling, but you also have your hands free to follow the numbers to recite for error-free entry. Unlike speech dictation software, the program is speaker-independent with no voice-recognition training required. In addition to voice access to the 16,000 preprogrammed voice commands that work with the specific program, users can also generate their own speech commands.

Printers

Most likely, you'll furnish your office with either a laser printer or an inkjet printer. Inkjets and laser printers have come down so much in price over the last several years that the choice, for most contractors, lies between these two types. Inkjets are the most popular in terms of units sold, leading lasers, with dot-matrix printers coming in third.

Dot-matrix printers

Dot-matrix printers, which work with fan-folded stacks of continuous paper, are old technology. They produce characters and images on impact, which transfers impressions of tiny dots (in the shape of the pin configurations) from the ribbon onto the paper. Dot-matrix printers almost always print larger dots than lasers and inkjets, resulting in less vivid, less impressive-looking documents. They aren't worth any price differential, unless you want to be able to print multicopy (carbon or carbonless) forms or fan-folded multipart forms.

Daisy-wheel printers

Archaic daisy-wheel printers have pretty much gone the way of manual typewriters (which they resemble in how they pound fully formed plastic or metal letters against a ribbon, which then impart ink in that shape against paper).

Laser printers

Laser printers use a laser beam, a mirror, a drum, and electrically charged toner powder to fuse an image made of tiny, evenly spaced dots on a page, working in a way similar to a photocopier. The higher the resolution—dots per inch, or dpi—the higher quality the printout. A printer resolution of 300 dpi is the bare minimum; 600 dpi is now the standard, with higher resolutions already making inroads.

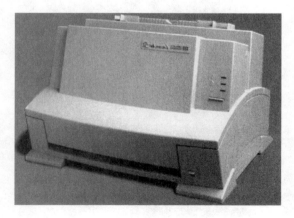

HP 5L Laser Printer.
Hewlett Packard

Inkjet printers

Inkjet printers produce printouts that in many cases are almost (but not quite) as sharp as printouts from most laser printers. They spray tiny drops of ink onto paper to create characters and graphics on the page. Cheaper than laser printers, they're also a little slower in terms of engine speed (the optimal number of pages printed per minute). The speed can vary, in this case according to how complex a document you're printing.

Color printers

The real news in printers is the rise in popularity of affordable color printers, especially inkjets, and the corresponding fall in popularity of black-and-white printers, both inkjet and laser. When users can turn out documents with color photos, vivid clip art, and charts delineated with contrasting colors at little premium in terms of cost, the black-and-white market gets infiltrated fast. Many consumers are opting for color inkjets rather than laser monochrome printers and paying about the same for them.

Prices for color inkjet printers have fallen dramatically recently, making it possible for even small contractors to be able to print in color. If you're thinking of buying an inkjet printer as a replacement for a dot-matrix printer or being able to print out pictures (perhaps taken by a color digital camera), the new Epson Stylus Color II inkjet printer (Epson America, 800-BUY-EPSON), which prints in either black and white or color, would be an excellent choice, especially if you use CAD software or print documents with graphics. You can print most of your daily work in black and white, while producing drawings, job photos, presentations, and sales literature in strikingly realistic color.

Epson Stylus Color II Ink Jet Printer. Epson America

The Epson Stylus II offers two resolution choices: a superfine 720 × 720-dpi mode for printing high-definition, near photographic images on specially coated paper and a 360 × 360-dpi mode for printing on plain paper, transparencies (for overhead projection), or Epson's special 360-dpi paper. (The coated papers reduce the amount of ink absorbed and produce sharper, clearer printing.) We tried every permutation and were very impressed with all the printouts.

This is a very user-friendly printer. The built-in auto sheet feeder holds regular- and legal-size papers, and envelopes. As both the color and the black ink cartridges remain in place, you can switch from color to monochrome printing almost instantly, anytime.

Though the relative low price of single-function color inkjets is, indeed, capturing many buyers who would otherwise opt for a low-end monochrome laser, if you're interested in speed, laser printers are faster. It's a judgment call on which type of printer makes more sense for your current and anticipated needs.

Portable printers

Portable printers are shrinking in size and price, while delivering quality output. Though portable models have been on the market for a few years, they've only recently achieved the weight, print quality, and printing speed that makes them a serious consideration for a total portable solution for contractor needs.

Multifunction machines

Multifunction products are the new kids on the block, an innovative category of devices that perform two or more basic business functions: printing, copying, faxing, or scanning, in various permutations. Most typically, they offer the first three. If you're tight for space or are furnishing an office from the ground up with electronic equipment, this might be a way to go. Most of these multitalented units print in black and white.

The Canon Computer Systems MultiPass 1000 document processing machine (800-4321-HOP) serves as a 360 × 360 inkjet printer, a plain-paper fax machine, a PC fax machine, a scanner (at 200 × 200-dpi resolution), and a convenience copier. A full-feature telephone is integrated with the unit.

The Brother MFC-4500ML 5-in-1 laser multifunction center (Brother, 800-284-4329) features a 300 × 300-dpi laser printer, a convenience copier, and a 400 × 200-dpi scanner. It also functions as a PC-based fax machine.

The HP OfficeJet LX personal printer/fax/copier (Hewlett Packard, 800-752-0900) acts as a monochrome inkjet printer with 600×300 dpi, a plain-paper fax machine, and a convenience copier.

There are also color-capable multifunctions showing up on the market, such as the Lexmark Medley (Lexmark, 800-891-0399), that are no more costly than many of the black-and-white entries. The Medley is a color-capable inkjet printer that prints in color at 300×300 dpi and in monochrome at 600×300 dpi, scans in black and white at 300×300 dpi, functions as a 300×300-dpi copier, and works as a plain-paper fax at up to 203×392-dpi resolution.

While the obvious upside of these multifunction units is that you get the capabilities of several devices in one box, the downside is that if it breaks, you might have none of the functions. Also, they aren't designed as high-volume copying and printing machines and are slower than many single-function units.

Plotters

Plotters are graphical output printers that work automatically, using moving ink pens to translate computer output into drawings and other visual data. Extremely useful for computer-aided drafting (CAD), they draw images on paper.

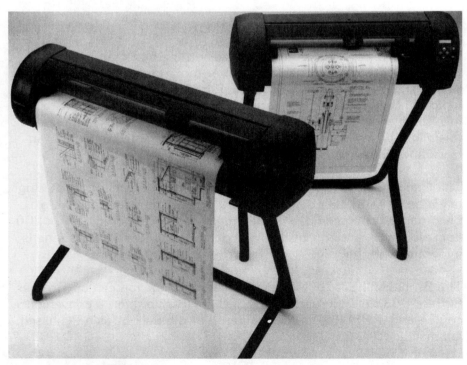

The CalComp DesignMate pen plotter offers large-format multiple-color plotting in a compact unit suitable for desktop, tabletop, or shelf placement. CalComp

There are two types of plotters that small- to mid-sized contractors are likely to encounter: pen plotters and inkjet plotters. The less expensive pen plotters are suitable for smaller contractor interested in producing professional-looking, full-sized CAD drawings. Much slower but more accurate than inkjet plotters, pen plotters generally come with eight-pen placements so contractors can print in either black and white or in up to eight colors. Inkjet plotters are usually much faster (up to five times faster), but are often less accurate. They feature much more memory, however, so they're better equipped to handle complex drawings.

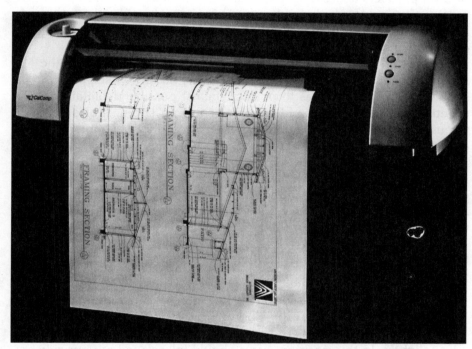

Available in D and E sizes, the CalComp TechJet Designer 720 inkjet plotter produces monochrome images at 720 dpi on cut-sheet or roll-feed media. CalComp

Ergonomics and repetitive strain

As computer use for business and leisure has escalated dramatically in recent years, so too has the volume of complaints by workers using them. Many millions of Americans, including business users, suffer from computer-related injuries, including those caused by repetitive motion. These are called either cumulative trauma disorders (CTDs) or repetitive strain injuries (RSIs), and are similar to the muscular strain you'd get from hammering nails all day or working with your hands above your head for long periods of time. They most commonly affect the hands, wrists, arms, neck, and back.

From keyboards such as Microsoft's Natural Keyboard (discussed previously in the chapter) to wrist rests and foot rests to ergonomically designed mice to adjustable keyboard holders and monitor pedestals, ergonomics has spawned a whole new industry of accessory products competing to save computer users from discomfort and disability. Though few companies will out-and-out claim their design reduces or prevents repetitive strain injuries, some of the designs by intent make it easier and/or potentially more comfortable for you to use computers over an extended period of time.

Several products address specific parts of the body and attempt to redress the problem of being too far away, too close, too low, too high, or too long at the workstation. One such product is an ergonomically correct lap rest that lets users literally bring the keyboard to their knees, with a built-in wrist support that holds the keyboard neatly in place and positions arms, hands, wrists, and shoulders in such a way as to protect against possibly debilitating repetitive motion injuries and neck and shoulder strain. It also keeps the user farther from the monitor and any potential radiation emanating from it.

For the lower body, an ergonomically designed footrest encourages correct placement of feet and legs to eases stress and strain on them as well as on the lower back. If the bottom of the footrest is curved, it will rotate as you rotate your ankle, for added comfort.

Here are some tips to minimize the possibility of CTD when using a keyboard:

> ➤ Position your hands above the keyboard at a minimum of of 90-degree right angle at the elbow. Wrists should be straight (with arms basically parallel to the floor) and fingers curled under slightly. In this position, arms should fall relaxed at your side. Don't hunch your shoulders.

> ➤ The monitor should be between 18 and 30 inches away, at eye level so you don't have to bend your neck while typing.

> ➤ When typing, avoid pounding away; maintain a light touch on keys.

> ➤ To keep typing to a minimum, use macros (programmed shortcuts) whenever possible.

Operating systems

Basic to every PC is an operating system (OS), the primary software that's the foundation controlling the launching and execution of applications, commonly referred to as software or programs. The operating system is the messenger between your computer and all its parts (the disk drive, the keyboard, the memory, the screen) and the applications you use. As the basic user interface, it directs your computer how to operate. Your software must match your operating system. The word *software* pertains to both the operating system and the applications that perform specific tasks, like data management, estimating, word processing, and spreadsheets.

The dominant desktop operating systems in the marketplace for IBM compatible computers have been DOS, Windows, Windows NT, and OS/2, the latter two not common in small businesses. The easier it is to run applications smoothly, the more productive your time. Therefore, your operating system matters.

The intent and promise of each new generation of operating system is two-fold: first to make PCs easier to use—less frustrating and more user-friendly, and second to maximize all the computing power that's inherent but often untapped or underused in your computer. New operating systems should always be backward-compatible with existing hardware and existing applications so users can make a smooth transition.

At the beginning there was DOS. MS-DOS is a single-tasking, single-user operating system. MS stands for Microsoft and DOS stands for disk operating system. It was the underlying software on all personal PCs, over which even Windows (with the exclusion of the self-contained Windows NT) were placed up until August, 1995 when Windows 95 was introduced.

Windows is a multitasking graphical user interface (GUI) environment for DOS-based computers. Introduced in 1985 by Microsoft, it features a pointing device (most usually a mouse) and drop-down menus for easy maneuvering and manipulation. Part of the inherent value of Windows is that it gives you visual controls to run many kinds of applications that share a consistent look, similar to Macintosh machines. In all Windows programs, the basic menus, buttons, and scroll bars are on corresponding "windowpanes" on every application. Once you learn the locations and functions, you can transfer that familiarity to other Windows programs. The learning curve comes into play, essentially, only once.

Windows NT is a high-end 32-bit operating system introduced in 1993 by Microsoft and designed for large computers and computer networks, rather than for small PC systems. It operates independently of DOS. You won't likely come across it in a small-business PC, though you might in a large company.

Windows 95

Windows 95, which also operates independently of DOS, is the current Windows operating system. The successor to Windows 3.1

and Windows for Workgroups 3.11, it will probably come loaded on any new desktop PC you buy. If it doesn't, install it or upgrade to get it. You'll want it. The Windows 95 interface is more intuitive than Windows 3.1 and more graphical. The visual cues are clearer, easier to learn, and more immediately understood.

Built-in multimedia

Windows 95 is designed to fully exploit 386DX, 486, and Pentium computers. Multimedia is built in and Windows 95 incorporates capabilities for smoother video playback. With built-in support for 32-bit applications, Windows 95 is ready to take on a new generation of more powerful and potentially easier and faster applications than those that already exist on the current 16-bit system.

Windows 95 is preloaded in many new computers. Microsoft

Plug-and-play compatibility

Windows 95 also incorporates plug-and-play capability, a new industry standard that—when all the requirements are met—lets the computer do all the compatibility configuration when you add a new hardware device. Plug-and-play capability supports almost 2,000 peripherals, including multimedia sound cards, CD-ROM drives, scanners, device drivers, tape drives, and game joysticks, without requiring any action by the user.

In order for this technology to work, you need, in addition to Windows 95, for the hardware device you're installing and your computer to be plug-and-play-compatible. If they are, a fully enabled, newly added, plug-and-plug device should work pronto.

Information-rich taskbar

The taskbar of Windows 95 is the multifunctional anchor of the user interface. First of all, it's a visual guide telling you what programs are open at any given time and enabling you to switch among any of those programs at any time. The taskbar also includes the Start button, which launches you directly into an icon-rich menu from which you can quickly launch your programs.

If you click on the icon Programs, for example, you get a listing of programs you have in the computer. You can launch any of them from there. If you click on Documents, you'll see a listing of the last 15 documents you opened. Click on the document you want and you'll automatically get it on screen. This ability of Windows 95 was specifically developed so users could easily use more than one application at a time. (It was possible in earlier versions of Windows, but wasn't intuitive.) In practice, switching among applications is almost as straightforward as switching TV stations.

Customized desktop

With Windows 95, you can put your current projects, e-mail software, word processing program, disk drive, and other frequently used items on the *desktop* (the opening screen) as icons. Then you just double click on a particular icon to open that item.

Primary interfaces

There are two core tools for managing your computer resources in Windows 95: Explorer and My Computer. Either can serve as your primary interface for viewing and navigating through information.

Explorer opens with two adjacent panes. The left pane shows all the disks and folders in your system. When you click on one of the items on the left, the right pane displays the contents. If the resource is a program, then the screen will show all the folders contained in it. Double click on that folder to display all its contents. If the clicked item is already a folder, then you'll immediately get the files and subfolders within.

My Computer, on the other hand, initially shows a single window that displays programs, files, folders, and drives. Double click on a particular item on the first window to open a new window, which displays the information contained within. You can then progress down through the layers to get from a particular disk, folder, or file into a particular folder, subfolder, or file.

With Windows 95, for almost every function and operation there are multiple ways of achieving the same results—different keystrokes for different folks. Users will soon enough find their own way of working.

Additional convenience features

Two much heralded (and certainly welcome) additions to Windows 95 include longer filenames and the recycle bin. The ability to use longer filenames means you can create names of up to 255 characters, using upper- and lowercase character, the comma, =, +, {, and } signs, as well as spaces between characters. This added flexibility should make it easier to name and recall files without too much fudging of titles. Your program, however, has to be written as a Windows 95 application to access this feature.

The new recycle bin, which can be set up as a Start-Up icon, will be the recipient of files you want to delete. The bin allows you to give your deletions a second thought. Choosing Undo Undelete will actually restore your files to their original location, or you can remove a file from the recycle bin, drag, and cut/copy/paste it to another location. (You can also permanently delete a file by using Shift–Del.)

Other new Windows 95 features include built-in fax and electronic messaging and access to the Microsoft Network online service. Another feature enables users to transfer files from a desktop PC to a notebook computer and back, in all cases saving the most updated versions of those files. This "briefcase" feature is very helpful if you frequently work with two computers.

Windows 95 also includes Wizards to guide you through initial hardware set-up options and installing new applications. They will also help you create shortcut applications.

Buying software: Vertical and horizontal programs

Your software decisions are as important as your hardware choices. Even with state-of-the-art hardware, the system is ultimately only as good as the software you have to run it. This is where the next set of important decisions come in. What applications do you want to use with the computer? How much are you willing to spend for each type of program? How much detail do you need from the programs? How much time do you want to spend on learning how to use specific applications?

Although, to paraphrase Abraham Lincoln, you can't please all of the people all of the time, there's something for everyone in the world of business software. Broadly speaking, business programs for contractors can either be general (horizontal-market) or industry-specific (vertical-market) software.

Horizontal-market software can be used across diverse businesses. General business accounting, project management, contact management, and most word-processing programs are examples of horizontal software. Vertical-market software is specific to a particular industry. For contractors, the vertical-market choices include CAD, specification software, estimating, contractor-specific accounting programs, and contract-writing and form-filling programs.

Horizontal software developers market to a much broader base and can therefore price their entries more competitively. Generally, the programs are upgraded more frequently and new features are added, both to keep up with and pull ahead of the competition.

Because of the smaller number of potential buyers for vertical-market software, the programs are usually more expensive than horizontal-market programs that perform analogous functions but within a more general format.

Off-the-shelf general business packages don't offer every industry-specific feature you'll find in comparable vertical-market programs. But because the price differential is so great, you have to evaluate the trade-off between the industry-specific features you're losing if you go with the general program vs. the much higher cost of the construction-specific program. Both types of applications have their place in a contractor's or remodeler's software library.

There are also high-end, construction-company-specific programs. These fill a niche market that's composed, primarily, of general contractors and subcontractors who do a large volume of business and who have dedicated personnel (and, ideally, back-up personnel) to use the software. (In many cases, software can end up as shelfware if it's too hard to learn or if there aren't dedicated workers to use it.)

Before you buy, be aware

All software, from operating systems to all applications, comes in versions. The initial version is almost always designated with 1 or 1.0.

Major upgrades are awarded a full jump, from 1.0 to 2.0 or from 2.0 from 3.0. Minor revisions in a program, such as changes, updates, and bug fixes, earn merely a tenth of point, for instance the change from Windows 3.1 to Windows 3.11.

When you're ready to buy any program, call the manufacturer or a couple of reliable computer software outlets to make sure you get the latest version of the product you're seeking. Versions up to a year old are often displayed on the shelves without any indication that newer updates or even completely revised versions have been released.

Productivity software suites

If you have Windows 95 as the operating system for your business computer, a very efficient way to load your PC with a full complement of easily accessible business applications is to purchase a suite of interrelated business programs.

One of the best is Microsoft Office for Windows 95, Professional Edition on CD-ROM (800-733-4411). This program integrates several leading Microsoft business applications, including Word for Windows 95 (a full-featured word processing program) and seven online reference books for a variety of fast look-ups, right from wherever you're working in any Windows program. The package, on just two CD-ROMs, is an excellent choice for small- and medium-sized contractors.

Rich in business applications

The business programs that make up the meat and potatoes of Microsoft Office include Excel for Windows 95, a comprehensive spreadsheet application that contractors can use for estimating; Access for Windows 95, a full-featured database management system for organizing and storing lists of information on inventory, contacts, employees, clients, and so forth, as well as seamlessly sharing information originating in Word and Excel; PowerPoint for Windows 95, a presentation graphics program that creates fully formatted presentations to show your work; and Schedule+, which is at heart a personal information manager. There's also a collection of ready-to-use solutions, Wizards, and templates designed to help small businesses plan new ventures, develop marketing strategies, and manage and track daily operations.

Users can easily work within multiple applications at once to quickly and easily load and review data, as well as create documents that combine text, data, and graphics. All the applications are integrated through OLE (object linking and embedding), which lets users either share updated information between applications or update information only where desired, as well as insert information from one application into another and edit it without affecting any other files.

References at your fingertips

The included Bookshelf puts a diverse seven-title reference library right on your desktop, for use any time you're in any of the programs—or, for that matter, working in any Windows program—via just a couple of clicks of the mouse.

The reference books, immediately accessible from an icon-based toolbar at the top of the screen, are *The American Heritage Dictionary of the English Language*, 3rd edition, with more than 350,000 entries and meanings and the correct spoken pronunciation for 80,000 entries; The Original *Roget's Thesaurus*, updated to include 1990s terminology; *The Columbia Dictionary of Quotations*; *The People's Chronology*, a comprehensive record of world events; *The Concise Columbia Encyclopedia*; *The Hammond World Atlas*; and the *World Almanac and Book of Facts*.

Word for Windows 95 also has integrated grammar and spelling checkers that help you polish documents. The software will spot typing or spelling errors and suggest corrections, and automatically correct repeated errors on the same words. You can customize the grammar settings, as well, to catch such peccadilloes as clause errors, double negatives, jargon, or overly informal usage. A particularly nice feature is a very forgiving 100-level Undo/Redo command so, if you start to revise in one direction and then, on reflection, realize your original intent was better, you can almost instantly get back to it. Word for Windows 95 also offers sophisticated capabilities for charting, graphing, and writing technical documents.

CAD for contractors

CAD (computer-aided drafting or design) programs replace manual paper-based drafting with precise electronic drawing. They offer speed, exactitude, and display possibilities previously unavailable at reasonable cost to contractors working in either their own offices or in clients' homes or offices. CAD software enables contractors and remodelers to create professional-looking, easily editable drawings for anything from room additions to full home designs, decks, landscaping, and commercial buildings. CAD is useful for designing a project, going from design-build preliminary sketches through final plans, creating working drawings for submission to an architect for approval, producing as-built drawings and change orders, and printing out drawings for incorporation into a bid or sales presentation. It's also a means of preparing drawings for filing with your local building department.

When CAD was first introduced, in the 1960s, it was an extremely expensive drafting capability that was implemented, if at all, only by large construction firms. Times have changed. Since the mid-1980s, computer technology in general and CAD technology specifically have filtered down and improved dramatically. While high-end CAD programs still require workstation power to work optimally, most of the CAD programs suitable for small- and mid-sized contracting companies work very well on today's newer desktop PCs. More power, expanded variety, lower pricing, and easier operation puts CAD front and center in the arsenal of viable tools for contractors, large and small.

In the past couple of years, a proliferation of affordable CAD programs have converted legions of new users with no previous CAD experience—or often no previous drafting experience of any kind beyond a quick hand-drawn sketch—to the concept of electronic drawing.

Firms that tackle a wide variety of building and/or remodeling projects might prefer to go with a general CAD system that's flexible enough to handle residential, commercial, and structural design, as well as HVAC, electric, and plumbing. Contractors who perform primarily in a niche market might find an off-the-shelf application-specific program that fits their needs directly—such as a single-focus deck, kitchen, and landscape program.

How it works

In electronic drawing, the screen becomes the paper and the mouse or other pointing device becomes the pencil and eraser. You draw to real size, to the true scale of the project, not to the scale of the paper. If you're drawing a 30-foot wall, for example, you continue the line until the screen measurement indicates 30 feet. This is a valuable assist if you aren't skilled in laying out a drawing on a fixed-size piece of paper. When you send the drawing to the printer, the program reduces the drawing to fit the size of your paper. Some programs will even print the drawing to true scale, such as ¼ inch equals a foot, so the plans can later be used by the crew to take accurate dimensions in the field. If you print to scale, either you'll need a full-size plotter or you'll have to tape your sectional sheets together to form the full-sized sheet.

Symbols are the building blocks

The common repetitive elements used to create structures are known as *symbols*, which you'll use over and over to compose your drawings. In the truest sense, symbols can be either geometric entities or object-oriented symbols.

Traditional two-dimensional (2-D) CAD drawing systems work by manipulating 2-D geometric entities: lines, circles, arcs, boxes, ovals, and points. Object-oriented CAD systems work by manipulating object-oriented symbols (2-D and/or 3-D) of items like walls, doors, cabinets, and furniture. CAD combines object-oriented graphics with distortion-free scaling or resizing in two dimensions to enable users to easily create detailed drawings.

Using symbols libraries

All programs offer architectural symbol libraries. Depending upon the program, the basic packages come with libraries ranging from a couple of hundred symbols to thousands of symbols that include at least a few specialty trade symbols, including HVAC, roofing, and electrical symbols. Many home design and architectural design programs include construction elements like stairways, doors, windows, walls, small and large appliances, electronic equipment, home and office furniture, landscaping, kitchen and bath; and commonly used electrical components like 110-volt and 220-volt outlets, wall and ceiling lights, and switches. Some higher-end programs also offer specialty symbol libraries as add-on packages.

In many design packages, when you're working within a receptacle room, clicking the electrical icon on an options or draw menu will cause the software to automatically place the 110-volt outlets in locations that conform to standard building practice. A fairly sophisticated program might even automatically place a 220-volt outlet for an electric cook top in the kitchen and convert a standard switch to a waterproof switch or GFI if located inside a bathroom.

Risk-free design changes

By using software tools to automate repetitive tasks both in creating designs and in making changes to those designs, CAD programs typically save contractors tremendous amounts of time in the initial drawing process and in revisions. Playing with what-ifs is risk-free. If you or the client don't like what shows on screen or in printout, you can quickly resume the design process with an earlier draft. You can also use alternative drawings to help explain to a client what's involved with other design possibilities and to justify cost. With any level of computer drafting, it's easier to move an object (whether it be a line, a wall, or a symbol) on screen with your cursor than with pencil and eraser.

Layers

Some programs let you draw on individual layers and then pick and choose various permutations for viewing. *Layers* are the CAD equivalent of individual blueprint sheets that show different views, the work of a single trade, or details of the same project.

In computerized drawing, layers can be put to use in two ways. You can use them to organize elements into groupings based on functions, such as demolition, foundation plans, steel work, electrical, and other components of a total project. Alternately, each layer can hold a drawing of a particular floor or section of a building.

You can mark each layer with either a distinctive color or a particular line type, or both. When you show multiple layers on screen at the same time, the different colors or line types help differentiate the various layers. You can also peel back the layers to reveal hidden or obscured details.

Software that allows you to show various views and take apart layers to show clients every aspect of the work go a long way to nipping in the bud clients' concerns that they don't know what the finished job will look like. Furthermore, you can view any area of a drawing by using a zoom command to get a closer look or to print out a detail.

Though you can view multiple layers simultaneously, you work on one layer (the active layer) at a time. The fact that the layers can be overlaid in any combination, according to personal preference, is a real aid in organizing the plans to show field personnel how to put the project together. These options can also be helpful when putting together a final presentation to clients that shows the overall scope of the job and how all the elements fit together.

Rotating to 3-D views

In addition to 2-D drawing capabilities, some packages can automatically convert the floor plan to an elevation along designated cut lines, create 3-D views that can be rotated, and even allow walk-throughs. You draw in two dimensions, but the programs can calculate the 3-D views almost instantly when you click on that feature.

Renderings

Several programs offer a variety of rendering capabilities, right down to adjusting the intensity and the settings of both indoor lighting and sunlight. As a side benefit, the resulting drawings are particularly valuable as selling tools (visual assists) in marketing value-added, upgrading aspects of a job or in selling new homes before they're built.

Generating material lists

Some CAD programs generate material lists, which will help you prepare your estimate. If you use one with that facility, you'll even be able to give clients a better-than-ballpark figure for any project early in the discussion stage, and modify the broad scope of the project to suit.

Starting with architect-provided CAD drawings

When you're bidding large-scope work for an architect, engineer, or any level of government agency, very often the job drawings are available on disk. This is an increasingly prevalent trend. If you're given or can get the project drawings in CAD format, you can load them into your computer and pull them up on screen both for estimating purposes and for establishing your own working drawings.

When all parties involved in the work have to provide working drawings and have CAD capabilities, the general contractor typically starts the process. The GC draws his or her work on the first layer or layers and then makes the disk available to subcontractors so each, in turn, can add work on separate layers. Because all the information is on disk, it's much easier to pass around the drawings, whether by modem or on disk by mail or messenger.

Unlike paper-based drawings, which usually consist of multiple sheets that need to be shuffled to get the big picture, all interested parties—in their respective offices—can look at all the computerized drawings on screen at once or in any logical combination. The general contractor and each subcontractor can see how all the work lays out, checking to make sure there are no conflicts.

For work in both the private and public sectors, final, approved drawings are then used as working drawings on the job site. With minor modifications, the drawings can also, in many cases, become as-built drawings when the work is completed.

If you can't get job plans on disk, you can use a scanner or digitizer to input the existing hardcopy plans in preparation of readying your own electronically generated working drawings.

CAD as a sales, marketing, and information tool

If you use a CAD program from the outset as a sales tool to develop the overall renovation concept with your client, you could maintain better control over the project and perhaps never even have to bid the project competitively. The working relationship starts when the project is in the talking stage. You can even offer the design work at no charge as an inducement to go into contract with a price cap, as part of a packaged deal. With the cap, the client feels protected and you're designing a job that you know your company will, most likely, build.

Off-the-shelf, entry-level, user-friendly CAD packages have found a niche with home-owners, so it isn't unusual for a client to bring a self-produced CAD sketch to the initial meeting with the contractor. You might even have to start your design process based on it. This works especially well with independent-minded clients with strong opinions on what they want in a renovation or addition. In no way do they want the look of the project dictated by an architect or designer. They might also not want to spend the money for design services. If clients know what they want, you, as the contractor, can facilitate it. If an architect is eventually consulted, the fees charged the client should reflect the work already done and be appreciably less than they would have been if the architect had started from scratch. Depending upon the local laws in the state and jurisdiction where you work, the filing requirements and the need for an engineering or architectural stamp vary. In some locations, your drawings might suffice. In other locations, clients might need an architect only for the stamp or possibly for filing purposes.

While any designing done by someone who isn't a registered architect or engineer should ultimately be checked by one, clients can save on hourly drawing time or on fees for preliminary discussion.

Change orders

A CAD program is also a good way to handle change orders once the job has started. It's usually a quick process to edit a drawing to reflect called-for changes or a range of possible changes. You can print out choices for client perusal, if appropriate. With a laptop and a portable printer, you might even depart from a face-to-face visit with a client with a signed change order and new drawings.

For jobs that consist of renovations of kitchens, family rooms, media rooms, home offices, and decks, clients might well be pleased to have to deal with only one company, rather than a contractor and an architect or designer. Furthermore, because the plan is developed in-house and you know what each phase (labor and materials) will cost, the project can more easily be held to budget first time out. Presenting a design-build sketch to a client can pretty much be a matter of "what you see is what you get."

Low-end CAD packages allow for almost instant room design, window and door placement, and furniture and appliance layout. They can give your client a conceptual understanding of what a project will look like without you having to show blueprints that might be beyond the client's technical capability to understand.

From a client/contractor perspective, using high-tech drawing skills is one more sign of your professionalism. When negotiating a contract with a potential client who is going to be paying your company thousands of dollars, it makes sense to assure that client of your professionalism, staying power, commitment to both your business and the project, reliability, and quality of work. All this adds to the success of getting the signature on the bottom line and the deposit into your bank account.

Programs

For home or office renovations or other relatively small projects, contractors who are inexperienced with drafting and/or CAD might do well to use low-end programs that provide 2-D and 3-D capabilities but not a depth of drawing features. This type of software isn't usually difficult to get started with and would be suitable as a marketing tool to illustrate a client's requirements in a visual format the client can readily understand. And if a drawing is worth many minutes of talk, then a walk-through is worth even more.

FloorPlan Plus 3D for Windows

As CAD programs go, FloorPlan Plus 3D for Windows (IMSI, 800-522-3279) is a handy stepping stone into CAD. It's an inexpensive computer design and estimating program that can work alone or interface with adjunct programs to form an integrated computer solution for the small contractor and remodeler. The design package allows contractors and drafters to draw floor plans fast and easily, and features walk-throughs.

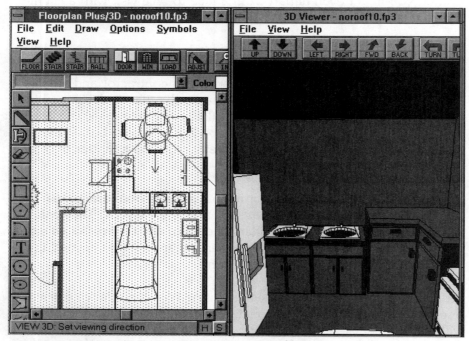

Split screen shows the floor plan and a camera view from FloorPlan Plus 3D.

Having evolved over the years from a DOS to Windows 3-D program, FloorPlan Plus 3D is lively-looking and offers intuitive operation. It has an icon-based interface, with the convenience of a toolbar that runs along the top and side of the drawing area.

2-D drawing and editing

You can draw and edit in the two-dimensional mode, then click on the 3-D button to automatically transform the 2-D plan into a 3-D illustration. Decisions such as inclusion or removal of interior walls, placement of new windows, and use of open or closed risers on stairways are easier to make when viewing the plan in 3-D because the direct effects can better be seen.

3-D stroll

You can create drawings, add furniture and other items from the object library, and then stroll through in three dimensions. (This type of preview is very convenient if, for instance, you're working on a renovation for a client and want to make sure the new room—with a new wall configuration—holds all intended furniture neatly.) The program supports drawing anything from a portion of a room to more complex multiroom, multilevel structures. Contractors can select which items to show or hide when doing a 3-D view.

Views from various vantage points

It's simple enough to cover all bases by altering view heights or vantage points for on-screen client viewing or printout, and even take into account user-positioned light sources. The 3-D drawings appear by default as wire frames, but another click will bring in selected styles of shading. You can view or print plans in any combination, up to 13 layers.

Special tools for stairs and roofs

A stair-drawing tool creates precisely straight stairs once you load in the attributes: width, total rise, total run, number of steps, and distance off the floor. (You can also opt for railings on either or both sides.) Spiral staircases require a bit more information; you need to define the pole height, pole diameter, stair height and diameter, minimum step angle, riser height, and starting and ending angles. But you'll reap accurate calculated values for step angle, number of steps, and headroom almost instantly.

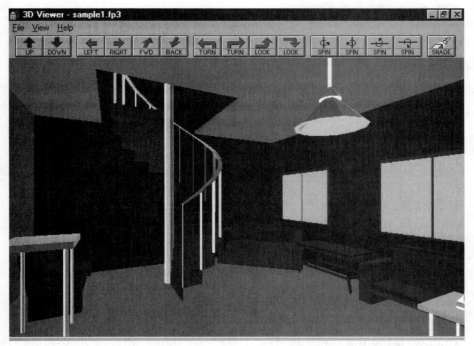

Three-dimensional view from FloorPlan Plus 3D shows possible custom design spiral staircase.

Though you can design your own style of roof, the built-in Roof Library offers several predrawn styles that you can either adopt as is or adapt to suit. The easy-to-manipulate Roof Editor facilitates easy addition of chimneys, dormers, and skylights.

Lots of symbols support skillful drawing

Other utilitarian features include an Undo command that allows you to reverse commands up to 20 levels back; the capability of supporting electrical wiring and plumbing in any or all building levels; up to 20 user-definable wall types, with automatic labeling of wall dimensions; the ability to rotate objects and add any sized text at any angle; and a library with over 300 objects, including furniture and appliances to simplify construction of drawings.

You can also create your own symbols and add them to the library. Layers are automatically supported so objects are instantly placed in the appropriate layer as you draw them. A zoom command allows you to magnify or reduce the drawings at different levels.

FloorPlan Plus 3D for Windows can also export plans to Windows .WMF files, and .DXF files for importing into 3D Design Plus, AutoCAD, and other CAD programs.

Chief Architect

Chief Architect (Advanced Relational Technology, 800-482-4433) is a sophisticated Windows CAD program for use by the home builder, remodeler, or architect. The package is object-oriented. You build by placing, sizing, and manipulating symbols. The symbol library is designed specifically for the residential home market and includes walls, doors, windows, roofs, furniture, and other items that go into designing a house. The symbols are editable to a degree, with dimensions and colors customizable through dialog boxes.

You select most of the drawing items and viewing controls from the icon toolbar. The toolbar is split by a toolbar information window that states which tool is active and lists the options for that tool on the bar.

Drawing information is stored in real-world scale. It's only when you're ready to print your document that you have to select a printing scale so it fits on your chosen paper.

You do basic drafting of floor plans from the Build menu in a Plan window, using the symbols. The 3-D menu shows interior elevations, exterior elevations, exterior prospective, and cross sections.

Multiple views for a complete perspective

You can have up to ten views on screen at a time, though the more windows you have open the smaller each is, so four is a reasonable compromise for a 14-inch to 17-inch monitor. The nine window types are plan; wall elevation; cross section; plan camera (an interior 3-D perspective view of a room); full camera (a 3-D perspective of the interior or exterior of multistory model); plan overview (an entire floor); full overview (an entire multistory model); materials (for a single floor); and layout (the arrangement of the other windows for printing).

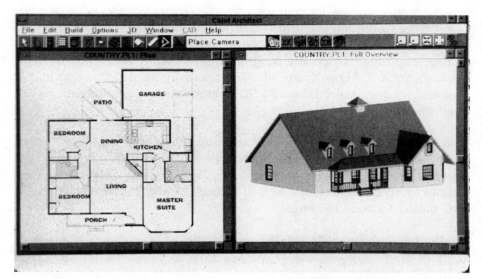

Split screen of Chief Architect showing floorplan and full overview.
Advanced Relational Technology, Inc.

Changes reflected instantly in all views

Chief Architect features associative editing, which means that editing changes performed in one of the view windows are reflected immediately in the others, if they show the same item. This is excellent for handling on-the-spot what-ifs, as well as other client- or contractor-generated stream-of-consciousness modifications. (Inexpedient programs that take a long time to redraw can be frustrating to work with and might cause clients to lose interest in the ongoing process. Chief Architect is remarkably speedy.)

The program can tackle various types of window designs, reflecting diverse glazing styles, the application of muntin bars, and other detailing accouterments.

If the characteristics of the items (objects) you want to place into the plan aren't built into Chief Architect, you have to produce them yourself using conventional CAD drawing tools (lines, arcs, circles, boxes, cross boxes, ovals, and points), which are available in the program's CAD facilities. (The program does not provide for building groups of associated items into assemblies.) Once created and placed into the plan views or elevations, they, too, are editable. The symbols aren't visible in 3-D views. For example, there are only two styles of cabinet faces that come in the symbol library: plain and framed. If you want to include more intricate details of the actual cabinet design you're planning to install, you can draw it in plan and elevation, but it won't convert into any of the 3-D views.

Automatic snap-together feature aids connections

For a sophisticated CAD package, the learning curve is remarkably short because you're drawing with building materials and because you don't have to rely on the grid system to put it all together; the program automatically snaps together items placed in close proximity that belong together. As the program doesn't work with a grid system (as most other CAD software does), you draw your walls by size in feet and inches. Walls default to 90 degrees and snap automatically at their ends.

You can, however, bypass default and build walls at 7.5-degree increments. The software automatically trims new walls so they connect properly, with one exception. A straight wall doesn't move or extend to accommodate the end of a curved wall. Rather, the curved wall moves to meet the straight wall.

Walk-throughs aren't totally automatic

Walk-throughs are a two-step process. First you take photos and save them to a file. Then you play back the images, in sequence, which gives the appearance of walking through the building. This process isn't as facile or spontaneous as a walk-through that's directed by cursor movement, as is available in many other CAD programs.

You can print out elevations and cross sections, but not camera views and overviews, in a variety of scales. If necessary, depending on the size of the drawing and the printer, the program will print the drawing so you can tape 8.5-x–11-inch sheets together to form a drawing drawn to scale. You can also use a plotter to print on a single sheet of paper.

Generating a material list

By going to the options/materials list you can get a list of materials used in the design. The program can't distinguish all types of materials, however. For example, walls are all built with wood studs and sheetrock. If you build some walls with block and others with wood studs and sheetrock, the program can't distinguish between the two forms of construction. Given the different building techniques around the country, the material list will vary in its usefulness. The list can be exported to estimating programs that import tab-delimited files. But the value of importing a list that might not be fully usable is questionable. You can export plans, elevations, and layout sheets as 2-D .DXF files to other CAD systems.

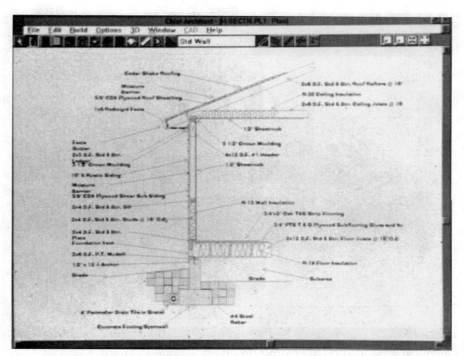

A typical cross-section from Chief Architect. Advanced Relational Technology, Inc.

Overall, Chief Architect offers an extremely strong combination of drawing, editing, and presentation facilities and screen redrawing (regeneration) speed. If you're looking for one program to serve both as a top-flight drawing program for working drawings and as a presentation tool, this is a hard entry to beat.

Home Architect 3D, CD-ROM edition

Home Architect 3D, CD-ROM edition (Broderbund Software, Inc., 800-521-6263) is a very competent yet inexpensive Windows CAD program. Though primarily targeted to the homeowner, it's an easy-to-use program that contractors can use to turn out accurate floor plans for anything from an addition to an entire home. The software comes with 150 professionally designed plans to help you get started, or you can start with a blank screen.

Object-oriented symbols and intuitive guidance

As with Chief Architect, rather than having to draw start-from-scratch lines and arcs, the program uses preformed shapes and object-oriented drawing principles. Instead of using a tool that draws a line, which you then have to designate as a wall, you use a wall symbol. Geared to novices, the program offers intuitive guidance every step of the way, even going so far as to prevent you from placing objects where logic dictates they shouldn't go. You're also alerted to obvious design problems; you can't place a sink within a door or window

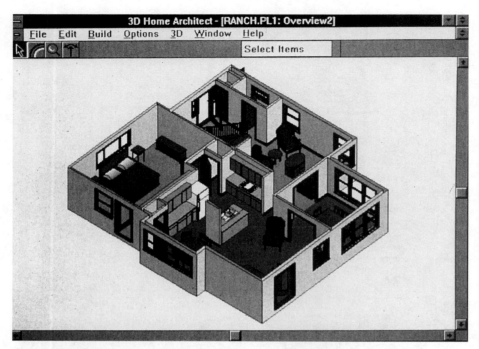

Overview produced by 3D Home Architect. Broderbund Software, Inc.

opening, for example. The program also has automatic dimensioning, calculation of area, and alignment of walls and objects.

There are hundreds of predrawn symbols for furniture, fixtures, electrical openings, and appliances in the symbol library to flesh out and detail every room. The objects are scalable and easily resized and rotated. You can even color customize the symbols to match the floor plan for clearer viewing. You can work with multiple windows, viewing up to four perspectives (2-D or 3-D) simultaneously. Working with a plan view adjacent to a 3-D elevation view allows you to see the effects of any editing immediately. When you edit in the 2-D plan view, the software reflects that change instantly in the 3-D view, and vice versa.

You can export an automatically prepared material list to any of several popular spreadsheet programs. The plans themselves can be exported in DXF file format to various CAD programs.

Design Search: Predesigned plans on CD-ROM

Buying predesigned plans for either spec building or custom building is an option that has been around seemingly forever. It was only a matter of time before someone went the electronic distance and put plans on a CD-ROM. Design Search (The Design Search, 800-447-0027) pulls together representative designs from about 20 architects and designers around the country, incorporating 2,000 designs in two dozen different house styles, from traditional, cape, colonial, salt box, and ranch to Tudor, Georgian, prairie, Spanish/Mediterranean, and vacation.

Seek and ye shall find

The selection mechanism works along the lines of a differential search, and the program includes selection boxes for over 50 criteria that you can use to determine the features or styles you want. By checking off what you want, you eliminate designs that don't fit. Within seconds, you essentially winnow down the choices to include only those designs that apparently conform to the requirements you've called for.

There are four major routes for conducting your search: house style, rooms required, foundation, and designer. Alternatively, using Quick Search Parameters, you can narrow the search by square feet (up to 6,300 square feet), width and depth, number of bedrooms, etc. This is convenient if you have a client who's open-minded in terms of style but has a limited budget and/or lot site. You can even search by position of the rooms in the house. This could be particularly handy if the land site dictates sunlight in the morning and moonlight at night or other specific room orientations.

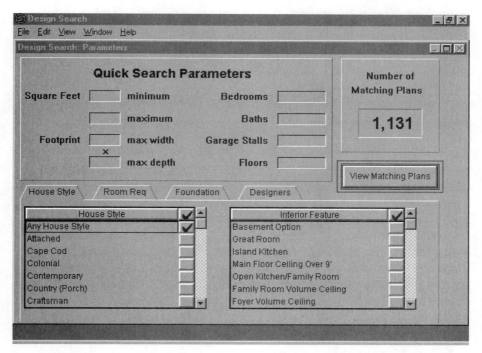

Logically laid out screen makes it easy to select the search parameters in DesignSearch.

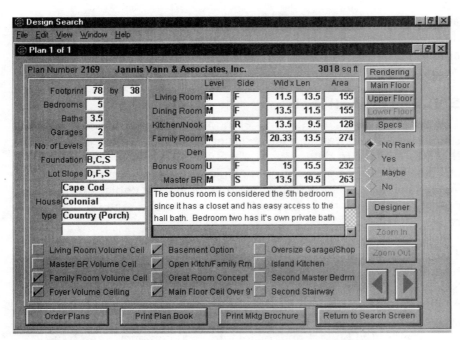

DesignSearch screen lays out specifications of a selected house.

The program doesn't offer a full set of plans on the spot. What you get is a rendering of the front view of the house, as well as floor plans of each floor. This is what you'll have in hand, after the selection process, to show clients. The plans and renderings print out at one full page for each floor. If you want to go further, i.e., build the actual house, you have to order the plans from the company separately, at additional cost.

Rendering of a 3,018-square-foot house, as depicted on DesignSearch.

Customizing floor plan printouts for each client

You can print out floor plans for each floor separately. If you want to use the plan as part of a marketing campaign, you could print out the rendering or floor plan, customizing the marketing sheet with your company name, address, a caption, and bullets indicating specific features. The developers have also made it easy for contractors to use the program to sell custom or spec homes by placing a rendering of the house into a preformatted template. All you do is add your company name and the price if you want it shown, and type in selected features and a real estate broker, if you're using one.

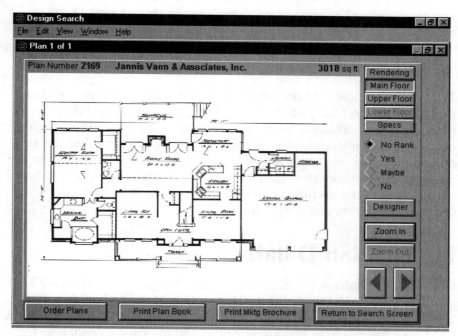

Representative first-floor plan from home included in DesignSearch library.

No doubt about it; you can find a house style fast that fits most requirements. This would most likely be fine for low- or medium-priced homes, but not for luxury houses, where customizing is usually a large factor, because the home renderings (and subsequently the plans) come as is.

The black-and-white printouts, along with a few color printouts, could also serve as a potent sales and marketing tool for dealing with a real estate broker, with respect to a piece of property you own on which you'd like to build a home.

You can print out various home renderings and print them up as marketing brochures, with the broker's contact information on it, and encourage the broker to use them to sell the piece of land with various building options (by your company) on it.

The program includes profiles of each of the 20 diverse firms' principals. Some are registered architects who attended architectural school and passed their exams; others are designers who have spent many years working for other firms before starting out on their own.

Ordering traditional sets by computer or phone

You can order the plans by fax and a credit card. The cost of a five-set package varies, depending on the design, between $325 and $475. Additional sets are available for a fee, as are line renderings, bills of materials, 3-D walk-throughs, color renderings, videos, and other sales and marketing aids. Some of the companies represented in this grouping also sell reverse plans, which are mirror images of the original layouts. With any of these options, it would be wise to confer with a local architect first to assure the plans conform to local building codes and to get them stamped.

The plans could be customized by the designing architects, but that probably wouldn't be cost effective. It might be better to bring the plans to a local architect for minor alterations such as, for example, moving a wall, changing the location of a sink, or increasing the size of a window. All the plans are of houses that have been built. The company plans three updates per year. The updates include additional plans by the same architects and designers, as well as plans by different architects and designers.

Home Plan Database

Home Plan Database (Professional Builder Magazine, 800-323-7379) is a CD-ROM package similar to Design Search that offers access to 2,500 designs, also from about 20 architects and designers. There's a floor plan (primarily in black and white) and an artist's rendering for each design, the majority of which are also in black and white.

Search parameters include home size, home style, number of bedrooms, number of bathrooms, location of master suite, type of home, land use (type of lot), width of home, and ceiling height. To purchase the actual home plans (five sets of blueprints per design) runs $400 for homes under 2,000 square feet and 20¢ a square foot for homes over 2,000 square feet.

DOS-based
SoftPlan Architectural Design

SoftPlan Architectural Design (SoftPlan Systems, Inc., 800-248-0164) is a three-module residential and light construction DOS-based CAD program. As industry-specific CAD programs go, SoftPlan is quite flexible, allowing you to configure the system levels and drawing levels based to your working style and needs. This includes setting up walls, material dimensions, header span tables and joist span tables, among others.

Like Windows-based Chief Architect, covered earlier in this chapter, SoftPlan is object-oriented: you draw walls, not just lines representing walls. This is advantageous to the CAD operator because it makes it easier to put together an entire room, home, or other building design.

A second notable attribute is the method of storage and retrieval. Each project is a chapter in a book. Within each chapter are your drawings for the project. Each book holds a particular category, i.e., two-story homes, split-levels, and large homes.

Fluid movement among modules

There are three modules: SoftPlan, for drawing in two dimensions; SoftView, which converts the 2-D floor plan to a 3-D elevation; and SoftList, for estimating costs.

The program relies on a hierarchical structure of function keys to get around from module to module and from screen to screen. These function keys are listed across the bottom of the screen, with explanations written below them. The functions are set up in three levels: Base menu, Draw menu, and Service menu. By selecting a key in the Base menu you automatically pull up the Draw menu keys, and you select a key in the Draw menu to enter the Service menu.

Selecting a basic function key provides a subset of options pertaining to the basic selected function. The screens are easy to follow, though there isn't the uniformity of commands that exists with Windows programs. After working your way down into the menu structure, you have to work your way out of the multitude of layers in order to enter another area or to exit the program. This regression can be tedious.

Keyboard commands, not icons

Because SoftPlan is DOS-based, it heavily relies on keyboard commands rather than icons. However, the program does make heavy use of shortcut key combinations. For example, the header table automatically selects the depth of a header depending on material used, while the joist table confirms the correct joist span length. You have to type in the correct figures, based on your local building code, to make them work for you.

Vertical-market CAD knows house dimensions and then some

Working with an industry-specific rather than a horizontal-market CAD program has its perks over a general CAD program. With SoftPlan, for example, you can set up material dimensions for various structural elements. You don't have to draw every dimension. Similarly, when converting a floor plan to a cross section, the thickness is automatically shown on the plan. Items for material thickness include nailer width, sill plate width, footing depth, brick offset, wallboard thickness, thickness of joist depth, and spacing.

Drawing a roof is often a complex procedure in horizontal-market CAD programs. SoftPlan lets you set roofing dimension parameters, covering 18 variables, including ceiling joist depth, pitch, overhang, facia, and framing style. This makes it a lot easier to produce a roof both on screen and on paper.

You can also set up how you want dimensions placed on your plans, establishing the starting and ending points from wall edge, surface, exterior stud, or interior stud. In addition, when using one of the wall types, the program automatically draws the appropriate pattern and wall thickness for that wall type.

In order to help you draw accurate representations of predefined standard sizes and styles of windows and doors, the program lets you set up product code libraries for various opening types (such as windows, doors, skylights, and bifolds). Product codes are libraries that you use to get predefined standard sizes and styles.

You can set up 10 libraries for each product, such as windows, doors, electrical, and kitchen, e.g., you can prepare up to 10 window product libraries representing 10 different manufacturers. Each product code library can, in turn, contain up to 500 items. Sixteen product codes appear on screen at a time; you page up or down to hone in on what you need.

Generous selection of detail-rich symbols

When you choose a symbol from the symbol library that's well defined by area, e.g., a kitchen, bathroom, or fireplace, a small picture of the symbol appears prior to installation into the drawing. These drawings are more detailed than those found in many less expensive CAD programs. The symbol library is extensive. Under fireplace, there are 56 options. The kitchen includes 95 options.

The setup procedures for the product codes or for any of the other reference sources is a time-consuming process and requires a good deal of organization, so it's best to have the information readily at hand.

When actively drawing in SoftPlan, you can select the product from the product code to insert into a wall opening. This automatic transfer of data not only saves a lot of drafting time, but also assures accuracy and consistency.

Group moving saves time

Moving segments within the drawings—for instance a whole wall—is efficient if you group items together. For example, cabinets and appliances can be grouped to a wall so, if you move the wall, all items connected move with it. The program has various methods of erasing your work, including Undo (last command only) and type erasure, which is a quick way to delete all the same items in your working drawing.

SoftView

SoftView is the 3-D module that's designed to take floor plans and convert them to cross sections, elevations, and 3-D drawings. It can also help prepare roof plans. You can generate 3-D presentation drawings from the exterior or interior of a building and from any angle or position. The 3-D model is viewable four ways: wire frame, visible line, shaded, and shaded and visible line. The module has the capacity for 12 cross sections drawings, four compass views, and a roof plan. The program follows simple steps to generate an elevation. Unlike simple 3-D walk-throughs, SoftPlan cuts the drawing along prescribed cut lines that you indicate.

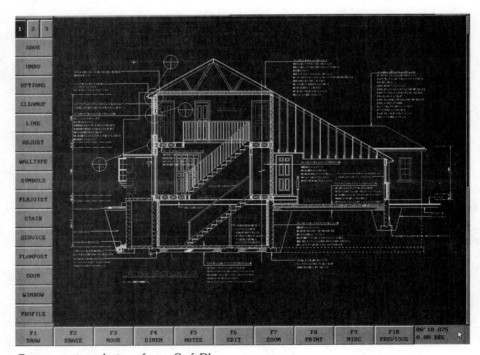

Cross-sectional view from SoftPlan. SoftPlan Systems, Inc.

Kitchen elevation from SoftPlan. SoftPlan Systems, Inc.

SoftList

SoftList is the adjunct estimating module that calculates material lists based on the detail provided in your drawings and the items you select for automatic inclusion in an estimate. This module increases the overall value and utility of this CAD program because you can automatically create a list of materials, price the material, and add the labor and markup. This is of value, however, only if and when you estimate projects off your own plans, as opposed to plans prepared by others.

The program, seamlessly linked with SoftPlan, works in the background as you design your structure by developing a linked database of items you want to include in the estimate. It automatically takes all items you designate for bid inclusion before you draw, thereby giving you, at the start, control of what you bid.

As an estimating program, SoftList is similar to a spreadsheet. It uses formulas to add calculated quantities, and the formulas can be for individual items or for assemblies. For example, you can create a formula that includes all items connected to a specific wall type.

The program includes up to 10 configurations for material calculations. The configurations you need could change depending on the type of work involved. With different configurations, you can specify appropriate methods of calculating materials and costs for new residential, renovated residential, light commercial, or other project categories. This differentiation can contribute to more precise estimating.

Flexible reporting opportunities

You also get very flexible reporting capabilities, with the ability to create 10 configurations of reports for a customized-looking estimate. Customizing the reports allows you to view the data from different perspectives.

The reporting capacity allows you to alter hours, overhead, and profit so, for your evaluation, you see the overhead and profit as line items but, for your client's printout, those factors are automatically added to each general category of the presentation. This is a method long favored by contractors and we're always pleased to see it as part of a program's modus operandus.

Keep in mind that, with SoftList, you don't get a preselected material and labor list of items to pick from to add to an estimate, nor do you work with a blank screen and add bid items, and you can't take previous projects and use the estimate as a template for other work.

No overlooked items allowed

Here's a neat built-in fail-safe alert: in the manner of a lit dashboard light indicating your seat belt isn't fastened, the word *zero* appears on the lower right edge of the screen if any bid item doesn't have a value assigned. As with spreadsheets, you can search for items and change column headings and widths. It's possible to change any value in a field and the calculation will automatically be recalculated. You can also add occasional items that weren't taken off of the plans to the estimate. This way you can include miscellaneous items that aren't drawn.

Though the program comes with a limited cost database, you must essentially develop your own databases and develop your own cost values. You set up a database configuration that includes the items you want calculated, the grade of materials, and how to calculate the values. (The coding doesn't follow any uniform construction standard.) You can configure the material list for any individual project or you can set the variables globally. You can set three costs for each item, which is handy for grades of material or for different wage rates.

The program comes with material formulas for calculating the costs. If you need to change formulas or create your own, however, be prepared for a learning session. Changing formulas is a very complicated process.

SoftPlan comes with a two-volume 33-lesson plan book. Working through the lessons, we found the material easy to grasp. The manuals for all three packages follow a consistent form and are well documented and illustrated.

Multimedia kitchen design with 3D Kitchen

Interestingly, the lower-end multimedia packages often provide sound and animation, while the mid-range and higher-end programs don't. This is often because multimedia packages are targeted at least in part to the homeowner and include articles, demonstrations, and animations that explain principles probably already known by contractors.

If you opt for a lower-end program as either a primary or secondary source of CAD, some of the animations might be nifty adjuncts to your own client-directed presentations. The two programs described in this and the following sections might serve you well on their own or might work for you as adjuncts to heavier-duty programs.

3D Kitchen (Books that Work, 800-242-4546) is a basic, innovative, kitchen walk-through program that could serve a small- to middle-sized remodeler well, not only as a kitchen design program but as an information and presentation tool for putting together layouts and showing clients what a personally designed kitchen would look like.

Three-dimensional view of a kitchen layout from 3D Kitchen, with working screen tools across the top and side. Books That Work

Full screen shot of a three-dimensional kitchen view from 3D Kitchen.
Books That Work

Renovating or remodeling a kitchen, like remodeling a bathroom, usually results in more personal or emotional involvement by the homeowner than other often more straightforward areas of the home. The term "dream kitchen" isn't bandied about lightly. 3D Kitchen affords contractors ample opportunity to address the emotional needs and personal tastes of clients.

This program was actually designed for use by homeowners, but contractors can easily use it as an easy-to-maneuver design and rendering tool, showing the evolving design both in plan view and as a 3-D walk-through.

Backgrounds set the stage

In quite a creative new wrinkle, the kitchen has been elevated out of the house so, when shown in 3-D view, it's suspended in air in front of either a black screen or in front of various outdoor settings. The kitchen hangs in space and you can select either a real-life background that approximates your client's home setting or a dream kitchen background. Choices include the Rockies at sunrise, a desert, or a tree-filled landscape. So you can either pick a setting that reflects the landscaping of the house or, in the manner that luxury cars are often displayed in a posh location, you can use a more exotic setting to add subliminal excitement to the kitchen design.

As you manipulate the 3-D view, you can zoom all the way in or out for a continuum of 3-D perspectives, from a bird's eye view of the entire room to details on individual cabinets. The bird's eye view is similar to looking at a TV show from behind the camera; you see the entire perspective of the set as an observer looking in. For a client interested in previewing a potential kitchen before it's built, the whole show could be very engaging. As you wander through the kitchen, you'd even hear your own footsteps.

Template layouts give you a head start

You might start your design process with one of five predesigned layouts or any of five different-sized empty rooms. The predesigned layouts include a narrow galley kitchen, as well as U-shaped, L-shaped, and center walk-through layouts. There's also a layout with a free-standing island. You can start with an empty room dimensioned to the actual site.

Object-oriented drawing with alterable symbols

Rather than working with lines, arcs, and other geometric shapes, you drag symbols, shown in elevated views, with your mouse in place on the floor plan. On the floor plan, they change into plan-view line drawings. You can alter each symbol to suit; for example, you could place a base cabinet or stove symbol on the plan and then increase or decrease its width to conform with the real-life model.

Drop-down lists for picking particulars

Every time you place an item on the plan, the Object Scope Sheet pops up. This is a very handy feature. Through this drop-down list you set the styles, finishes, colors, and materials for individual kitchen items. You can also set features globally for all categories. You can instantly change any element finish and color, and give your client the opportunity to see the finished plan. Floor selections are divided into tile, vinyl, and wood; under wood, for example, you can select from nine wood stains shown on strip, parquet, or random planking.

The program also has a color scheme coordinator. You or the client can pick from a range of color finishes based on professional color schemes. Use the Color Scheme Chooser to automatically change the colors based on the color groups in a color wheel. You can also change any item—wall color, wallpaper, doors, cabinetry—individually.

A built-in shopping list keeps track of all items placed on the floor plan. It tracks quantities, prices (low, medium, high, or yours), and subtotals. You can also manipulate a dimmer to control the kitchen lighting, emulating either various times of the day or various lighting choices.

Customizing touches fix up final designs

There are over 500 fixtures, cabinets, appliances, and other details to create and flesh out the layout. You can rearrange walls, windows, and doors, change cabinet tops and cabinet styles, add backsplashes and tiling, and change wall, floor, cabinet, and tile colors quickly.

You can do all of this either during the initial design process or as you walk through in the 3-D editing mode while your client sits next to you, hopefully suitably impressed by the whole process. Clients can make choices from all the options that are likely to fit in their budget; the program tracks the cost. You can alter any of the elements in size, location, or color before you start serious modification or redesigning from scratch.

The multimedia disk holds a lot of design tips and details

Because the program comes on CD-ROM, there's plenty of space left for an easy-to-browse design book that presents detailed information and advice, suggestions on room layout, general kitchen design principles, decorating advice, and previews of selected models of both appliance and plumbing fixtures.

If you, as a contractor, are new to kitchen renovations, the voluminous, easily accessible information on material, styles, and details of kitchen components can serve as a crash course in what goes into putting together a modern kitchen, whatever the proposed design style.

You can peruse the disk and do your homework before meeting with prospective clients. Then not only will you sound informed, but you'll be able to show the clients around what could be their new kitchen. Together you could design the space, without having to consult a professional kitchen designer. The easily navigated on-screen Multimedia Design Guide (the book part of the program) poses interview questions, the answers to which will help you prioritize options and the selection of materials, styles, and details.

For a small- or medium-sized job that doesn't require architectural plans, this could be a really nice selling tool. You can pick it up for about $50 at street prices, so it won't take much of a bite out of your budget and just might flip a few more jobs into your court.

Windows-based deck design with 3D Deck

3D Deck (Books That Work, 800-242-4546) is another package similarly targeted to the do-it-yourself market that can work very nicely for a contractor looking for a single-focus package to design a client's deck, fast. In fact, with a notebook computer tucked under your arm, you can just about design the project on your first visit to clients, showing them what they say they want.

Software streamlines the design process

Even if you've been building decks for years and know all the tricks of the trade, this is a handy piece of software. Using the Windows-based program for "bread and butter" decks can streamline design, speed up estimating, and give a quick and neat way to show clients viable alternatives. In short, the software can help you mass-produce decks. If you haven't built decks before, the instructional aspects of the program will serve as an excellent electronic mentor.

All the designing is performed via pull-down menus, on-screen buttons, and mouse clicks. The manual, which is just 13 pages long, only hints at the features available within and is almost superfluous after you've installed the program.

3D Deck integrates two components: an electronic design workshop with CAD capabilities in three views, and a comprehensive electronic book on building decks with hints and diagrams on time- and effort-saving techniques. You can also print out the text, but not the diagrams, of any screen for later reference.

On-screen desk-chair reading

The Before You Build section offers numerous graphics (including 40 full-color animated sequences) and tips for dealing with concerns your client might not have thought of but will be glad you took into consideration, such as wind and noise, desirable views, privacy considerations, traffic flow, furniture placement, and shifting shadows throughout the day and seasons. The animations use only one house and one fixed-location tree so you'll have to extrapolate for each client's actual site conditions.

Quick design, but just a few choices

Though more sophisticated CAD software allows designers to start with a blank drawing area, in this program you must begin with one of four predrawn models: free standing, attached to one wall, bound by two walls (an inside corner), and L-shaped (around an outside corner). Working from any of those styles, you can alter dimensions, notch the corners, and add 45-degree angles of any size.

The database includes seven wood species (in multiple grades); five deck, four joist, and four beam sizes; one post size (4 × 4); four common styles of railings; and 23 hardware items. You can't add to or change the items, but can edit the prices.

You can print a master shopping list (showing unit price and total price); a cut list showing components, description, and usage, but not prices; separate beam cut and joist cut lists; and a basic contract and budget sheet. As the program was written for the homeowner, no provision for labor, overhead, and profit is built in. You can easily add these costs at the end of the materials printout, however.

Material quantities are calculated either by unit price or by linear foot. The Workshop combines short boards of like species and grade so you can order the minimum number of longer boards of each description.

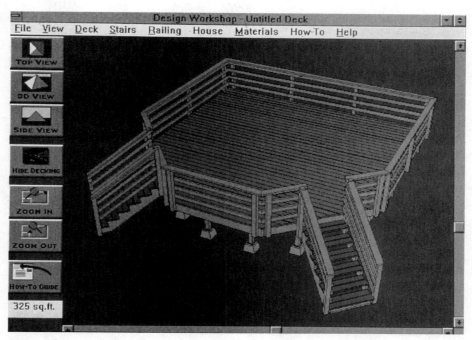

Free-standing deck design from 3D Deck. Books That Work

Three (fixed) available views

The program shows decks in three views: plan, elevation, and 3-D. (Unlike more sophisticated CAD programs, you can't rotate the deck in any of the views.) If you create a deck larger than the screen size, the program won't automatically redraw and resize the deck to fit the screen, but you can use the zoom feature to reduce the deck so it fits on the screen.

The program prints scaled plans showing the location of all joists, beams, footings, and rail posts. You can select between pier blocks or poured footings and can input the depth of the required footing. While it calculates various footing depths for material pricing, it doesn't convert in the elevation views to them.

The design principles are based on nationally recognized standard codes and practices. (Individual state and local building codes might vary.) The software doesn't automatically calculate beam and joist sizes for the deck you're designing, but rather adjusts the number of posts and spacing based on the wood species and sizing of lumber. You can easily see the substructure when viewing the deck without the decking. By altering your selection of materials, however, the program alters the spacing, modifying it to comply with code. The software can build decks up to 10 feet above grade, based on a live load limit of 40 or 60 psi.

Stair building, with open or closed risers, is straightforward. After you slot in the height of the deck off the ground, the stair editor provides a cutting plan and calculates the rise and run, which is revisable. (You can easily modify the stair location and width to suit taste and site conditions.) Then you can print out a diagram that reports the number of steps, tread depth, and riser height and shows the stringer layout.

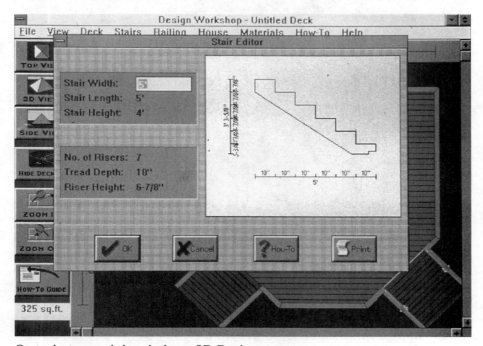

Stair design and details from 3D Deck. Books That Work

Design, then show and tell

Overall, this could be a great marketing and design tool for residential contractors during deck-building season. In addition to being able to design on screen, contractors can use selected animated demos and how-tos to help show clients how the deck goes together, and use the "mapping the environment" features to increase the overall project size to include some landscaping, electrical work, perhaps a new door or window, walkways, and other amenities clients might not otherwise visualize when they think of adding a deck.

LandDesignerPro for Windows: Way before a rake and a hoe

How does your garden grow? The 1990s answer to that "nursery" question can be made by a computer. LandDesignerPro for Windows (Green Thumb Sierra On-line, 800-336-3127) is a CAD program with an extensive set of features that contractors might find very useful for developing landscaping plans (and accompanying plant and material lists) for properties up to 170 acres.

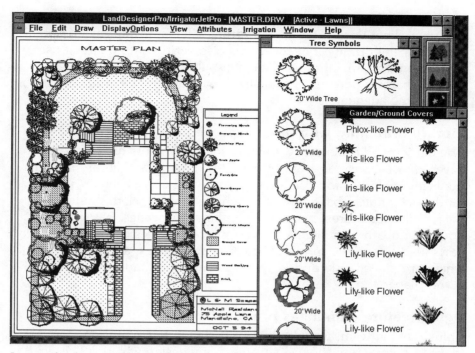

Layered screen options offered by LandDesigner Pro for Windows facilitate electronic garden design. Green Thumb Sierra On-line

You can draw your design on up to 24 predetermined drawing layers. The layers could include site analysis, foundation, sprinkler layout, walks, etc., which can be overlaid in various combinations or separated for optimal clarity and reference.

There are two ways to enter the base map: with the drawing tools, which are set up as icons on the top of the screen, or through Plot Plan Tool, which is advantageous if you're working off a preexisting blueprint or another design. With this time-saving capability, you don't have to draw the plan. Just type in the coordinates and then use lines, curves, and arcs to add to the newly created base map.

In this program, you draw with geometric elements. Draw menu options include lines, rectangles, rounded-corner rectangles, polygons, arcs, curves, ellipses, and circles. You can also add text to the currently active layer.

Lots of landscaping elements

The program includes 450 predrawn symbols for landscaping elements. The tree and shrub libraries contain symbols for several different styles and sizes of trees and shrubs, all automatically scaled into the drawing. They can be easily adjusted for size.

You can use the Sprinkler menu options to validate the design of the sprinkler system, which you must manually lay out. You must specify the appropriate initialization information, but before the heads and pipes are in the ground you can find out if the design will do what you and your client want it to. The program will test the sprinkler system design for uniformity of heads. It will also verify that no circuit uses more than 75 percent of available flow, that no single head uses greater than 60 percent of available flow, and that all desired areas are covered adequately.

Library brimming with hardscape choices

The garden and ground-cover library includes plants typically used to cover an area, such as grass or vines. The hardscape library includes nonliving materials for walkways, fences, and walls, such as gravel, sand, rock, mulch, bark, and wood chips. It also includes individual objects like sculptures, benches, fountains, barbecues, basketball hoops, birdbaths, and lights for fleshing out the designs. The sprinkler parts library features sprinkler heads, pipes, valves, and fittings, all of which are placed only on the sprinkler layer, no matter what your current layer.

Aging feature eliminates prognostication

Thinking long-term, there's also a nifty landscape-maturing feature that lets contractors show clients what any design will look like next year, in three years, five years, or anytime up to 30 years hence simply by pressing a key. This preview could be a great selling point for clients who can't visualize how their garden will age. It also helps ensure that newly planted trees and shrubs don't eventually grow too close to the house or cast too much shade. If they do, just modify the sizes or alter the locations of the plantings a bit and try the aging again.

Varied views of the garden, just like real life

You can show your design in both plan and elevation views. In the elevation view, you can automatically generate elevation or side views, generate walls of buildings, draw in details to the buildings for windows, doors, and roofs, and show the design from various angles and locations.

From the PC to the nursery

The software comes with an integrated, modifiable database of about 80 plants, classified by over 20 different characteristics, such as color, bloom season, height at maturity, and fire resistance, so you and your client can conduct plant searches along the lines of, for instance, "yellow flowers that can flourish in partial shade and alkaline soil" and come up with a list of best choices for the design. An optional, fully compatible, add-on plant library for your particular USDA hardiness zone lists up to 800 plants, also classified by those 20 characteristics.

The program also automatically calculates the amount of material needed to build and plant each design. If the design runs over budget, in some cases it might be easy enough to decrease plant sizes and increase spacing to fit the client's budget. Whenever changes are made to the plan, the program updates all associated estimation information.

Electronic xeriscaping

Here's an ecological and budgetary plus: if you search for sun, soil, and water requirements, you can apply the principles of xeriscaping and design a landscape that minimizes water use, which you can point out to clients as providing long-term savings. In LandDesignerPro, everything you add is permanently stored by wholesale, retail, and labor costs, so you're constantly adding to your database, in essence building reusable supplier files.

In addition to material lists, purchases lists, and client plant lists, there are a number of standard reports, or you can create templates for your own customized reports.

Automatic sprinkler layout

A second program, called IrrigationJetPro, which automates the sprinkler system layout by calculating and placing heads, circuits, sizing, and routing automatically, is also available.

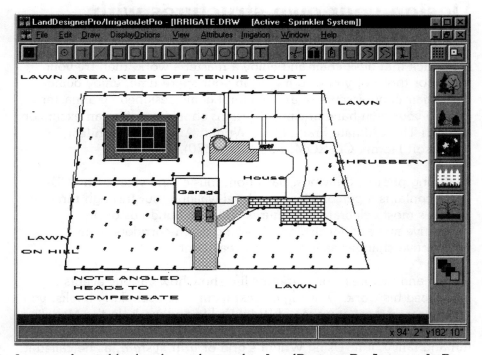

Layout of sprinkler heads, as depicted in LandDesignerPro/IrrigatorJetPro.

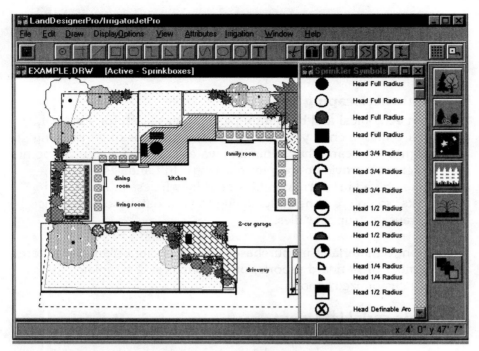

Active sprinkler boxes and sprinkler symbols, as shown in LandDesignerPro/IrrigatorJetPro.

Design your own structures with America's Architect

Kick back that desk chair and enjoy a master's work, then try your own. For those of you who might, in your spare time, enjoy being desk-chair connoisseurs of architectural gems designed by a master and try your own hand at similar designs should consider an excursion through The Ultimate Frank Lloyd Wright: America's Architect, (Microsoft Home, CD-ROM, 800-228-6270).

Featuring photos, drawings, narration, music, and videos, the CD-ROM contains a personalized eye-level walking tour through three of Wright's most celebrated structures and past hundreds of his decorative arts and furnishings. Walking down corridors, your perspective changes as it does on a real jaunt.

Videos and pictures from Wright's life show how various events influenced his work. Drawing on text from seven scholarly books, you can research most any area of Wright's life and work. In the Modeling Wright module, you can give full vent to creative longings just for the fun and fancy of it. Using Wright's grid or *unit system*, as he called it, you can freely manipulate the size and shape of geometric forms— actually simulations of Wright's building blocks—to design your own three-dimensional structure. With a couple of well-placed clicks, you can add such authentic architectural details as doors, windows, and roofs from Wright's early Prairie and Usonian periods.

Even without any previous familiarity with CAD, you can experience tremendous freedom of design and reap immediate visual results. As you alter the shapes on the upper half of a split screen, you see the changes reflected in elevation views on the lower half of the screen. When you click on Visualize, your drawing transforms into a three-dimensional wire-frame rendering that you can either shade or enjoy as is. You can zoom in and out, rotate the structure 360 degrees, and move in continuous degrees from a floor plan into an elevation. It's liberating to turn pie-in-the-sky conceptualizations and "gee what-ifs" into realities on screen if not in real life.

Specification software

A growing number of manufacturers of frequently specified construction-related products, from windows, doors, and skylights to sheetrock and tile grout, are keeping apace with technology and have either put out stand-alone design specification software or software that works inside CAD programs, or have passed along product information to third-party compilers.

These easy-access reference sources are potentially valuable for several reasons. They can inform you about unfamiliar products when you're bidding a project and need to determine installation procedures and estimated times for installation. If you get the project, the software can help you put together building product submissions to an architect or government agency for approval prior to purchase and installation. You can use these kind of programs to provide symbols to use in your own CAD program when you're responsible for designing the work. You can also use the drawings available in many of these programs to put together impressive sales presentations to clients. In third-party electronics catalogs (such as Sweet's), you can locate sources for the materials.

Product-specific software

A specifier's life isn't always an easy one. Product-specific software, whether compiled by a third party or put out by the manufacturer of the building component, can make your row a little easier to hoe. There are two good ways of getting product-specific electronic information: either directly from the manufacturer or from a Sweet's catalog, both on disk.

Building manufacturers' product programs are fall into a category of software that benefits both provider and recipient. It's advantageous for the manufacturer because it gives the company an excellent medium through which to display its product line, and makes it easy (and maybe even more likely) for a contractor to select a product from that manufacturer. It's advantageous for the contractor because it's easy to find needed information. The data can be straight specifications, product photos, illustrations, a calculation system for determining quantities or dimensional factors, or CAD drawings to be used in a CAD program.

A manufacturer-sponsored program typically holds visual and textual information on a company's full line of products for easy referencing and incorporation directly into bids, contracts, or other printed documents. Some programs also offer libraries of CAD symbols for instant copying and pasting into CAD drawings, which is a substantive assist when you're designing a project and want to include accurate details of the products you intend to use.

Typically a program of product listings uses differential searches to help you select appropriate products for each job. Some of the manufacturer-supplied software will also produce accompanying blueprint-type drawings. The following sections comprise a sampling of design specification software that contractors and remodelers might find extremely useful for spec'ing common types of jobs.

Marvin Design System

Marvin Design System (Marvin Windows & Doors, 800-346-3363) is a very comprehensive design specification package, free for the asking, that can go a long way to streamlining the design and specification of Marvin products. Most screens offer catalog choices directly from scroll boxes. The software throughout takes full advantage of the interactive software tools in Windows, and is very easy to work with.

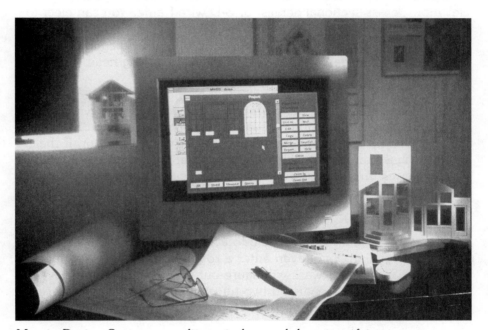

Marvin Design System expedites window and door specifying. <small>Marvin Windows & Doors</small>

The program is set up for designing through the project concept, which is your selection of windows and doors placed into a project database and given a filename. The catalog is divided into three categories: window, door, and magnum. Units or multiples are chosen from the screen catalog and added to the project database. The subcatalog for each category shows the name and rough opening sizes for each selection.

Once units are added to the project database, you can pull up that database and create your configurations, change sizes, and add features. With the various editing tools and your mouse, you establish a work surface (a section of the screen), move the selected units into a desired configuration, and, possibly, mull them.

There are six separate editing dialog boxes, each for a category: unit, sizing, glazing, finish, jamb, and casing. In each, you can modify the units to suit. For example, under glazing, you can pick type, thickness, and color. The program then checks your combination of selections for validity, verifying that it can be built. In fact, whenever you're in the custom design mode, every time you save your selections to the project database, the program checks to determine that your design doesn't exceed structural limitations and that it can, in fact, be built by Marvin—thus assuring viability of the design. You can specify whether the glass should or should not be tempered and select from among several hardware, screen, and casing choices.

Your work is viewable in a variety of geometric formats: plan, elevations, cross-sectional details, or 3-D wire frame. You can elect to show the unit by the architectural Design Level or by the more detailed Construction Level. With cross-sectional detail views, magnified sections from four perspectives are available, including head and sill.

For clients who are unsure what window configuration or even what style of window to go ahead with, you can specify front elevations showing custom shapes and standard-sized options, in two different drawings, and either show them on screen or print them out. If the client, because of cost considerations or other factors, decides to use standard sizes throughout, you can automatically change all the windows in the project to standard sizes at the click of a key.

Marvin Windows also manufactures custom windows and doors, so the program was developed to be able to accommodate drawings custom window designs. You can even enter a rough opening and a frame size width, and the software will figure out the unit dimensions. A compact loose-leaf manual and two tutorials, one for AutoCAD users the other for Windows users, round out the package.

VELCAD

VELCAD (Velux-America Inc. 800-88-VELUX) is another Windows software program that reflects considerable design effort on the part of the manufacturer. Operable both in and out of AutoCAD, the free package has a very easy point-and-click user interface to help you electronically select, specify, manipulate, and document roof windows and skylights.

User responses to preformatted questions

The program allows you to access specs and product drawings in two ways. The first way, suitable for novices, requests answers to prescribed questions. The software uses the responses to narrow the choice down to the specific product. For example, after entering a project name and number the selections include: framing type, roof pitch, roof material, configurations, product category, and type.

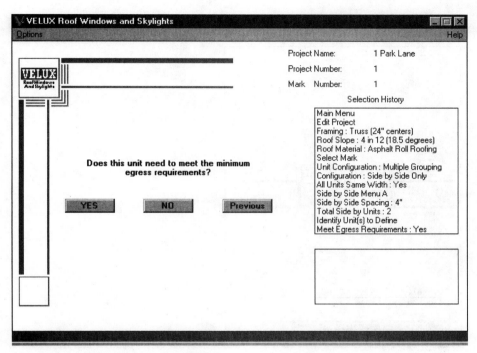

Narrowing the search with VelCAD.

The particulars are entered sequentially and added to the Selection History box, which remains on the screen throughout the process. From this information, the program produces a graphic chart highlighting the possible sizes. Once the unit is selected, further defining choices, such as exterior cladding, control mechanism, glazing, and sunscreening, are made.

Expert users can bypass the assist steps and more quickly and directly access specifications and product drawings for desired windows and skylights. Both modes show and print window and skylight details and schedules.

Savable files for later projects

Built-in tracking lets you access the product information culled during the design phase in a later construction phase. Also, you can create prototype projects to generate duplicate information for similar projects at a later date.

Detailed drawings show more than just windows

The software has many productivity-enhancing features. You can print out a drawing in either horizontal or vertical sections, or by elevation.

The impressive detail drawings show not only the unit but also the roofing materials, rafters, interior trim, insulation, flashing, and dimensions, along with installation notes.

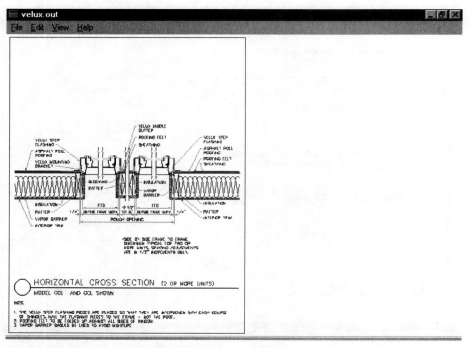

Horizontal cross-section from VelCAD.

Technical specifications are accessible through the Windows notepad. You can edit them to suit and add them to documents. You can also print out a schedule in table format, listing selected units and features, and print out the Selection History box, detailing the choices you made using the Expert System.

The nifty zoom feature allows you to take sections of drawings, increase their apparent size on the screen, and print large-scale views. The Help menu, a hypertext-based program, permits you to quickly access any item by selecting key words.

Andersen CADD-I

The free Andersen Windows program, Andersen CADD-I (Andersen Windows, 800-426-7691) can be used in DOS, Windows, and Macintosh environments. It's a symbols library that comes either in .DXF file format that presents 2-D plan and elevation details or configured for AutoCAD. Both versions contains the full Andersen product line, including windows, patio doors, and Flexiframes, along with detail section files, options like extension jambs, accessory details such as casings, and joining details. In the AutoCAD version, the program creates 3-D plan/elevation symbols, 2-D elevation symbols, and cross-sectional details, all on the fly. It also includes specification text files written in CSI format for every Andersen product. It can generate a list of Andersen products that have been incorporated in a CAD drawing.

There are 13 window and patio door types (casement, awning, double-hung, etc.) and several subtypes within these divisions. The software offers three views of each selection: elevation, horizontal detail, and vertical detail.

.DXF format

Marvin Design System, VELCAD, and Andersen CADD-I all use the AutoCAD .DXF file format. (.DXF files allow you to exchange drawings and information between different CAD programs.) If you don't use any CAD program, you can still use any of these programs. If you do have a CAD program, however, then once the files are in the host CAD program, they're converted to the host symbol format, thereby allowing easy incorporation into CAD drawings.

Pella Designer

Pella Windows and Doors also puts out a free program to qualified users, Pella Designer (Pella Corporation, Architectural Services, 515-628-6433) that works exclusively within an AutoCAD 12 for Window, AutoCAD 12 for DOS, and AutoCAD 13. It has the full Pella catalog for windows, doors, and skylights available to pull into drawings. You can build the plan and elevation at the same time, using a quick-draw feature. The elevation can be toggled back and forth between 2-D and 3-D views. The program gives you the ability to build window schedules and door schedules of the Pella line.

For contractors who don't use AutoCAD 12 or AutoCAD 13, Pella also puts out Pella Selector CAD Library, which consists of over 2,000 .DXF symbols that are elevations and cross sections of standard Pella products.

USG Action

U.S. Gypsum's USG Action (CD-ROM, Electronic Product Information System, 800-621-9622) is product information/specification software for those who specify USG's wares. Essentially a CADD and specification library amplified by lots of helpful ancillary information, it's designed to give construction specifiers, architects, and others quick electronic access to detailed data, drawing, and specification information on all U.S. Gypsum interior and exterior building products and construction systems. The program also encompasses the products of another USG Corporation subsidiary, USG Interiors (ceiling tile, grid, access floor, and wall partition products and systems). The CD-ROM versions (one disk) supplants an earlier 13-diskette version and carries much more material to boot.

The disk is primarily targeted to architects who are developing specifications and need detailed design information, but contractors who are called upon to make submissions of products will find it very useful for both their own edification and for creating specifications.

You can copy product specifications, descriptive copy, illustrations, and CADD drawings into the Windows clipboard for use in design documents, memos, etc., or for export into architectural plans and spec sheets. You can also search tests based on your selected criteria, and export details and text to the clipboard.

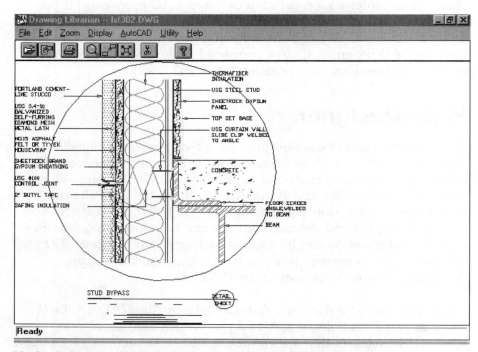

Under light steel framing, a drawing of intermediate floor from the drawing library of USG Action.

The program includes specs and drawings for fire-rated and sound-rated wall, ceiling and floor assemblies, and a compilation of over two dozen technical in-depth articles on a wide variety of relevant topics such as Joint Finishing: How to Get Blemish Free Surfaces in Critical Lighting Situations and Residential Fire Separation Walls: How to Select the Best. . . . The software also features abstracts from model code reports, and an electronic version of the company's 520-page Gypsum Construction Handbook, with full text and graphics, searchable by key word. The printable drawings show clear architectural details of how the products are installed.

The software is well planned and well organized. Products are listed under eight standard divisions: general, concrete, masonry, metals, moisture/thermal control, finishes, specialties, and equipment. The specs are written in formats compatible with both CSI and AIA MasterSpec (SM). The library also includes SAFETYDATA, CLG Plan, and a complete ceiling planning and installation guide.

SmartTools speed spec'ing

Among the SmartTools is DesignTools, with easy-to-use design functions that facilitate stud sizing, unit conversion, and tables. Unit conversions are especially rewarding; we haven't come across such extensive charts elsewhere. There are instant conversions from metric lengths and weights to English lengths and weights and vice versa, and from Celsius to Fahrenheit and vice versa. There are also handy volume conversions for solid and liquids. You might even want to use these conversion capabilities independent of the program.

The five tables are also highly utilitarian. In one, if you select the penny size of a common nail, you can get the length, gauge, and number of nails per pound. Other tables include interior stud framing, limiting heights, and curtain wall, non-load-bearing, limiting heights. Also under DesignTools are various manuals, including one for installing U.S. Gypsum ceilings.

FireTest also falls within SmartTools, and that it is. One of the three options, for instance, is Search for a Fire Resistance Assembly. You

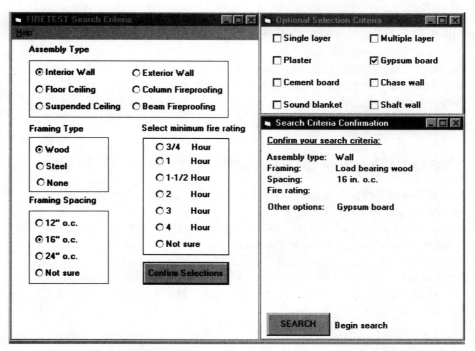

Under SmartTools, FIRETEST search criteria, from USG Action.

pick the assembly type, framing type, framing spacing, minimum fire rating, and other optional selection criteria like gypsum board, shaft wall, and plaster. Then the program will give search results and show all the ways you can build the wall, along with the respective fire ratings. You also get a printout of all components right down to weight per square foot. It even shows caulking locations.

SoundTest works in a similar fashion for both STC and MTC criteria. After you select the criteria, the results are shown on two screens: a schematic drawing of wall construction and materials list; and a results screen, which displays test numbers for the wall found during the search, along with related acoustical data (frequency and sound transmission loss) in tabular and graphic formats.

CADDTools offers easy-to-pull-up drawings of all kinds of products. Just click on representative icons to view the details: a blow-up line drawing, with clear-captioned naming of all parts. You can change the size of the picture for viewing or printing; you can put it on the Windows clipboard, zoom in or out, rotate it, or alter the viewpoint to any angle. CADDTools also provides access to standard cut-and-paste details of USG-recommended good construction practices. The details have hidden attributes useful for automating various functions, including specification generation.

Library listings facilitate locating information

If you want clarifications on anything, just look in the library. With a couple of clicks, you'll be able to quickly locate who to call from the electronic directory—phone and fax numbers—of the company's sales and technical offices. Color maps of the U.S. and the world show orders, sales, technical, and plant sites of U.S. Gypsum and USG Interiors, with addresses and phone numbers a click away. A planned upgrade includes the addition of two online options: Back Talk, for two-way communication via modem so you can directly ask the appropriate company personnel questions and receive answers, and News Link, for updates on the latest tests, as well as new products and systems.

WoodWorks Software for Wood Design

WoodWorks Software for Wood Design (American Forest & Paper Association, 800-463-5091) is a niche program intended for an audience that includes builders, engineers, and architects who build or design with wood and have the technical background to design wood structures. The software uses the AF & PA's current National Design Specification for Wood Construction. It performs quick, accurate sizing of structural members such as joists, studs, beams, and columns for various load conditions.

The Windows program starts right off in concept mode, with a graphical design and analysis work area for the preliminary design of structures considering gravity load.

The software is usable in two different ways. You can look at a given beam, span a given size and specify load, then click on various icons to see what size and members to use. Or you can put in a stud wall, for instance, put a joist or floor on top, then load it, and the program will give the suggested size and spacing of stud wall or joist.

Essentially, you can use WoodWorks as a substitute for span tables. It allows you to try all kinds of wood beside lumber: glue-laminated timber, wood I joists, parallel strand lumber (PSL), and laminated veneer lumber (LVL). The choices include all species and grades available, such as southern yellow pine, SPF, and Douglas fir.

Wood Beam Sizing Professional Package

Sometimes precision counts for a lot, and precision isn't always easy to come by in estimating a project. In many new construction and remodeling projects, wood beam and light steel sizing can be a major factor in both building a project safely and efficiently and in saving money on selecting the right size lumber. Wood Beam Sizing Professional Package (Northbridge Software, 800-766-3514) doubles as both an educational program designed to help builders and remodelers visualize how wood-framed structural systems work and a highly utilitarian package that can handle your calculations and size both lumber and steel, helping assure secure loads. The company also puts out a similar, scaled-down version called Wood Beam Sizing Basic Package.

The programs are visual calculators with dimensioned drawings of the item to be calculated. You can save all job calculations to a project file, and print out the results in detailed fashion.

On-screen testing evaluates performance possibilities

On-screen *testing* lets you hone in on the best combination of loading conditions, different wood types, and sizes, and see how a beam will perform. (Over 60 different species and grades of wood are included.) The professional package assumes you have some knowledge of structures and wood framing, and allows for detailed calculation of multiple loads, light steel beams, glue-laminated and LVL lumber, wood posts, and concrete footings. You can print out or save all your findings on disk.

Under the Professional Loading window, you can enter up to 10 separate loads. The operation is straightforward. You change the span

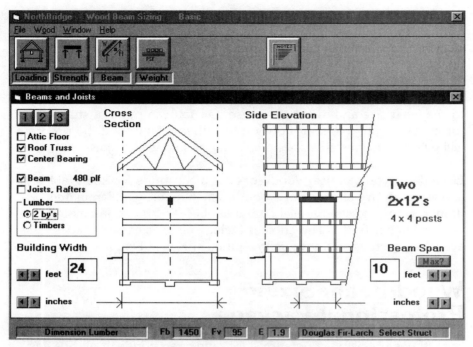

Beam and joist calculations for Douglas Fir-Larch in Wood Beam Sizing.

at any time merely by pressing the Span button. For each load, you enter the load pattern, load type, dimensions, and weight. The reactions for each load are shown at the bottom of the screen. To record the load, press Add. For changes, just press change or delete.

The built-in program prompts are very handy. For example, if the Add button appears, then you know the load shown on screen hasn't been recorded. When you've entered all loads you want information on, press Recalculate for moment and load combination calculations. The total reactions from all loads will appear at the bottom of the screen.

Formulas do the calculations for you

Under Wood Type, the strength of wood for construction is measured in three different ways:

Fb = maximum permitted extreme fiber stress under bending

Fv = maximum permitted shear stress parallel to grain

E = modulus of elasticity (deflection)

The typical base values for many woods are already listed. All you need to do is select the strength window and the type of wood. The software notes suggest you use the program values with discretion and that you obtain the actual values for the wood available to you from your supplier or from the NDS supplement.

Within the wood type section, you first select Dimension Lumber or Beams and Stringers. Then change the four boxes under base values to reflect the correct numbers. You can enter your new values into the list either permanently or temporarily. You can also delete any selected item. The maximum permitted working values will automatically be calculated based on your selected adjustments. You always enter the base values for 2 × 12s, and the size factor is automatically calculated.

For a simple span beam, once the total moment on the beam has been determined, click on the beam button to calculate the beam size. You can return to the loading window to change the beam span, width, or depth at any time for recalculation.

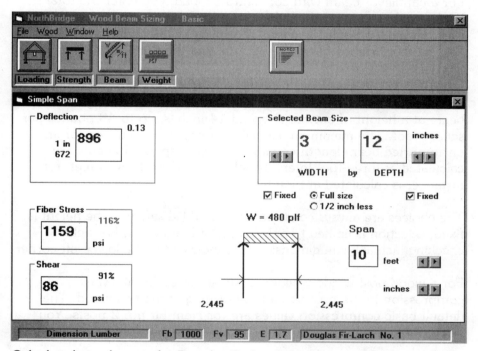

Calculated simple span for Douglas Fir Larch No. 1 in wood beam sizing.

Manual adjustments are possible

Regarding actual lumber dimensions, you can manually adjust for the actual size of the lumber being used. Select Dimensions under the Wood window and the default setting will select the current standard for dressed dimension lumber.

Custom work is also calculable

For custom work, all you need to do is change each window for the actual amount to be deducted. For example, if you're dealing with nominal 12-inch-deep stock that's actually 11¼ inches, change the 7 inch setting to 0.75. Wood Beam Sizing will remember your settings until you change them again. For LVL or glue-laminated lumber, the software defaults are set to the nearest industry standard size.

Cantilevers? No problem!

The program also handles cantilever beam windows (extending beyond the support at one end with the beam load either concentrated at the end of the overhang or distributed along the beam). Note that there might be uplift at the right support, and the left support would therefore carry the sum of the total load, plus the result of the uplift, plus the weight of the beam. Deflections usually govern. (Wood Beam Sizing does not calculate cantilever beams that extend at both ends).

For a cantilever beam with concentrated load, you enter the total load, which is combined dead and live loads. Deflection is calculated for the total load only. The load is applied to the end of the beam. You set the distance between supports and then press Recalculate.

Choices reflect safety considerations all around

For a steel beam window, the program selects a wide-flange steel beam at a height of between six and 14 inches, up to 48 pounds per square foot. The maximum allowable moment is calculated for an unsupported beam length equal to the beam span. Moments are calculated at three-foot intervals only, so a span of seven feet, for instance, is calculated at nine feet.

The choices are always conservative, for added safety. If the height is fixed, selection is limited to only beams of that height. For field checking, actual beam dimensions are indicated in the lower left corner.

For a wood post window, wood posts are sized for allowable compression in the post as well as crushing at the beam end. The default basic compression values are for Hem-Fir no. 2 posts. You enter the actual basic compression values for the wood you're using.

If the posts are a different material than the beam, you can still get calculations. Just enter beam value for perpendicular compression (for end crushing) and post value for parallel compression. The height is the maximum unbraced height. (No allowance is made for load eccentricity.)

Regarding concrete footings, the program will size an unreinforced concrete footing for light loads. For heavier loads, the software will size up to 10-x-10-foot square footing, with appropriate steel reinforcement. Your job is to enter the total load in kips, allowable soil-bearing pressure (2,000 psf suggested for light structures), post size or bearing plate size (from 4 × 4 to 14 × 14), and percent load, which is live load (typically 70 to 80 percent) and concrete strength (suggested 2,500 psi). Almost instantly, the program will produce the sizing. In addition to printing the results, you can either save the results and calculations to file for later use or view them on screen.

Woods of the World Pro

Wood users who are environmentally aware or who have clients who are environmentally aware might want to consider taking advantage of Woods of the World Pro (Tree Talk, Inc., 800-858-6230). Tree Talk is a nonprofit educational organization located in Burlington, Vermont, which deals with wood and forestry issues and is dedicated to assisting the forest products industry manage the world's forests on a sustainable basis. The interactive, multimedia database on wood and wood products covers all the world's well-known, commonly traded woods, as well as hundreds of lesser-known wood species, for a total of over 900 species and 50 wood-based composites. Here—on one disk—is everything you ever wanted to know about wood species you've heard of, as well as hundreds of species you probably haven't.

Helping wood users become environmentally aware

The intent of Tree Talk is to get wood users to discover lesser-known alternatives to endangered and unavailable species, i.e., to find woods available from sustainable instead of overused sources. Though there are over 25,000 extant tree species, only about 500 are in widespread commercial use. Most of the full range of natural species in both temperate and tropical forests are under-valued and under-used. Yet many of them have characteristics comparable to the overused or endangered species. Woods of the World Pro helps you find them.

There are 35,000 fields of information compiled from over 100 books and periodicals, professional institutions, and wood users worldwide. The software identifies the best woods for almost any application, or the best woods to meet a particular set of criteria (like color, bending strength, and hardness). You can access information on just about any timber by knowing its common name, scientific name, or what characteristics the wood you're trying to locate should have.

Search by specific characteristics

You can also use the software to find almost any characteristic of wood, regardless of its environmental standing. The database includes scientific and common names of the species; strength properties such as hardness, impact strength, shearing strength, compression, and static bending; geographic origin and environmental status; more than 20 common uses per species; physical characteristics such as texture, odor, grain, weight, shrinkage, toxic constituents, heartwood and sapwood color, and natural durability; and woodworking characteristics including sawing, planing, turning, carving, splitting, sanding, and gluing.

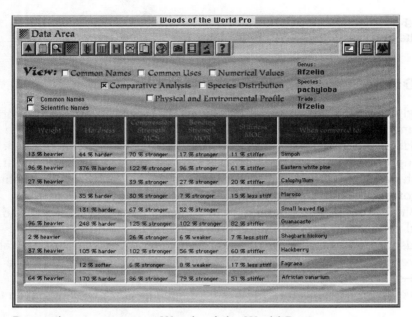

Data selection screen in Woods of the World Pro. Tree Talk, Inc.

All this data lets you quickly locate and identify a particular species to match any combination of up to ten variables. You can compare the appearance of up to nine woods at a time and compare five basic physical properties of one wood to any other nine species. The database will also hold your own entered notes on any species.

Pictures, tables, maps, and video clips

The program's database contains full-color pictures of all the wood species, showing color and grain patterns, along with 40 tables and

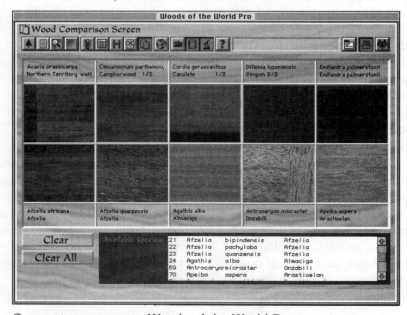

Comparison screen in Woods of the World Pro. Tree Talk, Inc.

graphics on wood weights and moisture contents, 3,500 maps including geographic origin maps, one hour of video clips, and a variety of other handy visual and text-based reference material.

There's also a directory of sources for purchasing temperate and tropical wood products obtained from well-managed harvesting operations, and over 250 environmentally oriented wood-based structural products and composite wood products. Also included are the names and addresses of companies with products listed in the database.

This is a thoughtfully formatted program that includes help windows, picture-display windows, command palette, and separate woodworking and environmental windows. The program also lets wood users know which woods, regardless of endangerment status, are harvested in a responsible manner. In fact, in addition to demonstrating how various wood products are made, the CD-ROM video segments also show what responsible forestry looks like.

Compu-Coverage

Laticrete (800-243-4788), manufacturer of high-strength, shock- and weather-resistant installation systems for ceramic tile, pavers, brick, and stone, has a free software program, Compu-Coverage, that calculates the coverage and consumption of installation materials for ceramic tile and stone. You can use it to establish quantities and thereby control costs of installation materials by not overbuying (or underbuying, which could require work stoppage).

The Windows-based program has three general categories: grout coverage; mortar, render, leveling coverage; and thinset (fixative CTF) coverage. After making your initial selection, you move to one of the three corresponding calculating screens.

For instance, say you select mortar, render, leveling coverage and choose an application such as leveling and patching. Once you insert the total area in square feet and the thickness of the bed inches, and press the Calculate button, the program will spew out the mortar requirements. If you want accurate estimates of material for grout coverage, thinset, or mortar applications, this a handy program you can use right out of the box.

Third-party compilations

Sweet's and Dodge, both long-standing stalwarts of the construction industry, now offer enhanced compilation of their standard-bearer products in electronic format.

SweetSource, an assemblage of spec'able products

Many companies have supplied information on their products to Sweet's, a third-party compiler, as a way to facilitate computer users in specifying their products. Sweet's catalogs have long been a hardcopy way for manufacturers to deliver information on building products to folks involved in the design and specification of commercial and other buildings. Many specifiers in architectural, construction, and engineering firms are familiar with leafing through multiple volumes to locate categories of products or specific brands of products. The CD-ROM, SweetSource (Sweet's Electronic Publishing, a division of The McGraw-Hill Companies, 800-442-2258), is a 1990s complement to the printed Sweet's catalogs that gives your fingers an electronic way to search.

As is typical of CD-ROMs, a great deal of information is loaded into a small package that doesn't take up more than a sliver of shelf space. It's a lot easier to search through the single-disk SweetSource than Sweets' hefty books, once you get the hang of how the program works. The disk holds a complete index of all products in the General Building and Renovation Catalog file and many from other Sweet's files, such as Contract Interiors and Mechanical Engineering and Retrofit.

For a growing percentage of the products (about 45 percent of the print GBR clients)—and here lies a great deal of the appeal, as well— the CD-ROM also includes CAD drawings, product images (photos, renderings, and line drawings), and text explaining the product, any or all of which can be exported to other Windows applications and used in presentations and construction documents. You can also collect and organize product information about your selections into a project file that's relevant to each project in order to retain cumulative information about product choices.

Finding specific products or every product in a category

This high-productivity Windows-based software tool allows you to quickly locate either a specific product from a specific manufacturer or every product (from those included on the disk) that meets a particular set of requirements. There are several quick, easy paths to narrowing down, comparing, selecting, and storing product data. Rather than having to thumb through pages and pages of products in a paper-based catalog and compare characteristics mentally or on paper, the program enables you to point and click on qualifying criteria, refining the possibilities down to a manageable number of products. You can call up detailed company or product information on a wide variety of options.

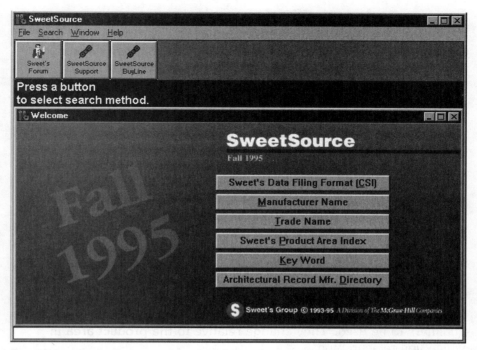

Search method selection screen of SweetSource, featuring various access routes to products.

Text-rich and graphics-rich details

The electronic database includes indexed references to all products in the printed catalog, as well as an ever-growing number of more informative product snapshots and showcases of products. A recent disk held about 24,000 indexed products, over 2,200 CAD drawings, over 3,800 photographs and images, over 4,200 text files, 800 product tables, and 4,900 product screens. (The numbers grow with every quarterly update.)

Essentially, there are two kinds of searches. The first is a comparative search, to locate and compare similar products from competing manufacturers. You can conduct this kind of search via Sweet's data filing format, similar to the CSI index; Sweet's product area index, which classifies products in logical groups known as *categories*, according to their physical and functional characteristics; and key word (with selections numbering over 1,750), which shows products from all manufacturers and offers quite direct navigation to a product area from an index of conventionally used terms.

The second search method is by manufacturer (exclusive search), by either manufacturer's name or trade name. Architectural Record Directory, one of the initial menu options, brings you information on how to contact manufacturer representatives for approximately 5,500 building products that can be accessed directly or by CSI divisions. Five of the six search paths—Architectural Record Directory being the exception—bring you ultimately to a Product Summary screen.

From general to specific as you select options

Conducting a search is visually rewarding. You narrow quickly from the general to the specific and you can watch it happen. When you pick a product line within a category, the toolbox across the top of the screen changes to include new options, such as show product, show definition, physical/functional, and material finish.

The screen also tells you how many products are in Sweet's files that are indexed as that type of product. As you select characteristics you want matched, the total number of matching products shrinks. (By watching the box, you actually see progress in action.) You can show products at any point, but you'll probably want to narrow the search to a manageable number before you start evaluating products against each other. The top half of the screen keeps a running tally of all the characteristics you have picked so you know how you got to where you are all along the way, right down to—for instance—desired aspects of the actual material/finish.

When you get to Options, you can actually specify the attributes and qualifiers to be used. They change relative to the product area in which you're searching.

After the qualifying process, it's time for the Product Summary screen. A scrollable list of individual data windows shows all the products that meet the search criteria. Some but not all of the manufacturers have opted to offer more data in electronic format, in Snapshots and Showcases.

Snapshots show multiple information in mini-windows

A *snapshot* displays definitive information on specific products as provided by the manufacturer. It will include any or all of the four information types: CAD drawing, tables (in chart or spreadsheet form), images (photos, illustrations, other), and up to 1,500 words of text (product description, three-part specifications, compliance information, performance data, instructions, and more). Each data element is accessed as a unit within its own window (handy if you want to transfer information). A zoom feature lets you examine drawing details more closely.

Showcases cover groups of products in depth

The *showcases* (which work something like custom slide shows) are often multiple screens. They give more background information than the snapshots and might contain information about a group of products or company overviews. This is by manufacturer's option, so not every product has a showcase. Those that do, however, offer further details on product features, capabilities, and information such as warranties, ordering options, and installation requirements.

Some manufacturers also provide regional product data. You can use the showcase as a potent sales tool, displaying the screens at timed intervals like a slide show. If you want to create your own showcase of products for either in-house or client review, you can put together a user showcase (with data from any showcase or snapshot) that focuses on what you want.

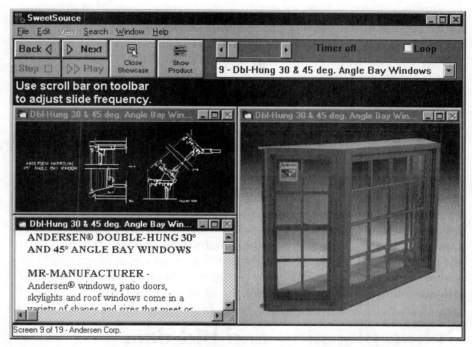

Multi-screen views from SweetSource, featuring a photo of product, a detail drawing, and text. Any of the views may be enlarged.

The products resulting from any of the first five search methods are represented by individual product data windows, each of which displays information available in SweetSource along with the print catalog reference. The product data windows might also include the manufacturer's name and logo, where to find information in the print files, the Sweet's buy-line number, and the trade name or product series. Icons for text, CAD, tables, and images represent the electronic data windows available in a snapshot. Another icon (a trophy) indicates whether or not a showcase is available.

Companies that don't provide electronic information but have information printed in Sweet's GBR catalog files are noted, and the product is indexed (no icon display). You're then referred to the relevant printed catalog for specific information.

Side by side by side comparisons

You can select up to nine products for product comparison. Though you can compare any number up through nine, comparison is best done two by two, for then the windows are relatively large and easy to read. You can compare data elements side by side, even if they're from different manufacturers, but you have to keep changing the pairs.

Transferring text files maximizes the use of material

You can transfer information to a variety of Windows applications quickly and easily, enabling you to add manufacturer's product illustrations, text, and specifications to your presentation or contract documents. You can save text information in Windows Write as a text file, and use it in non-Windows text applications. Even more time-saving, you can transfer drawings directly to AutoCAD for Windows right through the Windows clipboard without having to save the drawing as a .DWG file first. (Non-AutoCAD users can access drawings by saving them as a .DXF file.) You can, of course, also fax any of the information directly to a client, subcontractor, or other interested party.

Lots of help available

The online help system provides information and illustrations for product searches. Follow two or three paths and you'll get the hang of it almost immediately. (The mini User's Guide is a 16-page 3½-x-3½-inch pamphlet. Coupled with the extensive online help you can print out, it's enough.) If you have questions that aren't addressed in either source, SweetSource will provide a free support line where you can probably find an answer. SweetSource is issued quarterly.

Online planning and bid data with Dodge DataLine²

Targeted information often confers a competitive edge. As the English writer Samuel Johnson said over 200 years ago, "Knowledge is of two kinds; we know a subject ourselves, or we know where we can find information upon it." True then and just as true now, and valuable counsel for those who face the competition, one way or another, in the construction business.

F.W. Dodge, which has been managing construction information for over 100 years, has greatly enhanced the power of their reporting capabilities by commanding the electronic medium, via computer and modem, with an electronic bulletin board of listings. With Dodge DataLine² (F.W. Dodge, 800-426-7766), you can retrieve construction information regarding projects in all stages of development along with valuable facts about your competitors almost instantly.

This easy-to-navigate, power-packed, online service for general contractors, subcontractors, architects, engineers, designers, vendors, and other construction professionals is an easy way to access a vast network of timely and specific construction project data for both competitively bid and negotiated jobs.

Fast retrieval of new listings

By hooking into the Dodge database, you can learn about potential contracts as soon as they're listed. The more information you have when making key management decisions, the better. This well-constructed sales and marketing tool is designed to help you get your maximum share of the work.

DataLine^2 is intended to be referenced by management either daily or at other frequent, periodic intervals as a decision-making tool. It offers highly useful information that can be acted on right away, as well as historical data for several types of analysis.

You determine geographic scope and monthly online hours

Typically, a company subscribes at a fixed fee based on two factors: a specific geographic area and a designated number of monthly online hours. So customers can learn their way around the database and master techniques to manage online time efficiently, there's unlimited access for the first 30 days.

After that initial break-in period, most users generally confine access time to the contracted hours each month (usually three to five). As the system allows for customized access, specialty contractors and specialty vendors can sign up for limited access to the database with correspondingly lower pricing per month.

Plain-English choices

The program is extremely user-friendly, no more difficult to navigate than the ATM machine at your local bank. The menus are a series of plain-English choices. Just type in corresponding numbers or letters to activate commands; there are no keystrokes to memorize. Everything on screen is self-explanatory.

DataLine^2 offers its information through paths established by hierarchical searches, working from the general to the specific, thereby narrowing the database to your needs. It works under the same general premise used in the movie *The Fugitive*. The character played by Harrison Ford uses a computer to help locate a man with a particular type of artificial arm. Gaining access to computerized hospital records, he refines his search on screen and quickly reduces the possibilities down to just a handful of people. Working with DataLine^2 might not be as exciting, but your search can move along at an equally brisk clip, and hone in on results just as effectively.

You conduct searches by using one or more of 12 user-specified search criteria. These include text (with ten subcategories and sub-subcategories), such as firm name text or product/facilities involved;

project type; geography; minimum and maximum valuation; square footage; story height; stage of development; bid date; ownership (public versus private); trades/material/equipment involved; search filters (e.g., only new construction or building permits); and type of bid (negotiated or competitive). By using DataLine[2] regularly, you can winnow down the numbers and target your bidding efforts only to projects that meet your specific criteria.

The software gives you a 12- to 13-month backrolling database and just about everything you need to know about upcoming and recent jobs except the blueprints (not yet, at least!). And as a subscriber, you have free access to Dodge reports plan rooms (like Dodge hard-copy subscribers). The main menu offers eleven immediate options, including Search Subscription Territory (an opportunity to look outside your designated territory at additional cost); AutoSearch, so you can set up the system to run the same searches via a macro whenever you hit the keys; Flash Update by Dodge project number (the ability to specifically track up to 10,000 projects within up to 10 customized tracking lists for daily updated information); and construction activity updates.

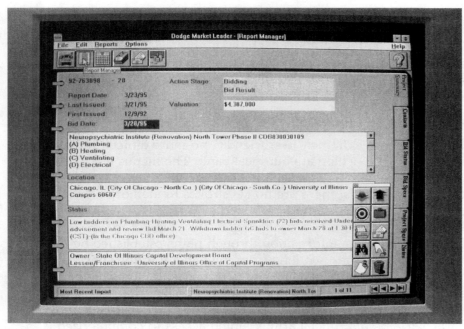

Lots of detailed information about biddable projects is available on Dodge DataLine[2]. F.W. Dodge

Short term, medium term, or long term

DataLine[2] has a trio of databases from which to cull information upon request. The most timely is the Flash Database, which accesses reports issued within the last five business days. The News Database retrieves data starting from the first day of the previous month and forward. The Research Database—excellent for historical searches—references backward through the previous 12 months.

You can customize access to instantly find projects from the 109 project types that fit your particular parameters. When you're familiar with the system, you can opt to set up PowerSearch to bypass menus and speed up the search process even further.

When you pull up a prospective project, it's possible to instantly determine current status, names of bidding competitors, times updated, current bid date, overall estimate and breakdown of specialty subcontractor estimates. The screen also gives structural and material/equipment information. You can download a full report, a two-line summary, or both into the database of choice. (To save online time, most subscribers log off before perusing the information more closely.)

Checking on the competition

Other nifty retrieval capabilities let you key in a company name and use text search to pull up all job activity Dodge has on file for your competition—whether for architects, general contractors, subcontractors, or engineers—and prepare historical reports on their bidding patterns. It's almost like having a private eye on staff! You can even find out whether they're primarily after competitively bid or negotiated work, how many jobs they've won recently, and how many jobs they're bidding on currently, so you can determine how hungry they are and how tied up their resources probably are. If desired, you can create macros to access this information instantly.

Contractors long familiar with Dodge reports shouldn't look at the online service as just an electronic version and leave it at that. There are several advantages of online versus hardcopy Dodge reports: you can keep current at your own convenience, not just when the mail comes, and note changes or updates almost when they occur, thus providing what could be crucial extra days to contact the appropriate parties, prepare a quote, or meet the bid date. (A network of over 1,300 reporters and correspondents feed in over 5,000 updates daily.) Most significantly, you can manipulate all the electronically retrieved information into meaningful formats or reports for evaluation. You can also export the data into your own database program, such as dBASE, Paradox, FoxBase, Access, Approach, ACT!, and TeleMagic.

Finding your way to optimal use

General contractors who primarily bid rather than negotiate jobs will be able to easily build a list of projects coming up for bid in the coming several months in the exact geographic location of interest. You can set searches by state, county, or even zip code.

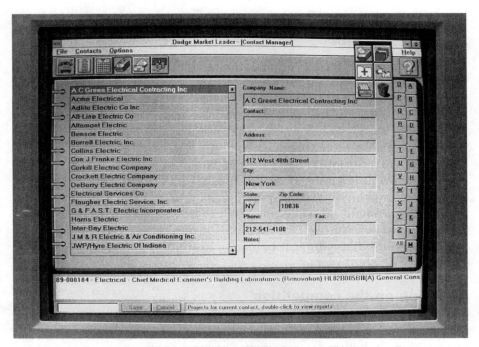

*Contact Manager screen from Dodge DataLine². F.W. Dodge

Project management firms or contractors who prefer to negotiate opportunities or get in at the planning stages can search preplanning, planning, and final planning stage projects for key information like owner or architect, with the intent of possibly heading off the competition before it becomes a factor.

By navigating through DataLine², subcontractors can save a lot of leg-time, phone time, and other sleuthing. They can find out which general contractors are bidding a project and get their prices out to everyone. Materials vendors can search for projects using their types of products and assure themselves of not missing a quote opportunity.

Here's a capability that's possible only electronically: using the Square Footage screen to narrow down a search for projects falling within selected square footage. This is especially helpful if you rely on square footage as a main factor, for jobs such as painting, flooring, or roofing. Similarly, you can define projects by story height, which might be useful for elevator manufacturers and scaffolding companies.

Help however you need it

A DOS-based program, DataLine² comes with its own communications software, user documentation, free training, phone support from a company consultant whenever you need it, an 800 technical help number, and free access to Dodge plan rooms around the country.

Dodge Market Leader

To facilitate use of the information downloaded from DataLine^2, Dodge also offers Dodge Market Leader as a companion integrated software product that serves as a marketing support. Market Leader is an organization tool with a built-in report manager that sorts information automatically to various databases, contacts, and schedules.

The software comes with an integrated word processor for customized form letters, and a function that allows contractors and subcontractors to mail-merge letters and labels for mass mailings. There's also a built-in spreadsheet for performing quick quote calculations. It also organizes project information for imports into your Windows-based applications for further use in marketing or sales campaigns.

Electronic estimating

L ONG before there were PCs, the pundit Oscar Levant observed about an eminent decision maker, "Once he makes up his mind, he's full of indecision." While he wasn't referring to contractors and remodelers putting together bids—he was actually talking about Eisenhower—he nonetheless neatly summed up what must be the feelings, at least some of the time, of many estimators. When it comes to estimates, the best kind—before they're submitted—are those that are easily put together and easily revised. (Estimators, like clients, are entitled to second thoughts, too.)

Fast, accurate estimating is one of the key factors that can make the difference between reaping a reasonable profit and running in the red. An electronic estimating program well-matched to your company needs can greatly reduce the time it takes to perform take-offs and prepare bids, increase calculating accuracy, and create a professional-looking estimate. It can also improve your buying power by combining material lists from several jobs running in roughly the same time period to allow for volume purchases. Furthermore, electronic estimating can offer you an easy way to evaluate job profitability.

If you're an old hand at manual estimating—using pencil and pad, past experience, and a good solid eraser—no doubt you can probably "guesstimate" costs even before you put your first quantity take-off on paper. You might even be inclined to lean toward sticking with the tried and true. But once you make the transfer, both emotionally and literally, and learn to build an electronic estimate on screen, you'll be able to turn out more estimates, faster, with less chance of making an error, and analyze and manipulate numbers before you finalize your bid. An electronic estimating program can also help give your firm a more professional persona by standardizing the look of your bids.

PC-based estimating for rough and finished bids

If you closely match your company needs with a software estimating package, you'll soon wonder why you ever hesitated to make the transition. Electronic estimating works equally well for rough, quick bids and for finished bids.

Although the trend in the computer industry is toward the Windows platform, most estimating programs are still DOS-based. Some companies have kept in step with filter-down technology; several software developers sell their estimating software on CD-ROM, with quarterly database updates available by modem.

Using the mouse-driven Windows interface is easier, in general, than working in DOS, and the learning curve between programs is shorter because the keystrokes and general looks don't change much between

Windows programs. Windows programs also allow you to make quick and easy graphical analyses (pie charts, bar graphs. etc.) of your bids.

Though you can use a spreadsheet program to build your own customized estimating template, unless you're quite computer-savvy it's easier to use a dedicated package already formatted for estimating that produces professional-looking bids automatically.

Evaluating your choices

What type of program you go with—basic, inexpensive estimating program; larger, more expensive estimating program; or fully integrated estimating, job costing, and accounting program—depends upon the size of your firm and the type of work you perform. Smaller contractors usually don't require programs that can do just about everything but the on-site work and take more than a bit of time to learn. They should rather consider starting with an inexpensive, easily learned, dedicated estimating program.

As your business grows and you need more functionality, you can move up to more encompassing software that ties in with other application programs, like accounting and scheduling. Furthermore, the experience you gain with an inexpensive program will help you decide which features you need in your next program.

Before you buy, it's important to determine whether any program you're considering estimates the kinds of contracts you bid and, in theory, reflects the way you do business. Evaluate your needs with respect to how your firm bids work. If you estimate primarily by time and materials, you surely want that capability in the program. (No need to change a winning strategy in midstream.)

Likewise, if you estimate by cost-plus contracts or fixed fee contracts, look for that ability in the software. Some programs offer multiple options. Also, look for software that's flexible in the way it handles overhead and profit, sales tax, and bonding requirements so you can put together bids with everything easily included.

Many estimators find it easy to use software that replicates standard, manual take-off sheets. A program that mimics traditional-looking manual bid sheets makes it easier to make the transition. (This is why the checkbook program Quicken is a top seller in the small office/home bookkeeping market; it mimics checkbook entries and other forms.)

Template-based estimating

One of the easiest ways to work with electronic estimating is with templates. Templates are preformatted documents designed to be used to create other documents, e.g., fresh estimates. Each template could list items typically used in a specific kind of project. You can set up several different templates that fit the different types of work you generally perform.

When you're ready to estimate a particular job, pull up the appropriate template, save it as a new estimate, and add labor and material quantities for the items used. This way you'll have a printed estimate in short working order. By using a template, you won't inadvertently omit any components; they'll all be there, ready for the numbers. And if you don't need any items, just leave them blank; you might need them in the next estimate.

If and when you need more functionality, you can move up to more encompassing software. By then, you'll know which added features you need.

Preformatted databases

The size of the database is another consideration. Some estimating programs come with extensive databases of thousands of items priced out with labor to install them and the cost of the material. Others come with small databases that require you to either insert the numbers or change them to conform to your prices. The advantage of a database of thousands of items is that the items are already laid out in a logical sequence and coded according to standard industry coding. Starting a database from scratch can be a tedious process and overwhelming if you use more than a few hundred items regularly.

Many software estimating companies buy their databases from third-party companies that specialize in producing databases. Often, these are the same companies that have been producing annual cost books for years, so the numbers are fairly close to target. But the costs in any database can't be as accurate as the quotes you get from material vendors, even though some programs localize rates for your individual city via cost-correction factors.

Flexible, updatable databases

The easier it is to make multiple adjustments to numbers pulled into the estimate from a database, the better. Being able to globally change the costs (material and labor) with a percentage is a worthwhile feature. It's also very convenient if you can use the database to produce both individual line items and assemblies. For estimating purposes, an *assembly* is a group of items that are used together in a part of your job. Using assemblies in your estimating saves time because you have fewer items to enter, which potentially increases accuracy because there are fewer opportunities to make mistakes when entering numbers.

The more often database tables are updated throughout the year, the better they will reflect true costs, so look for a package that mentions frequent updating either by update disk or by modem.

Estimating and more with modular software

The more encompassing estimating programs—marketed as fully integrated systems that tie into accounting, job costing, inventory control, payroll, and other modules—typically require a day or two of training to get up and running. If you want to tie other functions into estimating, you'll need a modular package. Job costing, in particular, can be very valuable in helping you determine, even daily, where you are in terms of making or losing money on any individual project.

Generally, packages of this type require trained personnel to run them. It's prudent to consider not only the cost of any fully integrated program, but also the cost of training an employee to learn to use the program productively. Truly comprehensive programs usually require that you use them for a prolonged period of time to become comfortable with them. If you're contemplating buying a full-blown, integrated system, have a sales representative come in and demonstrate the software in your office. At trade shows, salespeople demonstrating programs often take prospective clients through the estimating process at a steady clip, apparently effortlessly. But it's never that easy. If you can, take a good look at the software and make sure not only that you want to take on such a large and complicated program but that it works in a way that's at least somewhat compatible with the way you work. Otherwise, learning it will be an upstream swim.

What-if capabilities

Rarely is an estimate fixed in stone before it's accepted and turned into a bid. Once the bid is put together, what-if analysis can and should come into play. The easier it is to be able to fine-tune the final numbers—changing a percent or a cost line and having the bid automatically recalculated—the better. Look for that type of capability. Also, it's a plus to be able to edit the description on a bid summary to easily accommodate alternate prices, exclusions, or any other bid breakdown.

Being able to analyze a bid from different perspectives is also useful. Some of the more sophisticated software packages are capable of breaking down estimates by labor code, cost code, job phases, and even by drawing numbers.

Some estimating programs allow only one mark-up on the total cost; being able to apply multiple markups either on the whole job or on components is better. The program should also be able to calculate sales tax for capital improvements following your state's requirements. Otherwise, it can be time-consuming to break those numbers out.

It's also convenient if there's a way to record short notes that can be tied into the line items of the bid or that would help you recall pertinent information when you perform bid analyses.

If you're working on large projects that have thousands of items to take off, to save time and minimize the possibility of errors, you might want to use a digitizer that ties in electronically with particular estimating software and can transfer quantities directly into the bid. For smaller work, you can use an electronic roller that directly enters quantities into some estimating programs. Other links include project management and CAD software.

Considerations before you buy

Try to buy an estimating package from a company with a proven, relatively long-term track record and a good reputation so, if and when you need help down the line, the company is likely to still be in business and have a phone line available for technical support. In fact, check out the access to and availability of software support before you buy to see how easy it actually is to get your call through and receive help. No matter how straightforward the program seems and how reassuring the manual is, most of us need the reassurance that technical support is there, at the end of the line.

Change orders: Going your way?
Another important consideration when evaluating estimating programs is how the package handles change orders. Will the change order become part of the original estimate or will it be a separate estimate? If you have a distinct preference, look for a program that does it your way because fixing it can be time-consuming and confusing.

Review the program and the manual
Sample onscreen estimates help you gain risk-free insight into the operation of the program, and work with sample numbers without jeopardizing real numbers. You can use the sample estimate to experiment, trying out different techniques while teaching yourself the program until you feel comfortable.

In all programs, context-sensitive help screens are more convenient than general help. Also, preview the manual if you can. Look for a prevalence of screen shots and other illustrations. These graphics will help you master the various screen components. Try to judge whether the developers have a clear working knowledge of the construction business and use terms precisely. If they use them incorrectly or not at all, learning the program could be very confusing.

Look for a good track record and technical support

As with all specialty software, it's wise to select a company with a proven track record. Many software companies have failed within a few years of releasing programs. If the developer of the estimating software you buy disappears and you have a problem with the software, you'll have no one to turn to for technical help. Look for longevity as part of a program's curriculum vitae.

Also, check out the access to and availability of software support before you buy. Call and see how easy it is to get through. Having to leave your name on voice mail and waiting a day or two to get a call back can cut into a program's effectiveness. You want prompt responses to your calls, as if they were emergencies. When you're estimating a project on a tight deadline, help the day after tomorrow won't win the bid.

Programs
Spreadsheet-like estimating program: Add-Vantage

The Remodeler's Add-Vantage (Add-Vantage Software, 800-287-5247 in Massachusetts, 800-768-5636 out of state) is a Windows-based, stand-alone estimating program that actually evolved as an outgrowth of the developer using the spreadsheet program Excel for estimating. The program doesn't require any knowledge of that or any other spreadsheet program, and is quite easy to learn.

The package includes ten templates for various types of residential remodeling projects, including one-story and two-story additions, basement, bath, kitchen, and wood sundeck, as well as a repair category for items such as siding, painting, replacement windows, and roofing.

Each template looks like a spreadsheet, with rows and columns, and is a detailed sectional breakdown of many possible items for building the bid. You have a great amount of flexibility in changing templates, creating new templates, or simply changing the items for an individual estimate.

Well matched to a stick builder's style

The software is essentially intended for use by experienced stick builders who are accustomed to estimating all items in a project; it doesn't work for estimates put together by the square foot. It has a material and labor database of items, but doesn't list any cost factors. You enter all prices for material and labor on your master database and the program automatically places the numbers on all the templates for different kinds of jobs. Then when you build a particular

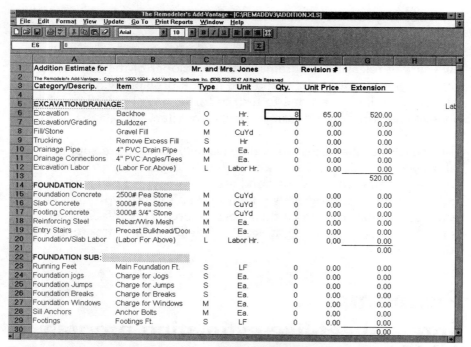

Estimate, laid out by categories in The Remodeler's Add-Vantage.

estimate, the database prices are used and the materials and labor extensions are automatically calculated. You can even edit the database to add alternate labor rates.

As the templates are formatted, you add the labor cost at the bottom of each category as a total for that category. The program concept is based on the premise that overhead is part of your labor rate. The remodelers who developed the software used a fixed unit price for all labor and you can do it that way. Here is where experience in small remodeling estimating is important.

The line items don't include labor prices, so it's beneficial to have a feeling for how much time the work will actually take. If the projects you perform are similar, this shouldn't be difficult. Alternately, you can change the line items to reflect individual labor costs simply by changing any listed unit to labor rate. You can then establish as many different labor rates as you need.

Detail-rich choice of printouts

The program prints out three forms: main estimate, executive summary, and schedule of doors and windows. In addition, you can cut and paste parts of the estimates into a Windows word processing program for inclusion in a proposal or contract. The executive summary lists totals for each category, before tax on materials and margin on total cost.

The three printouts show great detail. Everything on the screen prints out except totals for labor costs, labor hours, and material costs, which appear on the screen version of the estimate for your evaluation. These types of detailed printouts allow contractors to show clients detailed estimates (minus costs) rather than just grand totals. This could be a real plus in cases where you sense that, when clients know what they're paying for, they could be more apt to accept the project cost.

For a remodeling contractor who has been using a pencil and paper to estimate by line items, is new to electronic estimating, or doesn't want to work with large coded databases, this program provides an easy transition.

Making the most of graphics with BidMagic

BidMagic (Turtle Creek Software, 607-272-1008) is a stand-alone Windows program that takes a very graphical approach to estimating for both residential and light commercial construction. Probably because the developers had written Mac software for many years before moving into Windows territory, the program is icon-rich. Macintoshes have always had a very strong graphical orientation, and this package shows the benefits.

The software handles both rough estimates and finished bids. (You select the category at the beginning.) Extremely versatile, BidMagic is easy to use for anything from new construction and guts/rehab to room or wing additions and remodeling projects. By entering additional items into the price book, you can actually use the program for just about any other type of construction, as well.

Using cards to simplify data entry

BidMagic is built around a sequence of *cards*, or screens, filed under six main menus (File, Edit, Navigate, Bid, Data, and Help). Estimating is a four-step, onscreen process, and you can use up to 40 different cards to enter information about the bid. Each card covers one specific aspect and you can move right through the cards in sequence to complete the entire estimate.

The software uses a unit price approach to estimating, with each line item representing a specific cost. You add, change, or delete unit price line items and the suggested quantity, labor adjustment, and material adjustment formulas. The program comes with a built-in price book of over 1,000 construction items. You can change any cost, adjust labor wages, and add your own prices easily.

The first step in putting together an estimate is to enter operating costs into the basic costs, overhead and profit, and soft cost. Unlike the modus operandus of many other estimating programs, you aren't locked into a single way of doing business. Overhead can be calculated as a percentage of hard costs alone, a percentage of hard and soft costs, or as percentage of the overall amount of the bid.

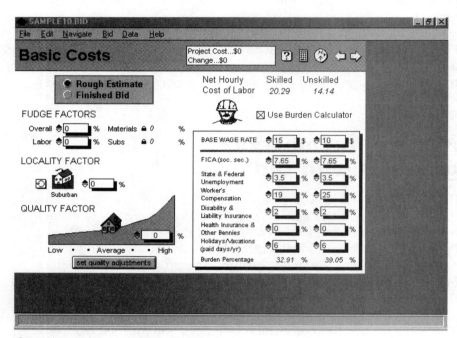

Sample card screen from BidMagic.

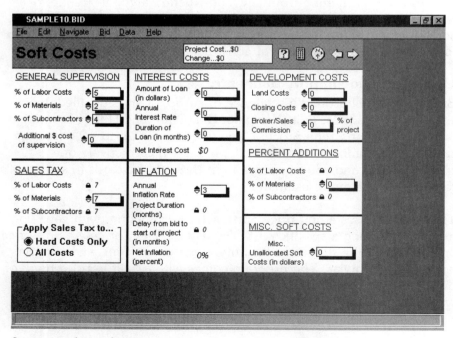

It is very clear where to input your soft costs in BidMagic.

The second step is entering the project measurements. Like other good estimating packages, the program uses "smart" dimensioning; you enter simple dimensions like walls, length, floor areas, and ceiling heights, and the software calculates measurements such as framing, trim, siding, and wallboard quantities. Changes in any factor are reflected in a new bottom line almost instantly. The program delineates very clearly just what is needed. Under the roof dimensions card, for example, you first select from nine different roof styles and click on whether the roof will or won't have a parapet and/or an overhang. You won't likely miss any measurements with this program.

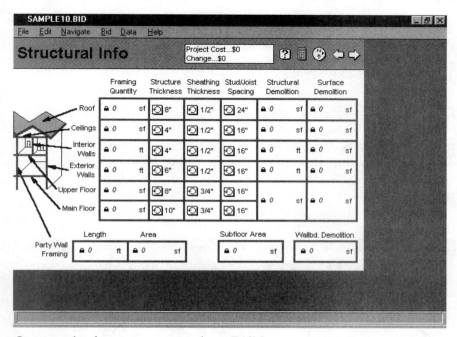

Structural information screen from BidMagic.

Fudging and fixing

The third step is to enter construction choices. This is where you get to play with the numbers. The program includes three quick-fix factors—locality, quality, and fudge—to adjust project costs up or down depending on your particular situation or on a gut feeling. You adjust the factors in percentage increments via a Nudge button.

The locality factor (covering remote, rural, suburban, small city, or big city) lets you adjust by neighborhood in the finished, but not the rough, estimate bid.

The quality factor—running from low to high—is another way you can work with BidMagic to hone in on numbers that will come in right for your company on finished bids. Unlike the locality factor and the four fudge factors (discussed in the next paragraph), the quality factor is weighted, so some items increase in price faster with an increasing quality of work. Each cost category has its own sliding scale for labor and materials.

The fudge factors are extremely effective for handling job-to-job variations in cost (and picky clients), and are available for both rough and finished bid estimating. The four areas are materials, labor, subcontractors, and overall. Each fudge factor is a percentage adjustment applied across the board to every item in every cost category. The overall fudge factor is applied after the first three and adjusts all prices, including soft costs.

The last step is viewing the final contract price on the Bottom Line card, which shows a detailed cost broken down into either 31 categories that match the different specifications cards, or 16 cost divisions that match the system used by CSI and AIA.

Clicking right and left arrows will change cards one at a time in a forward or backward direction. You can also work on the bid out of order, which is very convenient if you want to change a project detail midstream or if you forgot something. When you've made the change or addition, one click gets you back to your most recent card.

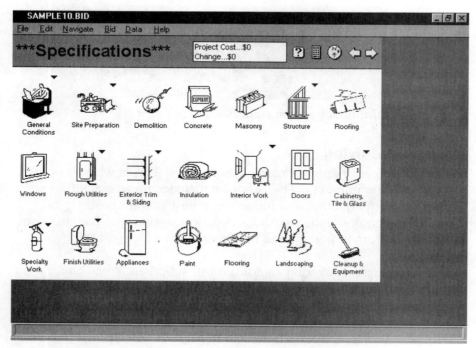

Pictorial icons ease the way in setting up Specifications in BidMagic.

An optional material take-off module gives you a complete material take-off list for any part or all of the project. It also produces price request sheets to pass out to lumberyards.

You can create and store estimating templates for the different types of projects you normally do. Working with templates not only saves time and effort on subsequent estimates, but it also helps assure you won't forget the basics. You might even save two or more templates for similar types of work, reflecting high- and low-end quality, union and nonunion labor, or different types of construction methods.

Program perks

The icons allow you to easily identify just where you want to enter data. Under Specifications, for example, one screen in particular shows 21 drawings. From site preparation (a bulldozer) and structure (framing) to insulation (a roll) and exterior trim and siding (siding), a quick look assures correct placement.

Even more valuable, perhaps, you can choose to hide soft costs among actual hard construction costs, or you can show them as individually itemized in the estimate, whichever works best for you.

CD Estimator

Craftsman Book Company, publishers of cost estimating books that have long been mainstays in the architectural/construction industry, have put together the 1996 CD Estimator CD-ROM (Craftsman Book Company, 800-829-8123). The disc includes over 2,000 pages' worth of 1996 cost estimates from five Craftsman 1996 cost reference manuals, the National Estimator (an easy-to-use estimating program designed to access the various cost databases), and a 40-minute video tutorial. The manuals from which the cost databases are replicated are *National Construction Estimator*, *National Repair & Remodeling Estimator*, *National Electrical Estimator*, *National Plumbing & HVAC Estimator*, and *National Painting Cost Estimator*.

Subcontractors can use the numbers in the databases that relate to their fields, while general contractors and builders who rely on subcontractors can use the specialty numbers to spot-check or create rough estimates in addition to using the program for their own estimates.

The instant access toolbar puts Quantity, Craft, @ Hours, Unit, Material, Labor, Equipment, and Total right across the top of the screen. You can change any price or description in an estimate, copy costs from one estimate to another, and add tax and markup. Contractors can print out completed estimates directly or export them to many popular Windows or DOS word processing or spreadsheet programs.

The Windows-based National Estimator, included on the CD-ROM, makes it a smooth procedure to use the cost data to compile construction cost estimates. The pricing tables on the disk are organized in logical categories following industry-standard practices. When preparing an estimate—whether for a renovation or addition—you work with a split screen. One half shows your estimate while the other holds information pulled from the database.

Picking up a line item from the database is very quick and easy, either by page number or by keyword search. Using Windows copy and paste commands, you can copy a line from the database and paste it into your estimate. Costs are extended and columns totaled automatically.

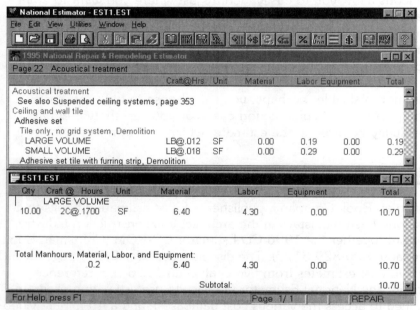

Split screen showing database on top and estimate sheet on the bottom, in 1996 CD Estimator.

You can use the listed cost adjustment factors to reflect the labor and material costs for your locality. In California alone, for example, there are 37 cost regions. It's also possible to add markups (the contractors' profit) and even transfer the estimate to a word processing or spreadsheet program for inclusion as part of a larger finished document. Updates by modem from Craftsman's Contractor's BBS (issued three times a year) are free.

Drop-in cost data programs for spreadsheet users

R.S. Means and Saylor Publications, both long-time publishers of cost data for use by contractors in all construction trades, as well as by architects and engineers, offer estimators the ability to estimate with electronic data and spreadsheet programs.

Bringing compiled costs into a construction estimating template

R.S. Means (800-448-8182) has long had a reputation for being right on the money for providing cost data for the construction industry. Though not designed as a true estimating program per se, the latest version of MeansData for Windows Spreadsheets builds on their constantly updated compilations of cost data.

The program is designed to integrate any of over 47,000 unit prices and 10,000 assembly line items into one of three popular spreadsheet formats (Lotus 1-2-3 for Windows, Quattro Pro for Windows, or Excel for Windows) so you can, in essence, use your spreadsheet and Means' cost tables for estimating. If you already know how to use a spreadsheet, this is a convenient way to work with familiar Means cost items. The pricing information is updated quarterly. MeansData for Windows Spreadsheets also features preformatted estimating spreadsheets and built-in report capabilities.

Customizing by individual cost data files

To customize the software, you have to purchase up to 15 separate construction cost data files. Individual unit price cost data files include building construction; concrete; electrical, interior cost, light commercial, mechanical, plumbing, repair and remodeling, and residential. All cost data files except the light commercial and residential are based on union wages.

Open-shop rate adjustments are possible

If your business operates using open shop rates, you can buy an add-in file that will slot those rates into any of the union-based programs. Composite unit price cost data files (commercial, civil, and facility) are also available, along with six different assemblies cost data files (rel. 10, concrete, electrical, heavy construction, mechanical, and plumbing).

Three search routes

The software has lots of user-friendly features. You can search unit costs by keyword, CSI, or UNIFORMAT number. Your estimate total changes instantly as you add or subtract items. Line item costs and division totals are calculated automatically. The program features one-step adjustment to reflect local costs for 209 cities, applies the quantities, and then calculates the final estimate using the contractor's own markups.

If you don't want to use the Means data files for some of your costs, you can create your own data file and thus include your true costs when you make an estimate, essentially using the program as an estimating template.

One drawback is that the format adds markups only on the total value of the estimate. You can get around this by adjusting your user files to reflect overhead, profit, contingency, or any other conditions you might not want shown, or by adjusting the numbers in the spreadsheet. Likewise, when the estimate prints out, it prints each standard construction category separately, with the markups at the end. But if you adjust the data and enter zeros in the template for the markups, each category subtotal would be ready for presentation. The estimate also calculates worker hours, a nice feature that might help you plan and schedule a project.

The software could be particularly useful for preparing change orders because it prints R.S. Means on the printout. As that name has industry-wide recognition, it's a way to validate a potentially higher price for change-order work if you can actually do the work for less than what's printed out. Also, any items in the estimate can be used as subcontracted items.

The small spiral-bound manual provides what you need to start estimating quickly. It also includes three lessons to guide you through the basic steps for creating an estimate, creating a user data file, and creating an estimate from assembly data. There's free, unlimited technical support on an 800 number.

Estimating tables customized for end users

For over 30 years, Saylor Publications, Inc. (800-624-3352) has published estimating manuals that list cost data for use by estimators in the construction field. The five books, published yearly, are *Current Construction Costs* (the base volume from which other cost data is derived); *Residential Construction Costs*; *Remodeling/Repair Construction Costs* (with labor and therefore total unit cost data broken down into four degrees of difficulty—the greater the degree of difficulty, the greater the costs); *Commercial Square Foot Building Costs* (assemblies combined to come up with final cost—the components are listed within, as well); and *Residential Square Foot Building Costs* (likewise for dwellings). The books have cost-factor adjustments for 118 cities, based on union wage rates, productivity, and practical experience.

To keep apace with the latest modern information processing technology, electronic estimating, Saylor Publications has replicated the data in these books in a standard electronic spreadsheet format that's compatible with most spreadsheet programs, in two separate databases. Each database is complete and comprehensive in logical CSI numbering format.

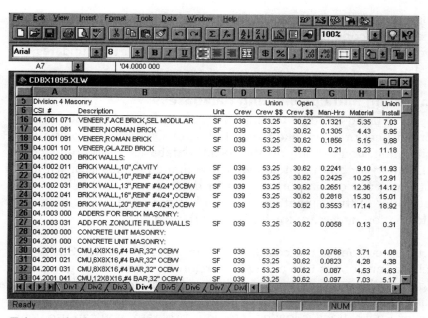

Tabs on the bottom of the screen make it easy to move around in customizable Saylor electronic databases. Saylor Publications

Two database choices

The first database, Commercial Construction Costs and Remodeling/Repair Construction Costs, includes almost 13,000 cost items. The second database, Residential Construction Costs (with a Remodel/Repair macro option), has almost 6,500 cost items. Each item in both programs comes with a CSI number, stand-alone description, unit of measure, crew code, crew dollar rate, work-hour rate, material cost, and installation cost. A timesaving one-stroke macro converts spreadsheet files to remodeling/repair construction costs for commercial and residential use.

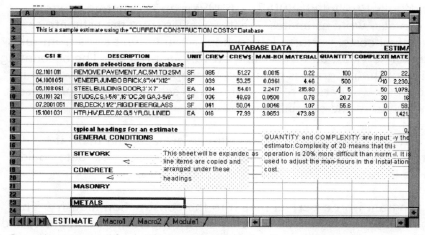

Sample estimate from Saylor Database for Spreadsheets. Saylor Publications

You can edit the cost and the wording of the description to fit your needs, and copy both to your work area. You can also adjust or override costs. A yearly subscription includes quarterly updates of costs.

Importing and customizing databases

If you're using a recent version of an off-the-shelf Windows spreadsheet program like Excel, Lotus, or Quattro Pro to do your estimating, you can import the Saylor databases. If you're using an estimating program that comes with a limited database or without a database, you can import the Saylor databases as long as the developer of the estimating program has provided Saylor with information necessary for formatting the files.

You can customize the cost tables from three of the five Saylor Publications books into a private version for a particular geographic region and area of expertise, with the kind of item classifications that suit particular company needs. Once the imported database from Saylor Publications is loaded into your program, you can use your own personally designed estimating templates for the various types of projects the company bids. This customizing also saves hard disk space on your computer.

The customizing works in the following fashion. Current Construction Costs uses the 16 major divisions of the CSI and is broken down into major subtrade categories within those divisions, with the codes in an all-numeric system. You can limit the customized database to include just the specific CSI divisions your company works with. Within those divisions, you can also expand for greater itemization.

QuickBooks Pro

QuickBooks Pro (Intuit, 800-781-6999) is an accounting program that can also write estimates, create invoices from the estimate or from actual costs, perform job costing, separate unit costs from sales prices for services, and track time on various projects. The accounting portion of the program is discussed in chapter 7, so the coverage in this chapter will pertain to the estimating, scheduling, and progress billing features and capabilities.

You can use QuickBooks Pro to estimate projects and then, if awarded the bid, convert the estimate into invoices. The data could then be incorporated into the accounting program.

The program isn't a perfect match to the construction industry. The forms don't reflect the way contractor's estimates are traditionally laid out and calculated, and the estimating screen looks like a typical invoice rather than an estimate. You enter items on a line-by-line basis as if you were filling out an invoice.

Limited calculating abilities

The program has refined the use of drop-down lists for tracking material and labor costs, but material and labor aren't bundled together. Furthermore, QuickBooks Pro can't do material calculations. You're limited to multiplying the quantity by the cost. You can't set square, linear, or cubic dimensions or other units of measure when calculating quantities, and the program multiplies quantity only by unit cost. You can add a column that indicates what unit of measure you use for the quantity, but you still have to do the calculations off the screen. This is partially due to the layout of the estimating sheet, which resembles a traditional material invoice. The database likewise follows a format that seems more suitable for a retail establishment: item, unit price.

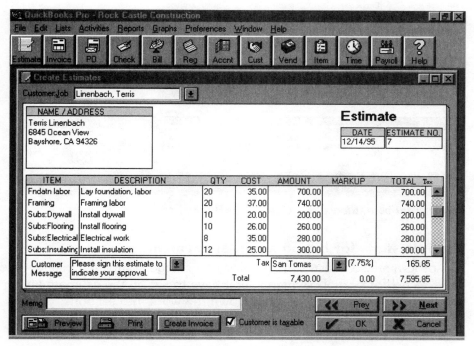

The Estimate screen in QuickBooks Pro resembles a materials invoice.

You can either arrange your estimate as a single line or create a detailed estimate. You can combine labor and material as a unit and come up with a unit price to perform an aspect of the work, but when you put together multiple line items you lose the ability to track the individual units. The program is set up so labor and material for each line item are entered on separate lines, rather than following the construction industry standard of estimating labor and material on one line.

As it's probably important for you to know how well you estimate the cost of each type of work that goes into a job, you won't want to use a single line item to represent all the work of a project in your own internal reports. If you're working a project as a subcontractor, you might want to show only a single price to the general contractor, but for your own records you probably need to prepare a more detailed estimate, with a separate line time for each specialized task. Then, as the job proceeds, you'll be able to create reports comparing your estimated costs with actual costs.

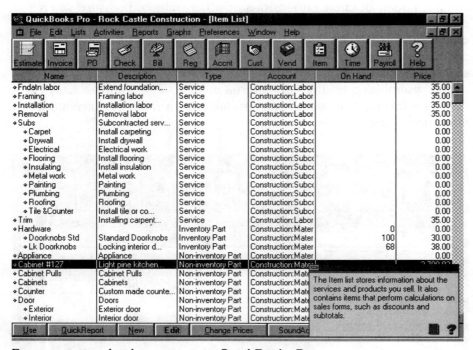

Representative database screen in QuickBooks Pro.

Multiple steps for billing a partial payment

The program also doesn't provide for percentage completed billing. In order to bill for partial payments, you have to set up the estimate and invoice into sections. By breaking down the work into sections, you can bill for each section as an installment. When you bill at established time intervals by percentage completed, you can maintain your billing cycle and adjust for delays or speed-up of any segment of the work.

Memorized transactions act as editable templates

Memorized transactions of all sorts permeate the program, speeding the estimating process while reducing the possibility of categorizing an item under two headings. When doing work similar to a past project, you can pull up the estimate and treat the memorized transaction as an editable template.

The estimate form is fairly customizable. It includes a notepad onto which you can add commentary pertaining to the project. You can add or delete columns, change the headings, and control which columns print out for customer viewing. For example, you can see line markups on screen, yet exclude them from printed copies you might show your client.

Nifty job-tracking capabilities

Job tracking is quite comprehensive and includes job type, job status, and start and completion dates. You can track employees' hours on a seven-day calendar, indicating which jobs the work was performed on and what tasks were performed, and the status of each project. If jobs are tracked by type, you can later prepare reports based on the job type to determine how profitable over time you're doing with the work. When you categorize your work from your estimates, you can transfer the costs to track both the expenses and the income for these items by job type. When you track time on specific jobs, the program also includes payroll costs.

	Est. Cost	Act. Cost	[$] Diff.	[%] Diff.	Est. Revenue	Act. Revenue	[$] Diff.	[%] Diff.
Parts								
Counter top	1,900.00	1,900.00	0.00	0.0%	2,185.00	2,375.00	190.00	8.7%
Cabinet	525.00	575.00	50.00	9.5%	577.50	577.50	0.00	0.0%
Total Parts	2,425.00	2,475.00	50.00	2.1%	2,762.50	2,952.50	190.00	6.9%
Service								
Installation	320.00	190.00	-130.00	-40.6%	384.00	480.00	96.00	25.0%
Painting	120.00	76.00	-44.00	-36.7%	144.00	192.00	48.00	33.3%
Total Service	440.00	266.00	-174.00	-39.5%	528.00	672.00	144.00	27.3%
TOTAL	2,865.00	2,741.00	-124.00	-4.3%	3,290.50	3,624.50	334.00	10.2%

Job-costing information from QuickBooks Pro. Intuit

Job tracking includes keeping accounting tabs on services, materials, and other charges. When you set up an item, you can select how it's handled. For example, you can set up a service performed by a subcontractor or a material item for a specific client or job. You can pass through the cost with a markup to the client and track the expenses and incomes in separate accounts that are set up for the jobs. When using time tracking, you can transfer the data to payroll and print out checks. The seamless data flow among integrated estimating, time tracking, payroll, and job costing functions assures that accurate, consistent data flows automatically throughout the program, requiring you to enter the information only once.

The program is available both on CD-ROM and on disk. The disk version comes with softcover manuals. The CD-ROM version doesn't; the manuals are on the disk. Even better, though, when you click on a SoundAdvice button available on many screen, you get step-by-step, well-thought-out, audio instructions on just how to proceed in that area of the program. The sample database is, conveniently, set up for a construction company and includes estimates, an estimate database, a progress schedule, and typical bills.

Precision Estimating for Windows

Precision Estimating for Windows (Timberline Software, 800-628-6583) is the first Windows estimating package by Timberline Software, long-time providers of DOS-based software for the construction field. While many of the features from their DOS estimating program are included in this new Windows product, there are many entirely new features. The program was written from the ground up to work under Windows 95, taking advantage of that operating system's strengths.

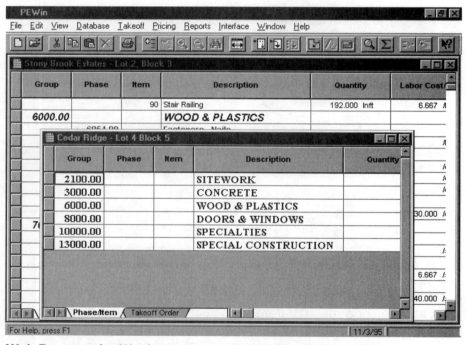

With Precision for Windows, you can build your estimate on a graphical, interactive spreadsheet. Timberline Software

Precision Estimating for Windows is a spreadsheet-type estimating program. Unlike many conventional programs, however, which require you to save your work as you go along, Precision Estimating for Windows continuously saves the estimate on which you're working to the hard disk. This is a valuable asset because incidents happen and not always right after you save your work. When you start a new estimate, you give it a name. Then the program constantly saves the file to disk. (Therefore, the Save and Save As commands found under the File command in other Windows programs don't appear in this program.)

Easy resequencing of estimate screens

The estimating screen resembles a spreadsheet in appearance and is formatted with the usual columns for labor, material, and quantity. The layout is customizable on a job-by-job basis to your own general format or to the format set up by Timberline. You can instantly (with no sort down-time) resequence the estimate screen in four ways: by phase/item, by take-off order, by location (such as first floor, second floor, building A, building B) or by work breakdown structure (WBS), which is user-definable.

A choice of take-off methods

Precision Estimating for Windows lets you use any of three types of take-off methods: quick take-off, item take-off, and assembly take-off. With the quick take-off method, you drag and drop desired items from the database to the estimate or spreadsheet screen. With drag and drop, you select an item with your mouse and, while holding the mouse button down, move the item over to the spreadsheet. It will automatically be placed correctly within the sequencing.

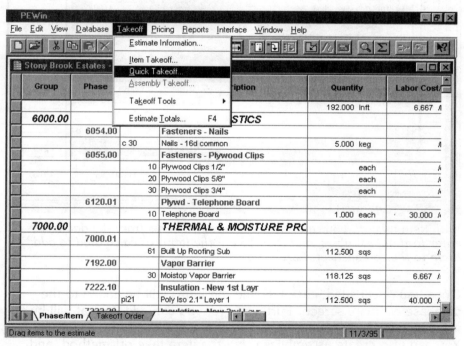

Precision for Windows offers three takeoff methods. Timberline Software

With all three estimating modes, items dragged and dropped from the database to the estimate are automatically listed in the proper hierarchy, based on CSI codes or any other user-defined structure. As additional items are added to the estimate, they're automatically inserted in the proper order. This feature is particularly helpful if you're building estimates based on take-off rather than by category.

While in item take-off mode, the database screen is superimposed over the spreadsheet estimate and holds three smaller windows: the database, the parameters for the highlighted item in the database, and a miniature spreadsheet that shows the items selected until accepted onto the spreadsheet. When you enter an item on the mini-spreadsheet, you can accept the default parameters set for the item, including unit and unit cost, or you can alter the defaults. The program automatically calculates the extension with any item you select—such as sheetrock or studs—with the built-in formulas. You can change the formula variables and the recalculated item on the miniature spreadsheet.

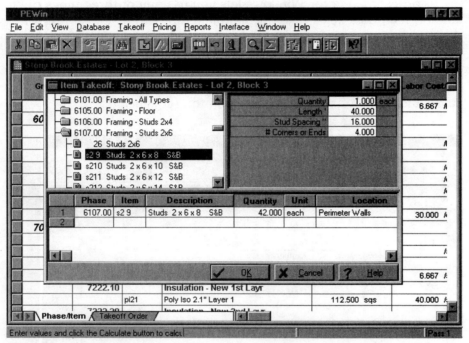

With item takeoff, you can select one or more items from the database, enter formula variables, and then accept the items as calculated to add them to the spreadsheet. Timberline Software

Once you're satisfied, click OK and the items will be added to the database estimate screen. Furthermore, you can add item at will by using personalized coding or coding that comes with the program. You can also create assemblies using the item take-off method, and save all components by clicking the appropriate button on the main menu bar. This is a graphically easy manner of making assemblies. Using assemblies can greatly increase estimating speed and efficiency.

General and specialty databases

The program comes with nine databases of about 1,000 items each: general contractor (commercial), home builder, remodeling, sitework/demolition, concrete/masonry, steel fabrication, interior finish, mechanical, and electrical. It might be wise to customize the values to fit company circumstances. The company also offers ten advanced databases, ranging from 2,500 to 17,000 items each. Options include acoustical/drywall, conceptual, and home builder. Third-party databases ordered from Timberline and produced by R.S. Means and Richardson Engineering can also be integrated with the software.

As items are entered onto the spreadsheet, they're automatically inserted in CSI chronology. This handy feature frees you from having to compile all like items beforehand. As you enter them on the spreadsheet, they're dated and timed both on screen and in an audit trail, so you can see precisely when each item was taken off or changed. There's a provision for several lines of miscellaneous detail for every item.

Another small but significant perk is that the software has combined in one cell both the value and the unit. This makes it easier to recognize the nature of the quantity in the cell, such as dollars, rates, square feet, and units.

The program uses file tabs in a logical fashion to store information in subcategories within categories. For example, on the Estimate Information screen, you can click on tabs for client, architect/engineer, job classification, and even bid results, among other choices.

Omissions are automatically detected

Scan mode is another nice feature. In a lengthy estimate, where it's possible to forget to add a number or extend a price, scan mode— operating something like a spell checker in concept—scans the estimate for any missing prices, rates, or amounts. If it picks up any omissions, it alerts you and allows you to make the corrections.

Precision Estimating for Windows takes ample advantage of the Windows 95 MDI (multiple document interface) capability. MDI facilitates the opening of documents into separate smaller windows within the larger window. This expedites working with the information from more than one estimate at a time. You can drag and drop lines or sections of estimates between estimates.

Following the work flow with WinEst Pro

WinEst Pro (WinEstimator, Inc., 800-950-2374) is a potent, high-end Windows estimating program that couples the advantages of current computer technology with logical estimating procedures. It's powerful enough to easily estimate projects ranging in the seven figures.

The program follows a *work-flow format* in developing bids; you start by opening a new job file and follow a suggested sequence in developing the bid, e.g., perform detailed take-off, analyze labor and material pricing, get totals, and add markups. Two of the program's strongest features are the variety of ways you can customize how you bid and the many filters you can apply to the data when doing bid analysis.

Toggling among screen views

The program has a logical layout and large-size icon buttons across the top of the screen. The icons represent item take-off, estimate sheet, totals page, print report, add items, unique items, activate digitizer, activate calculator, and edit items. It's very easy to switch among item take-off, estimate sheet, and totals page.

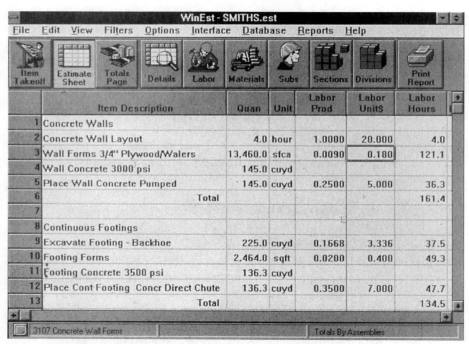

WinEstPro uses a graphical icon bar, for easy selection on the estimating screen. WinEstimator, Inc.

Automatically indexing added items

The program uses the Construction Specification Institute (CSI) coding format for all items in the database, in organizing the estimate, and in all reports. The database items come with formulas for calculating the item value. For example, the program will calculate the number of studs or volume of concrete automatically. When adding a new item to the database, the program prompts you to place it according to the CSI code. This automatic indexing allows for proper insertion of additional items, and proper placement in any report or summary you call up. You can also add a unique item to the cost database after it's added to your estimate.

Bid take-off screen

You access the database and do your bidding through the bid take-off screen. This is actually a powerful spreadsheet with about 40 columns preconfigured to automatically calculate the designated item. The database items are accessed by CSI number, name, or assembly. For general items, the CSI numbering system takes you from the general to the specific in four split screens. Click on as many items as you need, when done select Add, and the items will automatically be inserted into the bid sheet. Some of the values are calculated; others require additional unit pricing or labor rates to finalize the row. This is a good, straightforward, database access method.

The WinEstimator databases aren't kept current, so don't expect accurate prices. Though updating labor rates is relatively easy, updating a large material database requires getting prices on potentially hundreds of items. Sometimes, then, updating isn't really worth the manual effort. You might do better buying a third-party database designed to work with the program, created by either R.S. Means or Richardson. WinEstimator sells them specifically for their programs.

Global changes save time

With some programs, you can change only the database values for the current estimate; in WinEst Pro, you can change any value globally. You can also create customized templates for specific types of projects, selecting how and in what order the information is displayed, as well as which column headings you want to use.

It's easy to add items to a bid that are unique for a given job, or even add your own frequently bid items to the database. You can bid a project by listing individual parts or various assemblies. There are three categories of assemblies: conceptual, detailed, and parametric. A *detailed assembly* consists of a group of specific individual items used together to complete a task. A *conceptual assembly* consists of a group of general items used together to complete a task. A *parametric assembly* consists of mathematical averages used to calculate, in either detailed or general scope, construction relationships.

The software offers options to print out various estimate summaries. Go back and change a number and the program will automatically revise the entire estimate.

Software tie-in with CAD packages

WinEst Pro integrates with various CAD programs, allowing you to directly enter items with a digitizer. You can also move data into a scheduling program to analyze your bid. If you get the project you're bidding, you'd already have the job scheduled with the proposed work flow optimized for the best allocation of resources. The item take-off gives you access to the database. The estimate sheet is where you view the collection of items you put together to create an estimate.

The Totals page allows for markup and bonding costs, and lets you view the totals in summary fashion. If your office estimates large projects involving multiple estimators working on separate segments, you can merge their estimates together. WinEst Pro also lets you calculate markups on the totals page in a manner that allows for burden and maintenance calculations or fixed hourly add-ons to labor and equipment. An option in the Markups dialog multiplies a fixed dollar value by the total quantity of labor or equipment hours in the estimate.

Work breakdown possibilities

The work breakdown structure, within which you can define an estimate line item by up to seven subcategories, is user-friendly. You can change the seven pre-defined categories, and use the categories to sort items for bid evaluation, work scheduling, or material ordering. The different categories are location, bid item, system, sublocation, uniform sequence, material class, job cost phase number, scheduling task, CAD reference, and company internal format. And under the seven categories you can set up subcodes.

You can attach notes to any line item in your estimate, which is handy for recording information from vendors or subcontractors. The manual is both comprehensive and well written. Illustrations abound. Learning the program should be no problem.

Technical support over a toll number is available, for the price of the call, for 90 days. Support goes into effect from the date of purchase, not from the date of your first call, so it's wise not to dally getting the program out of the box.

In addition to WinEst Pro, the company also offers WinEst Pro Plus, which is a multiuser version, and Residential, a scaled-down version of WinEst Pro. The optional databases are by R.S. Means and Richardson, and you can also order additional WinEst Pro databases. The company also has an electronic bulletin board (BBS), from which you can download a demonstration disk, technical support help files, and product information.

A trio of easy-to-learn estimating programs for DOS

The expression "to each his (or her) own" is never truer, it seems, than when it comes to estimating. When it comes to pricing out a job, how estimators work is often a matter of how they were taught, their specialty, and outright personal preference. When it comes to computer estimating software, sometimes it's hard to find a match to your own particular style. Not surprisingly, if a program's developer has estimating experience, the software created will often reflect past estimating practice. Whether it matches yours is another story.

With that in mind, the trio of estimating programs by Turbo Construction Estimator (800-321-1624) might be particularly helpful in satisfying a wide range of residential remodeling contracting, subcontracting, and new-home building needs because they offer a variety of choices in ways to estimate. In order of capabilities and prices, from low end to top of the line, they are: Rapid Estimator, Lightning Estimator, and—the flagship product—Turbo Construction Estimator.

The three programs share the same overall look and style of operation. The primary differences include variations in the size of the databases and the numbers of database categories, estimate sections and capacity for items per section, and printing capabilities.

Across-the-board easy operating

The programs, unencumbered by complicated database codes, have color-coded screens for easy identification of where you are, familiar pull-down menus, and appropriate function-key choices for each screen listed across the bottom. Each is menu driven—you can select either the first letter of a menu choice or highlight a choice and press Enter—and features pop-up menu windows and several convenient hot keys for quicker access to choices.

The on-screen instructions make sense on first reading—no mean feat in itself—and expedite easy learning and quick estimating, even the first time out. The last estimate worked on is filed on top of the estimate directory, so you're set to proceed as soon as you start the program.

Each program has its place

If you're a subcontractor or if the projects you do are small and repetitive in nature, the entry-level Rapid Estimator, with room for 500 items in the database, might be a good fit. Lightning is well-tuned for light commercial and large remodels, and Turbo for all sizes of commercial and residential estimating.

In any of the programs, you can start estimating by selecting new estimate as either a new construction project or a remodeling project. The label headings conform to the nature of the work. The software is set up to categorize jobs, using section titles called *phases* for new construction and *rooms* for renovation projects. Phases can be excavation, foundation, etc., while rooms are just that: kitchen, dining room, living room, etc. Selecting a phase or room opens a full-screen worksheet onto which you add all line items pertaining to the category.

```
┌ Grand Total ┐        ┌ Sub Total ┐
Jan/17/94   10:24am    │ 273,292.99* │    │  30,143.08* │

═══ Estimate Window ══[ Building Phase:  MECHANICAL ]═══
Estimate Name:  NEWCONST                        Unit       Total
Quantity    Unit  Work Description              Price      Price

 2,286.00  SF    Rough in electrical             2.01    4,600.58
    27.00  Ea    allowance on electric fixtures 75.00    2,025.00
     1.00  Ea    Set Fixtures allowance        812.50      812.50

                 --------Appliances--------
     1.00  Ea    Install refrigerators GE #TFX24RL  1,718.75  1,718.75
     1.00  Ea    Install range hood             468.75      468.75
     1.00  Ea    Install Cooktop Dacor #GGC365 1,030.00    1,030.00
     1.00  Ea    Oven Dacor # 305            1,718.75    1,718.75
     1.00  Ea    Install dishwasher GE #1130   623.75      623.75

                 --------Heating--------
 2,286.00  Ea    Wishbo Radiant Heating system   7.50   17,145.00
                 To be verified by Wirsbo estimate

[Enter]=DataBase    F1=Help  F3=Custom  F5=Copy  F7=Delete  F9=Calculator
[/]=Options Menu    F2=Save  F4=Change  F6=Move  F8=Next    F10=Dimensions
```

Estimate screen in Turbo Construction Estimator. Turbo Construction Estimator

Old estimates can serve as templates for new ones

You can also build a new estimate by taking a previous one and using it as a template, then saving the newer one under a different name. As you proceed in putting together the project, both the total for each section (phase or room) and the grand total are always shown on top of all the worksheets.

The databases aren't exhaustive, but are meant rather as a starting point. They're indexed by categories, and you can pull data from any category into any phase or room, providing great flexibility in your estimate design. The building phases or rooms and the database categories aren't linked, so you can retrieve any database item for inclusion into any worksheet. All items in the database can be altered. You can also change database entries without leaving an estimate in progress.

The Custom Estimate Input window allows you to add any item at any juncture into the appropriate worksheet. A nifty extra feature in Turbo: when in the Estimate Input window, you can add global room dimensions and overall project dimensions that are used by the program in calculating quantities and prices.

Turbo and Lightning allow for user-defined trade categories, which makes these programs particularly flexible and attuned to your own terminology. Turbo alone features section resources, so you can save part of an estimate to a resource file for reuse in another estimate.

By developing your resource file, you can pull entire predefined sections into new estimates for repetitive estimating. This is a particularly powerful capability that gives you, in effect, a third way of estimating.

All three programs have pop-up calculators, the ability to change databases while working in an estimate, and a variety of print options. Turbo and Lightning also allow you to either show or hide all levels of pricing, and hide profit and quantities from clients and competitors when printing. One drawback is that you can't view the reports on screen before you print.

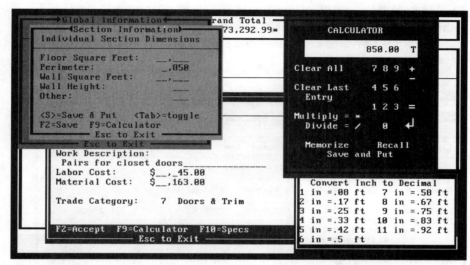

Calculating options abound in Turbo Construction Estimator.
Turbo Construction Estimator

Top-of-the-line Turbo Construction Estimator confers several very handy flexibilities beyond the first two programs, including the ability to mark up or discount automatically, reuse parts of past estimates in current estimates, and total subcontractors individually. It also offers automatic backup and numerous database print options, including a special printout for subcontractor job and material lists.

You can try out the software yourself at minimal cost; the company offers full working copies of Lightning and Turbo for $15 each, with built-in clocks that disable printing ability after 30 days. If you want to go ahead with the program, you just call the company and arrange for full payment and an access code. The company offers free technical support.

Fast Track Estimating

Fast Track Estimating (Northwest Construction Software, 800-368-6335), which is geared directly to the needs of remodeling contractors, is a versatile and flexible program that offers a direct and quite fast route to preparing remodeling estimates. It's customizable and therefore suitable for any size or type of project. The program is easy to master; it has only four general divisions: Do Estimates; Print

Estimating and Bid Reports; Maintain Standard Cost Database (for labor, materials, and other cost variables); and Systems Parameters, which includes a hierarchy of password protection.

The program comes with a material database of hundreds of items and over one thousand assemblies, and virtually limitless expansion capabilities in either category. Each assembly includes all components needed to build a specified section of the work. Entering or updating any estimate is a streamlined process of either pulling in the database items and using the standard computed costs or substituting your own prices.

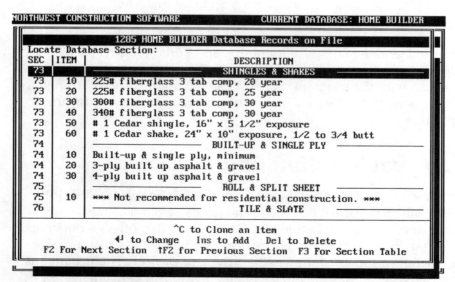

```
NORTHWEST CONSTRUCTION SOFTWARE                CURRENT DATABASE: HOME BUILDER
┌─────────────────────────────────────────────────────────────────────────┐
│                       Enter/Update Estimate Line Item                      │
│                          Record will be Changed                            │
│                                                                            │
│  Line Number      :   5      Database Item    : 064.0010                   │
│                              ──── DESCRIPTION ────                         │
│       2" x 4" x  8' int. L.B. wall  = studs/nails                          │
│                                                                            │
│  Number of LF     :   12.00      Standard Pricing? Y (Y or N)              │
│                                                                            │
│  Labor Cost       : 0.3 hrs of Carpenter, Rough @$16.00/hr or $4.800/LF    │
│  Material Cost    : $5.388/LF                                              │
│                  — PER UNIT COST —    —EXT. COST—   — MARKUP —  — PRICE —   │
│                  STANDARD  COST USED               STANDARD ACTUAL         │
│  Labor             $4.80    $4.80      $57.60       1.15   1.15    $66.24   │
│  Material          $5.39    $5.39      $64.68       1.15   1.15    $74.38   │
│  Subcontract       $0.00    $0.00       $0.00       1.15   1.15     $0.00   │
│  Other Cost        $0.00    $0.00       $0.00       1.15   1.15     $0.00   │
│                                                                            │
│     Total                              $122.28                  $140.62    │
│                                                                            │
│  ^↵ to Save    ^Esc to Cancel    ^M to Toggle Multi-Add   ~C for Calculator│
└─────────────────────────────────────────────────────────────────────────┘
```

Estimate line item detail from Fast Track Estimating.
Northwest Construction Software

```
NORTHWEST CONSTRUCTION SOFTWARE                CURRENT DATABASE: HOME BUILDER
┌─────────────────────────────────────────────────────────────────────────┐
│                  1285 HOME BUILDER Database Records on File                 │
│  Locate Database Section:                                                  │
│  SEC │ITEM│                        DESCRIPTION                             │
│  73  │    │                   SHINGLES & SHAKES                            │
│  73  │ 10 │ 225# fiberglass 3 tab comp, 20 year                           │
│  73  │ 20 │ 225# fiberglass 3 tab comp, 25 year                           │
│  73  │ 30 │ 300# fiberglass 3 tab comp, 30 year                           │
│  73  │ 40 │ 340# fiberglass 3 tab comp, 30 year                           │
│  73  │ 50 │ # 1 Cedar shingle, 16" x 5 1/2" exposure                      │
│  73  │ 60 │ # 1 Cedar shake, 24" x 10" exposure, 1/2 to 3/4 butt          │
│  74  │    │                   BUILT-UP & SINGLE PLY                        │
│  74  │ 10 │ Built-up & single ply, minimum                                │
│  74  │ 20 │ 3-ply built up asphalt & gravel                               │
│  74  │ 30 │ 4-ply built up asphalt & gravel                               │
│  75  │    │                   ROLL & SPLIT SHEET                           │
│  75  │ 10 │ *** Not recommended for residential construction. ***         │
│  76  │    │                   TILE & SLATE                                 │
│                                                                            │
│                        ^C to Clone an Item                                 │
│              ↵ to Change    Ins to Add    Del to Delete                    │
│        F2 For Next Section  ↑F2 for Previous Section  F3 For Section Table │
└─────────────────────────────────────────────────────────────────────────┘
```

Database screen from Fast Track Estimating.
Northwest Construction Software

Five comprehensive report formats, all viewable on screen before printing, offer some choice in how you present the numbers. The reports show in both detail and summary fashion items such as a full detail list with all costs, price, add-ons, and tax; estimated costs, before markup by room/area and by type of work; bid reports of marked-up prices to show clients, also by room/area or by work type; detailed or summary-only material order lists for purchasing and field use; and a labor cost report that shows estimated costs by craft.

Companion program for fast proposals

Northwest Construction has a companion program, Fast Track Proposal Writing, that, when used in conjunction with the estimating program, practically puts together your proposal for you. If the program is installed into Fast Track Estimating, then, while you're working up your estimate, you're also—in effect—putting together your proposal. By pressing the appropriate keys, you can simultaneously copy to your proposal the very paragraphs referenced by the database items you select for your estimate.

Fast Track Proposal Writing helps you produce proposals, which upon acceptance by a client, can easily be turned into a contract. Working like a topic-specific word processing program, the software is packed with a smorgasbord of 300 preformatted boilerplate paragraphs of proposal language describing most common remodeling tasks, which you can cut and paste wherever you choose.

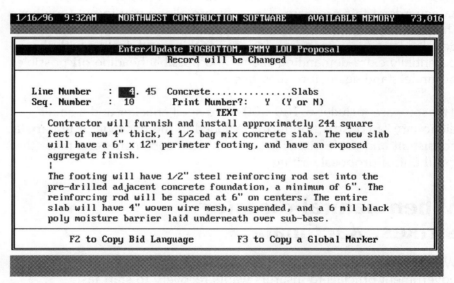

Representative screen, on concrete mix, using Fast Track Proposal Writing. Northwest Construction Software

```
1. Contractor will furnish all necessary plans for the completion
   of this job.

   Plans will include the following drawings as needed:

   Plat, foundation, floor plan, elevations, sections, layout,
   soffit layout, plumbing, electrical, H.V.A.C., schedules, and
   general job information as needed.

2. Contractor will furnish a sum of money as required by the local
   public authority to provide assurance that any work on the
   public street, sidewalks, or streetside curbs adjacent to the
   Owners property will be completed.

3. Contractor will pay for and obtain all necessary permits to
   complete this job.

4. Contractor's scope of work shall not include the
   identification, detection, or removal of lead base paint from
   the home.
```

```
↑↓↔ Scroll   PGUP Page up   PGDN Page down   END bottom   HOME top   ESC Quit
```

Representative screen, regarding boilerplate text in contract form, using Fast Track Proposal Writing. Northwest Construction Software

In creating your proposal, you can use the language as is or modify to suit. To expedite the whole process even further, you can even create maxi-templates that link a number of commonly used paragraphs that you can then copy as a group into any proposal.

The program has aimed at crafting the master proposal language in order to preclude contractor/client misunderstandings. If you've ever experienced a gut reaction along the lines of "Uh-oh, here comes a fussy client," then you'll appreciate the built-in precautionary safeguards of this program. The software allows you to put together a short-form proposal, adequate for typical prospects, or a more detailed long-form proposal, for approaching and dealing with those potentially extra-demanding clients and possibly heading off possible misunderstandings before they occur.

The software includes a 100,000-word spell checker and a small dictionary of construction terms included in the package. It imparts a consistent and professional look to finished documents and takes the grind out of proposal writing.

When natural disaster strikes, Xactimate

When natural disaster strikes, everyone from property owners and government officials to insurers wants recovery to start fast. Rebuilding becomes top priority. A major part of beginning the assessment and recovery process after devastating floods, hurricanes, earthquakes, or fires is preparing accurate damage estimates. Faster estimating means faster claim settlement. Xactimate (Xactware, Inc. 800-932-9228) is a high-end structural damage appraisal and reconstruction estimation software package that can help remodeling and restoration contractors, adjusters, and estimators at insurance companies estimate material and cost for repairs, reconstruction, cleaning, or replacement of damaged residences, commercial buildings, offices, and other sites.

Popular package with insurance companies

This software was originally developed for builders, but is also widely used by many insurance companies. If you work frequently with insurance companies frequently on recovery work and want estimating software that's in sync with insurance companies, this is a good bet. Check and see if they use this package. Even if they don't, of course, you can.

Suitable software for on-site processing

Many estimators using this type of software find it expedient to move through a site with a laptop in one hand and a stepladder on which to position the laptop at each stop in the other hand. Loading in the data is almost instantaneous and the calculations are essentially complete at the end of the on-site visit. If you really want to take advantage of the latest technology, you can carry a laptop loaded with Xactimate, a portable printer (usually a bubble- or inkjet) to print out the estimate on the spot, and even a portable modem to fax out the estimate. If you get approval on the job order, you can even print out the estimate and get authorization (for work approval) on the spot from the property owner. This could really speed up the recovery process!

Hardcopy scope sheets and flip charts

You can also use, on site, the traditional paperbound scope sheets (or tick sheets) that come with the big black portfolio packaged with the software, and then systematically transcribe the data to Xactimate when back in the office for immediate printouts of estimates and reports. The flip chart at the top of the portfolio lists all the commercial and residential price list items by abbreviation, alphabetized by categories, e.g., acoustical treatments, cabinetry, cleaning, wrecking, and hauling through a total of over 60 divisions, and then alphabetically within those divisions. The flip chart also includes printouts of the built-in formulas for odd-shaped rooms or slope-ceiling rooms.

You can also use a separate Contents Cleaning scope sheet with 16 categories, for a total of over 250 separate listings of furniture, equipment, appliances, floor coverings, and water extraction services, to list every item that has to be cleaned.

Talk, tape, and transcribe

Another possible way to use Xactimate is to walk through the job site with a hand-held tape recorder and record the data. Then, when back in the office, you can play back the tape and transcribe the data into the program.

With pull-down menus, scrolling lists, WYSIWYG (what you see is what you get) screens, built-in interactive lessons, and context-sensitive tutorials, Xactimate is user-friendly from the outset. The lessons provide basic training for the novice with a step-by-step tutorial through an entire sample estimate. Once you're on your own, you can tap the special Help key (or use the mouse) to call up a tutorial for step-by-step help at any juncture. There's also standard context-sensitive help available throughout.

Key market customized databases

A built-in database listing prices for over 10,000 line items (materials, labor, taxes, soft costs, and other construction-related items) forms the core of the program. In addition to a database of national averages, you can choose from residential, commercial, and cleaning databases customized for over 475 key markets in the United States and most of Canada. Prices are updated quarterly.

Every price item in the database includes a description of the materials and labor. Many of the items also include illustrations. You can pull them up to see what the actual item is like and view a listing of what components are included in the price, so estimators, property owners, and insurers all recognize what's included or excluded on each item. For example, an illustration of a half-louvered door shows that pricing includes jamb, casing, and hinges, but not hardware.

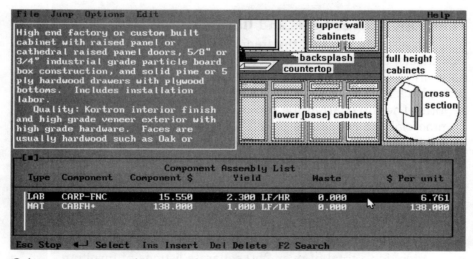

Cabinet component layout and assembly list from Xactimate. Xactware

There are also illustrations and formulas available for many price items that make dimensioning odd-shaped rooms or figuring complex assemblies such as joist systems, dormers, and rafters much easier. There are several roofing formulas to help you calculate the squares in several types of roofing systems, including circular, conical, gambrel, and mansard.

Four selection processes and two ways to compile data

You can select estimation items in four ways: by mouse, by manipulating tab and arrow keys, by keyword search, or by typing in simple codes. (Xactimate has thoughtfully used abbreviations commonly used by adjusters and builders, e.g., ½-inch drywall = DRY ½. You can work room by room, phase by phase, or both. When you enter dimensions and select price list items, the software automatically calculates necessary materials (including waste) and costs. You can opt for the summary screen to show an estimate summary by price list item or by trade, and you can edit while in the screen.

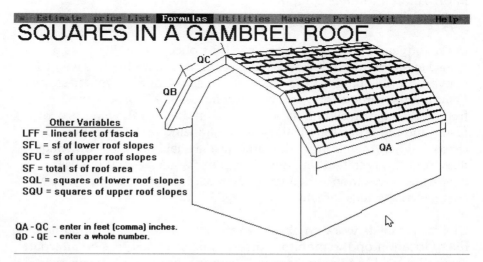

Roof formula screen for a gambrel roof from Xactimate. Xactware

Xactimate computes soft as well as hard costs, including workman's compensation, as well as overhead and profit. You can print estimates, price lists, formulas, and reference printouts, all of which are customizable. You can also select to print time and material breakouts, material bills, work orders, frequency of item usage reports, as well as estimator, performance, and other management reports.

The software has the built-in capability to handle digital images, either those taken by your digital camera or those scanned in. You can either view the images or print them with the estimates. You can fax estimates and worksheets directly from the program, as long as you have a fax/modem.

Quarterly updates for the price list are free during the first year, as are any program upgrades, and there's free technical support for the first year. The program is a 32-bit DOS-based application, but can be run through Windows 3.1 and Windows 95.

Golden rule

No matter what estimating system you use, if it doesn't come with automatic backup on a continuous basis, be sure to back up your work frequently as you go. You don't want to lose the time you save in performing electronic estimating by having to build and edit your database a second time around.

Digitizers

Contractors and estimators who want to enter graphical-based information into their computers conveniently in order to perform accurate and fast take-offs often use graphical input devices.

In recent years, graphics tablets, used in concert with digitizers and transducers (pointing devices), have become a cost-effective way to convert graphic data for modification, analysis, and computer storage. Contractors, remodelers, and others who use CAD programs frequently might well find data input and the whole drawing process faster and more accurate if they use a digitizing tablet with pen or cursor. (When the contract drawings are available as CAD drawings on disk from the architect, engineer, or public agency—and this is increasingly common—then you can bypass the digitizing process. Just install the files directly into your CAD program.)

Digitizing tablets work on absolute rather than relative positioning. Every location on the monitor corresponds precisely to a counterpart on the tablet. Using a digitizer for electronic take-offs is faster than performing manual take-offs. And because it's so precise, you can cut down on built-in "overages" to offset possible inaccuracies. (But don't exclude waste factors.)

Drawing boards from CalComp

The DrawingBoard III series of digitizers (CalComp, 800-458-5888) offers contractors a choice of three small and three large tablets for drawing, tracing, drafting, mapping, and other computer graphic applications at relatively low prices and with lots of time- and effort-saving functionalities. Each drawing board comes with a choice of 4- or 16-button cursors and standard two-side button pens, either corded or cordless, or pressure-sensitive, cordless, two-side button pens. All come with digitizer software.

Straight-out-of-the-box operation

These digitizers are preconfigured to work automatically with various hardware brands and software packages. They come with 18 user-recordable macro capabilities, plus up to 16 additional user-recordable macro buttons for the cursor or pen. The menu strip is removable so you can replace it with one reflecting customized configurations and commands. Resolution is extremely high: operator-selectable up to 2,540 lines/inch and accuracy to ± 0.005 inch.

The boards are available in six sizes, from a 12 × 12-inch tablet (weighing just 4.1 pounds) up through a 44 × 60-inch unit, in both corded and cordless units. Each tablet comes with an interface kit, cables, manual, power supply, and a choice of transducer. The software operates under DOS 3.0 or higher and Microsoft Windows 3.1 or higher.

The tablets now feature fully automatic installation so you can orient the tablet immediately to whatever software package you're using. In Windows applications, the digitizer offers dynamic windowing, which makes it easier to switch between applications and makes efficient use of the whole surface of the tablet.

EstiMat from CalComp

CalComp also has a new line of lightweight yet durable flexible digitizers, called EstiMat (EstiMat, CalComp Corp., 800-932-1212). They're available in two sizes—D, with a 30 × 36-inch working area, and E, with a 36 × 48-inch working area—so users can work on the entire document at one time, rather than in sections. EstiMat acts as a full-functioning conventional digitizer, but can be rolled up for portability or storage when desk or table space is at a premium. The two sizes of EstiMat, weighing just seven and nine pounds, are rugged enough to weather a variety of field conditions. Each model also comes with a cordless pen or puck for entering graphical data for either computer-aided design (CAD) or estimate take-offs. You can also use either of the tools as a conventional mouse.

Direct data entry is possible

Some estimating programs allow for direct entry of digitizer take-off information. You can use EstiMat in this capacity if your estimating software gives you that capability. When using EstiMat this way, place the blueprint on the EstiMat and trace the specific elements of the drawing. The estimating software will electronically convert the information into the appropriate section of your estimate. Sophisticated estimating programs automatically calculate quantities and costs.

You can also use EstiMat in conjunction with numerous CAD programs, such as AutoCAD and DataCAD, to draw architectural plans or trace existing plans into the CAD program. The digitized image is then available for manipulation, alteration, and printout. This can save you time if you're responsible for creating "as built" drawings by using original plans as the starting point. The digitizing surface of EstiMat is a sturdy, heavy, gray plastic mat with rubber backing. It's

Roll-up EstiMat. CalComp Corp.

imprinted with blue dots every square inch throughout and with $\frac{1}{10}$-inch hash marks around the perimeter of the working area. A grooved 2½-inch controller bar running along one short edge houses the electronic components and will conveniently hold the electronic pen. EstiMat can be connected by a standard RS-232 serial port to your desktop, notebook, or laptop computer.

Hand-use preference and pointing devices

To accommodate both left-handed and right-handed operation, users can set up EstiMat for two orientations, with the controller housing at either the left or the right edge. There are two menu strips, one for each orientation. Each strip has 18 user-recordable macro buttons on the surface, for configuring the tablet for your programs and playing them back by selecting the buttons.

CalComp offers two types of cordless, battery-operated pointing devices that interact with the conductors beneath the surface of EstiMat to pick up the signals: a two-side button and click-tip electronic pen (often used for rapid sketching, menu selection, and digitizing) and a four- or 16-button puck for accurate, detailed digitizing.

These devices look and feel like ergonomically sculpted mice with the addition, at one end, of a circular lens with crosshairs. (For increased accuracy, the crosshairs are etched on the bottom on the lens.) The buttons can be used for additional macros. With the 16-button puck, you can set up 16 additional macros.

Relative or absolute positioning

You can use the pointing devices on the tablet with either relative or absolute positioning. A traditional mouse works only on relative positioning—if you pick the mouse up and put it elsewhere on the tablet, the cursor on the screen hasn't moved. In absolute positioning, which is the way to use a digitizer when you're drawing, locations on the surface of the tablet correspond precisely to a counterpart on the screen. So every time you put the cursor on the upper left of the tablet, for instance, your screen cursor will always be in the same coordinate as represented on the tablet.

EstiMat comes with the very versatile CalComp digitizer software, which gives the pen or puck added capability beyond standard mouse and digitizing functions. For example, with the software, you can set up macros; tablet mapping for DOS programs; tablet configuration, intelligent configuration, which adjusts the tablet configuration to automatically run optimally with assigned DOS programs; and dynamic windowing, which allows you to assign areas of the tablet to activate Windows programs.

Safety in the field with Roll-Up

Roll-Up II (GTCO Corporation, 800-344-4723) is a roll-up digitizer with a unique feature called *redundant grid technology*, which uses multiple paths to carry electrical signals. This feature protects against inadvertent field abuse. If some of the wires embedded in the material ever fail or if the surface is cut, other wires that follow other paths will continue to function so the tablet won't develop a dead spot.

The unit, which works with many CAD and estimating programs, comes in three active area sizes, from 20 × 24 to 36 × 48, weighing between 4 pounds and a little over 7 pounds. The unit can be configured for either left- or right-handed orientation. As with CalComp's digitizers, both corded and cordless pointing devices are available, including a pressure-sensitive stylus pen. The pen can be set to 256 pressure levels and locked to your pressure preference.

You can purchase any size of the digitizer as part of the QuikRuler Measuring Workstation, which includes a pointing device, a measuring

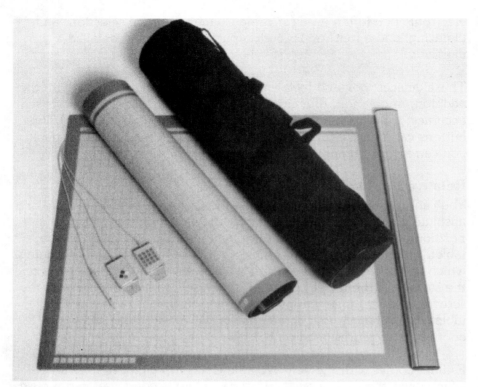

Roll-up digitizer by GTCO. GTCO Corp.

menu, an LCD display (for taking readings when you aren't hooked up to a computer), and a measuring program. The program allows you to use the measuring tools in conjunction with a spreadsheet or accounting program. It can calculate areas (including irregular areas), lengths, quantities, and units. The QuikRuler also performs standard calculator functions.

Scale-Link is an electronic ruler, plus . . .

Here is a clever comingling of two concepts: a hand-held, battery-operated scaler and bundled software for making fast take-offs and inserting those numbers into an estimating or spreadsheet program. The Scale-Link Computer-Input Plan Scaling System (Scale-Link, 800-653-3532) combines a digital plan scaler, Scale-Link, with two software programs, Take-Off and Take-Off Manager, to automatically scale dimensions into most applications, simplifying the estimating process and eliminating the risk of transposing errors. Barely larger than an oversized pen, Scale-Link works like any of the conventional free-standing scales when not connected to your computer, but has a built-in serial jack for connecting to a serial port in your computer.

Once plugged into your PC and working in concert with the Take-Off software, you set the scale to the plan, roll the device over the plan,

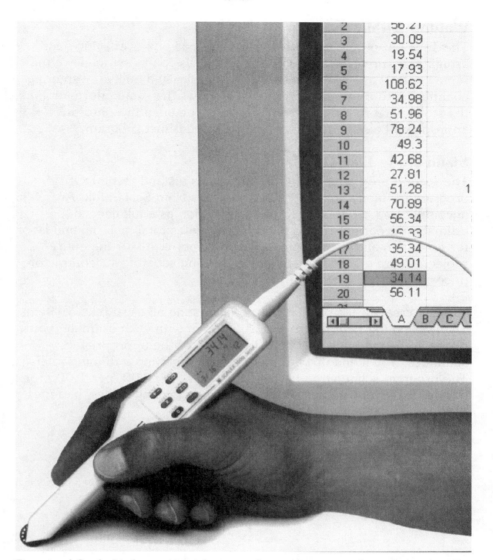

Pen-sized Scale-Link comes with two software programs for automatic scaling into software applications. Scale-Link

and your measurements are automatically entered onto the screen ready for insertion into your estimating or spreadsheet program.

Generous choice of scales

There are 52 preprogrammed scales, as well as three user-defined scale factors. Though it can measure regular areas and volumes bound by straight, perpendicular sides, it can't measure irregular areas and volumes. You can handle these, however, by breaking the irregular measurement into smaller regular measurements and then adding the results. Both DOS and Windows versions of this application are included in the package.

Window within a window

The Take-Off program is presented as a small box overlaying your estimate or spreadsheet program, and allows you to set many of the same controls as on the actual unit. It's basically a utility for entering quantities into estimating programs. It shows the same information as the scaler screen, but allows you to paste the quantities into the appropriate box of your estimating or spreadsheet program.

Stand-alone Take-Off Manager

The second program, Take-Off Manager, is a stand-alone DOS program for tabulating and saving take-offs from Scale-Link. An uncomplicated program that doesn't function as a full-fledged estimating program, it automatically calculates total material and labor for each item and adds the material and labor costs for the entire project. There are no provisions for entering separate subcontractor prices or overhead and profit.

You can create a file or master template listing all usual take-off items. Then, using the template as a starting point with each estimate, you can save the template as a new file and enter the appropriate quantities. You'll end up with a quick way of getting a running total. The program is limited to take-offs per each, per 100, per 1,000, or per lot. Scale-Link comes with software, connecting cables, batteries, and manual.

Project scheduling software

HENRY Kissinger once said there couldn't be a crisis the next week because his schedule was already full, a limitation no doubt often shared by hassled contractors on hectic jobs. Since no one has yet figured out how to get more hours in a work day, the best hope for getting everything done in the allotted time is still to maximize all possibilities. This is the focus of a special category of business software commonly called *project management programs*.

Hand tools were just the beginning

Noah's ark was the first structure to earn kudos from every sector. While we can't be sure whether or not it was built without conflicts or even within budget, that early architectural triumph was clearly built much as many of today's contractors would like to complete projects—on time.

In those days, all Noah had to rely on, in addition to dedicated workers, were hand tools, a healthy supply of wood, and faith that the weather would hold. Today, you can use a progress scheduling software program.

In modern times it seems that, despite the best intentions, no construction project runs smoothly. Somewhere along the way, obstacles, setbacks, slowdowns, weather, fickle decision-making, change orders, and priority shifts loom on most job sites. Conflicts surface and require resolution.

Automated progress scheduling

Progress scheduling software (which is also referred to in the computer industry as *project management software* is designed to help you manage projects and allocate resources (people power, equipment, and materials) for optimum time management and profit. A schedule is useful to help you organize your thoughts and intentions and share them with everyone involved, from direct labor and subcontractors to clients. Computerized scheduling presents schedule information quickly and easily on screen and in print through a variety of formats and reports. It also allows for quick updates to reflect actual job or project conditions and progress.

Formalized schedules

For contractors and remodelers specifically, project management offers an easy electronic way to set up work schedules, establish priorities, and adjust various scheduling elements to meet target finish dates and budget constraints, before and during the life of a project. It provides a formalized format in which you can manipulate the figurative building blocks—labor, equipment, materials, and funds—for maximum efficiency and the best bottom line.

Presenting a schedule to a client at the beginning of a project can be especially important if you use it as one of the qualifying documents to justify partial payment. If clients make alterations in the plans that require change orders, showing revised schedules helps justify the probable price and time increases. The schedule can reflect, visually, how any changes will affect the entire project. Not only should you bill for the cost of the change order, but you're entitled to recoup any additional cost incurred because of it. The schedule is a graphical representation to back up your charges.

Presenting a job superintendent or foreman, at the start of a project, with a schedule that's easy to understand and follow is equally important. Along with the right materials, tools, and workers, it's central to optimal productivity. Having a reference point for how and when various aspects of the job should unfold allows the foreman to plan the day (and week) carefully before the work has begun, arranging for equipment, auxiliary tools, and deliveries ahead of rather than when they're needed.

Project management

Before computer software addressed project management, it was a highly time-intensive, detail-oriented chore often limited to larger projects, or not formally done at all. Whether it replaces pad-and-pencil scheduling, "guesstimating," or just relying on hopeful expectations, the intent of a project management program is to put you in control of your projects, avoid conflicts, and solve problems before they arise by maximizing resources and containing costs.

A project management program helps you plan and control projects by setting up a dynamic schedule of how a job should proceed, and then helps you change that schedule to match a project's actual behavior when real life doesn't conform to the preconceived plan. Basically, you list all requisite activities, estimate the time necessary for completion, and link the activities in a logical fashion.

There are numerous competent scheduling programs that can work well for contractors, among them Computer Associates' SuperProject for Windows, Primavera's SureTrak Project Scheduler, Add-Vantage Software's The Scheduler's Add-Vantage, and Microsoft's Project for Windows.

Must-know terms

If you're thinking of going electronic for project management, here's a compendium of 26 commonly used project management terms and definitions to help you evaluate packages and determine whether or not what they offer fits your needs.

Activity An individual task that contributes to the achievement of the goal of a project; a basic component of a project.

Base calendar A calendar that determines when work for a particular activity can be performed; it lays out the work periods and the holidays for a project so activities can be scheduled within the designated period of time.

Baseline The initially planned project schedule, saved for later comparisons.

Constraint Restriction placed on start or finish dates of an activity, i.e., not earlier than or later than a particular date.

Critical activity An activity that must start and finish on scheduled dates, otherwise delays will occur that would push off the finish date of the project.

Critical path method Scheduling the entire project by determining the duration of a project based on a series of critical activities that must occur sequentially, from start to finish. Critical path scheduling calls upon and works in concert with your experience to develop time frames and interdependencies that determine start and finish dates for individual tasks. As you connect activities, you have to specify which part of the preceding activity, if any, controls which part of the following activity. The delay of any of the tasks affects subsequent tasks and thus the completion of the project.

Dependency The relationship between tasks, particularly when completion of A is necessary before start of B.

Duration The length of time a task takes to complete, in minutes, hours, days, weeks, months, or years.

Filtering Choosing particular activities according to specific attributes or combinations of attributes.

Float The amount of time a task can be delayed (slack time) without affecting the scheduled completion of the project.

Gantt chart A graphical bar chart depicting activities along a linear time scale, indicating—via elongation—the relationship between tasks.

The lengths of the bars are representative of the duration of each task, i.e., you can tell at a glance when tasks are scheduled.

Lag time The delay between two tasks that have a dependency expressed in hours, days, or a percentage.

Lead time The overlap between tasks that have a dependent relationship.

Leveling Resolving overallocation of resources by delaying various tasks according to priorities.

Link The logical dependent relationship between two tasks.

Milestone A durationless task that signifies an intermediate deadline date or important achievement of a specific phase of a project.

Overallocation The result of too many task assignments for any one resource within a particular working time period.

PERT chart Project evaluation review technique for evaluation and resource tracking, a network chart visually representing interdependencies among a series of linked tasks.

Priority Designating a particular task's availability for the leveling process. The higher the priority of a task, the later in the leveling process it will be delayed. Lowest-priority tasks are delayed first, working up the hierarchy in importance.

Resource calendar A calendar that delineates working time from nonworking time for a particular resource, whether that resource is an employee or piece of equipment.

Resource leveling A way to resolve conflicts when limited resources must be shared among tasks or projects. Program can often compare resource demands to available quantities in order to identify overallocated resources, and then delay lower-priority activities until higher-priority activities requiring those resources are completed. If you link your projects with resource leveling, you can easily see and manage the workload of each resource as it relates to all your construction projects. This is an excellent capability available in most, but not all, project management programs.

Fixed-duration scheduling When the length of time must remain unchanged. If you can't delay the deadline, then you juggle equipment, supplies, and work hours to get it to fit.

Resource-driven scheduling When the tasks' durations are based on the amount of resources assigned or applied to them. This is particularly useful when you have limited resources that must be shared among tasks.

Task The smallest individual unit or step of a project.

Variance The difference between the original plan the currently scheduled plan.

Work breakdown structure (WBS) A way of positioning tasks in a hierarchy for reporting schedules and tracking costs.

How it works

When you use a project management program to set up scheduling, essentially you're creating a project, adding activities, creating relationships among them, and assigning target dates and various constraints like expected start, expected finish, and mandatory finish. If some of the activities are constrained by factors such as material delivery dates, equipment availability dates, or other deadlines, you can attach the activities to specific dates by assigning those specific constraints.

As each project progresses, you can gather and analyze progress, document changes, and adjust remaining data. During the job and after its completion, many programs allow you to compare baseline plans against actual allocations to improve estimating skills for future projects. Most projects require some modifications as the job proceeds.

Passing out the schedule

Once you're comfortable working with your project management software, you can quickly schedule a $70,000 or $170,000 job, with printouts ready for distribution. Many programs provide templates for daily, weekly, and monthly work schedules, ordering material schedules, and delivery of material schedules. They might also produce a daily cash flow analysis. Printouts of a good, workable schedule offer contractors and remodelers an easy way to inform interested parties, beyond the foreman, of what's coming up when.

From workers and subcontractors to suppliers and clients, each recipient will have in hand a precise visual layout of the time frame of what's to come, short term and long term, and exactly when you expect it to be finished. Periodically printing multiple copies of schedules and passing them around is almost as good as taking out performance insurance. Each subcontractor or work group will understand the line of responsibility and hopefully avoid bottlenecks or, worse yet, stoppages. No one can pass the buck with an "I didn't know."

In a well-designed scheduling program, delays by others are easy to handle; just pick the corresponding dates of the delay and the tasks affected and a solidly constructed scheduling program will automatically move everything relevant down the prescribed time in the prescheduled format.

As mentioned earlier, a printed schedule presented to a client at the beginning of a project can also serve as a qualifying documents to justify partial payments. Also, when you keep your clients continuously apprised with updated schedules, they will have no easy justification for not meeting decision dates on appliances and other furnishings, paint colors, flooring choices, or other items not yet decided at the start of the job, or for not being in attendance for important deliveries.

By keeping watch of the bottom line, you can jockey payments, events, and billings to keep you ahead of—or at least even with—the client. It's easy enough to show the schedule to your client to document progress and therefore money earned to date.

Programs
CA-SuperProject

CA-SuperProject for Windows (Computer Associates, 800-225-5224), with a 16,000-task capacity, is a solid project management program for large projects or multiproject consolidations. It uses the finish-to-start dependency as the default link, though you can change that if you want.

The program can handle global changes by updating multiple projects linked together. The Windows Combine option puts together all open projects in a single task outline, PERT chart, and WBS chart for display purposes, as well as editing and reporting, while retaining them as separate projects. This improves the ability to share resources among projects. The Gantt chart of the Task Outline view shows interproject relationships with special symbols.

The software has beginner and expert modes, pull-down menus, pop-up forms for context-sensitive editing, lots of quick-key combinations and fast function keys, and extensive reporting capabilities. It shows schedules in four outline views: task, in increments from minutes to months to years, all of which can be used on any schedule; resource, any piece of equipment, material, department, employee, consultant, or anything else assigned to project that shows scheduled hours for a person or piece of equipment; date, which displays the project from a date perspective; and account, which organizes the project from a cost account perspective.

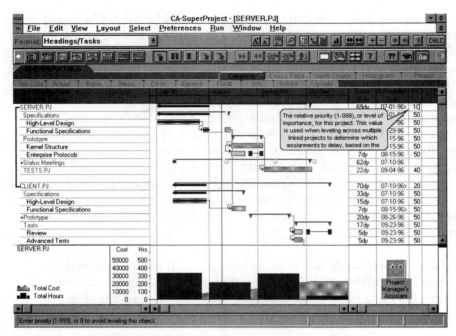

With CA-SuperProject 4.0 for Windows, interproject relationships are diagrammed clearly. Computer Associates

The program factors in efficiency ratings when it assigns resources; longer time periods are allocated for tasks that use less efficient resources. Gantt charts are displayed by default on the task and resource outlines. You can also order views of the schedule in the form of PERT charts, work breakdown, and calendar.

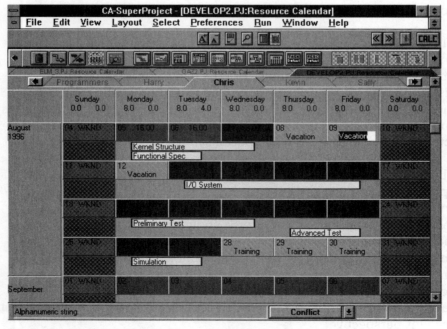

CA-SuperProject 4.0's interactive calendar views present lots of easy-to-read information. Computer Associates

In SuperProject, you can simultaneously chart up to 14 items, such as schedule, actual baseline, milestones, float, and late dates. You slot in such information as the scheduled duration of the task, task ID (to identify it numerically), scheduled start, scheduled finish, work breakdown code (for government contractors), units a day, whether or not the status is crucial or noncrucial, and a short description. You're asked if a particular task depends on another for start or completion. Arrows will then connect some tasks on the chart to show dependency. You can use any of the various view options to build your project, and customize the look to your taste. You can edit data in any view, and those edits will be automatically reflected in all other views.

The Project Manager's Assistant—which you can keep open in the background and switch to as needed—provides step-by-step guidance for all levels of users at any stage of project management. It features a Fast Start section, which gives on-screen guidance for each procedure, including creating a new project, outlining tasks, estimating their duration, linking tasks, creating new resources, setting up resource calendars, and assigning resources to tasks. Typically, through a selection process, the PM Assistant automatically provides the appropriate view and loads one of over 100 (customizable) layouts.

From any point in the project, SuperProject can provide "what-if" analysis of potential scenarios to help you optimize scheduling the remainder of the project. For easy interior comparisons, you can transfer current scheduled dates and hours to your choice of up to three different baselines.

CA-SuperProject also comes bundled with and linked to TimeSheet Professional for Windows (discussed later in this chapter), which is software dedicated to tracking time and material projects.

SureTrak Project Manager for Windows

SureTrak Project Manager for Windows (Primavera, 800-973-1335) is an entry-level project management program. The format provides an easy electronic way to manipulate the time frames and responsibilities of the pieces of the puzzle—labor, equipment, materials, and funds— for maximum efficiency and the best bottom line, using resource leveling and other techniques.

Basically, you outline activities, estimate time for completion, and link the activities in a logical fashion. SureTrak, like many other project management software packages, helps you incorporate the resources you have into a schedule and establish a baseline for later comparison. As a project proceeds, you enter data that reflects the actual progress. You can then fine-tune the project accordingly.

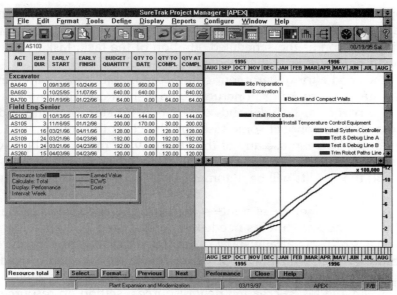

Activities are grouped according to their assigned resources in SureTrak Project Manager for Windows. Primavera

SureTrak offers a great deal of flexibility and multiple levels of selection (filter) criteria in how you can look at the progress of a project. The program uses time-scaled bar (Gantt) charts and time-scaled logic (PERT) charts to display information. You can view by critical path scheduling of key activities, by task, by budget, or by employee. There are more than 40 predefined reports and graphics through which you can view all your information.

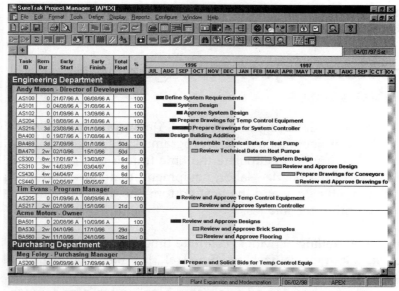

Screen from SureTrak Project Manager for Windows showing activities grouped by department, and within each department by the person responsible. Primavera

There's also a comprehensive on-screen tutorial to ease you comfortably into the program. The user manual is well documented and includes an extensive glossary of terms. For what is deemed to be an entry-level program, you get a lot of capabilities and choices.

The Scheduler's Add-Vantage

The Scheduler's Add-Vantage (Add-Vantage Software, 800-287-5247 in Massachusetts and 800-768-5636 out of state) is a dedicated, industry-specific, Windows-based program for home builders and home remodelers. Essentially, it's an electronic Gantt chart that lists all general, traditional categories in home building and home renovation. Though it lacks the more sophisticated capabilities prevalent in other programs discussed in this chapter, it provides the means—without the frills—of building a Gantt chart that shows basic start and end dates of each major task. The software is actually a manual critical path program intended to work in concert with your experience to develop time frames and interdependencies.

Basically, you use the preformatted scheduling templates. Across the bottom of the color-enhanced program screens are a series of 20 predefined buttons for selecting color-coded lines that represent various aspects of a project, such as excavation and electrical, plumbing and painting, all the way through to the punchlist. Slot in the time period you estimate for each task, click on the category, and the software will put it into the schedule.

Delays are very easy to handle; if you've had a day or more rain or snow delay, just pick the corresponding dates of the delay and the affected tasks and the program will automatically move everything relevant down the prescribed time.

Not only does the software provide a work schedule, an ordering of material schedule, and a delivery of material schedule, but it also provides a daily cash flow analysis. You can jockey payments, events, and billings so you don't perform work at your expense. (It's easy enough to flash the cash flow printout in front of clients to show them what is due.)

If a new job is similar to a previous one, you can pull up a copy of the schedule and use that as the basis for the new schedule, altering it as necessary to accommodate the differences. If you do a lot of roofs, bathrooms, or kitchens, for example, this can save a lot of time.

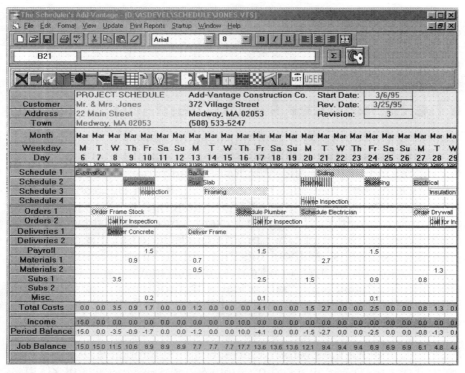

Work schedule and ordering and delivery schedules can be shown on one screen in The Scheduler's Advantage. Add-Vantage Software

Microsoft Project for Windows 95

Microsoft Project for Windows 95 (Microsoft, 800-426-9400) is a very strong program for both novices and experienced users. A 32-bit project management package, it fits into the Microsoft Office for 95 suite of programs with a common icon, integrating with Office 95's Schedule+ and Microsoft Exchange Server to allow you to view through those two without opening Project files. Because it uses the same title bar, tool bar, and menu bar as other Microsoft Office programs, if you use any of those, you'll find this an easy lateral move.

The program is extremely competent in creating and organizing a schedule, scheduling independent and linked tasks, assigning resources, and assigning costs to tasks and resources. It offers many computer-aided strategies for evaluating and adjusting the schedule for a single project or for multiple projects.

There are several kinds of help available, specifically geared to aid you in discovering the connections between tasks you need to accomplish. The program also features an Answer Wizard, which responds to user-formulated questions along the lines of "How do I . . . ," which usually lead to step-by-step or interactive answers, and "Tell me about . . . ," which generate visual answers or traditional help explanations. There are also pop-up screen tips that provide instant, in-context, information dialog box options, tool buttons, menu commands, and some screen elements. You won't get lost.

The reporting capabilities are very sturdy, with over 20 predefined views and reports to satisfy a broad range of communication needs. The reports, which are previewable, cover overviews, current activities, costs, assignments, and workload. You can also create custom views or reports to suit target audiences. The program comes with both a guided tour and a series of on-screen instructions, teaching you how to create a project schedule.

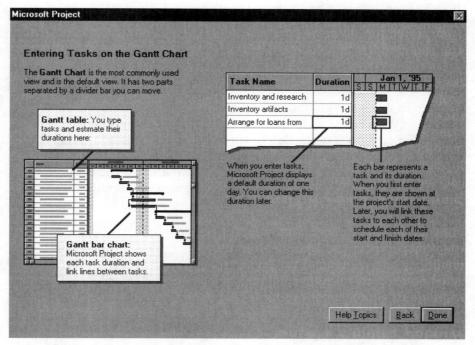

Lots of on-screen graphical instructions make it easy to learn your way around Microsoft Project.

TimeSheet Professional for Windows

Keeping close tabs of all expenses and material projects is often the key to justifying your billing, and can help you stay within budget if the project has a cap. TimeSheet Professional for Windows (Timeslips Corporation, 800-285-0999) is an easy electronic spreadsheet for tracking time and material projects. The program tracks the information by project, client, or activity and shows you at a glance daily and weekly time totals. You can even export data directly to a project management program and therefore track project performance over any time frame and compare budgeted with actual hours and expenses.

TimeSheet uses a spreadsheet grid format that's customized to look like a seven-day calendar. The system works by setting up a separate weekly calendar for each employee. Each calendar (or timesheet) represents the activities of one employee, with each employee definable by up to ten customizable fields that hold information like address, social security number, and other personal or business data. It's simple to switch calendars by clicking on the employee list and selecting from previously entered employees.

You can put together groups of employees for composite crew make-ups. Employees can belong to up to ten groups each. This can speed up selecting multiple workers for various projects, either to perform specific types of tasks or to work together on diverse tasks.

The grid is divided into vertical columns, one for each day of the week, and horizontal rows, one for each task. The left side of the screen holds the master tracking list for identifying the tasks performed. The tasks (basic entities for which you record and summarize time) are identified by the codes you set up for specific aspects of your work. You fill the cells with the actual time for each task performed on a given day of the week. Expenses and notes can also be affixed to each time cell. When times are placed into the grid, the weekly time totals for each task are automatically calculated on the right side of the screen. This total can help you identify tasks receiving too much or too little time. Daily time totals are calculated at the bottom of each column.

			Mon Oct 23	Tue Oct 24	Wed Oct 25	Thu Oct 26	Fri Oct 27	Sat Oct 28	Sun Oct 29	
Allison Meyers										
10/24/95		$25.00								
Arizona	Account	Developm				3.75				3.75
Arizona	Hardware	Training	7.00	1.00						8.00
Arizona	Marketing	Off-site								
Oper	Vacation					8.00				8.00
Con Rail		Meeting								
Con Rail		Sales			8.50			4.00		12.50
Con Rail		Training								
Con Rail	Inventory			1.00						1.00
ConRail	Marketing	Course	2.00							2.00
ConRail	Marketing	FocusG								
ConRail	Marketing	Plan								
ConRail	Marketing	Training		0.50						0.50
PacFax	Needs	Training								
PacFax	Inventory	Course				2.25				2.25
			9.00	2.50	8.50	6.00	8.00	4.00		38.00

Allison Meyers, Arizona, Hardware, Training.   NUM 02:43PM

Timesheet Professional 7-day grid. Timeslips Corporation

The program also incorporates a day-at-a-glance grid that allows you to view a daily schedule of events. The daily view capability supports data entry without a predefined task. A mini-sheet view lets you display either the time sheet or the day grid in a miniaturized window that "floats" over other applications, allowing you to enter a time or reference a task without exiting your current application.

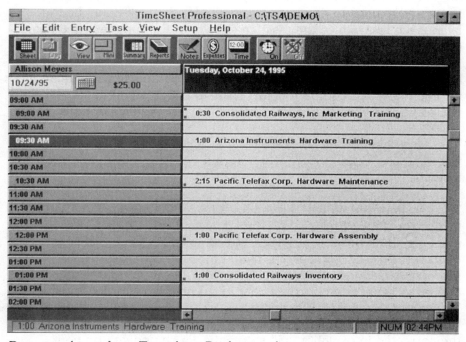

Day at a glance from Timesheet Professional. Timeslips Corporation

When setting up each employee into the system, you include the billable wage rates for the various tasks. When a cell is highlighted, the dollar value for the time in that cell is shown under the employee's name.

The program offers several useful icons that let you edit currently selected time sheet cells quickly. The note icon lets you attach a memo or other annotation of any length to the currently selected time sheet cell. (Cells with attached notes are marked with an upright black triangle.) The expense icon lets you attach an expense record to the current time cell, useful either for internal cost-tracking and reimbursement or for customer invoice purposes. (Cells with attached expenses have an inverted black triangle.) The expense table can automatically add a percentage mark-up, and calculate sales tax after the mark-up. This way clients can see only the marked-up price, without seeing the breakdown, including your mark-up.

The time icon lets you add or subtract time from the total time in the selected time cell. Time is billable by the hour or by selected intervals of minutes. A stop-watch timer, also selectable by icon, is handy if you bill for your time on the phone.

TimeSheet Professional also allows you to create four kinds of reports. You can report on budget vs. actual and percentage of completion; view time and resource project budgets; view work by project, activity, individual employee, and client; and review project notes and expenses. The software multiples the task hours by the billing rate to produce the task fee shown on the summary and detail reports.

If performing a project with a cap, you can put in estimated quantities for each task and compare actual costs to budgeted amounts, allowing you to keep a close watch on costs while you still have options.

The developers of the software have included a sample database so first-time users can explore the program via sample data and report formats.

You can import data without modification directly from TimeSheet Professional for Windows into any of several leading project management software packages, including CA-SuperProject, Microsoft Project, Symantec's Time Line, and others for more thorough tracking and analysis. Once you've set up your resources and tasks, you can import the data into TimeSheet for job tracking. You can then record the actual times for the tasks and resources. When you export the data back to your project management program, the corrected information will automatically be updated on your progress schedule.

7

Accounting and
job costing software

CONTRACTORS, like other businesspeople, need an efficient way to keep track of the financial side of their operation. It has always been important to know if a contracting firm is making a profit or heading into the red.

Many small contracting businesses not yet converted to electronic accounting have to rely on an accountant's occasional scheduled reconciliation of the books or on a part-time bookkeeper diligently maintaining manual up-to-date records, preparing invoices, writing payroll checks, and paying other bills. If a firm has no bookkeeper, the contractor has to find time to do the paperwork, on the run, while juggling job hats.

With small businesses, usually what gets done on a weekly basis is payroll, sporadic bill paying, and check depositing. Job costing, if performed at all, is done on a very infrequent basis, most likely at the end of a project to see how it went. By then, it's too late to use the information to its best advantage on that job.

On top of that, contractors without the benefit of electronic accounting often make intuitive decisions based on incomplete financial data or no financial data at all. If, for example, you know you're running over on labor while the job is still in process, you can determine the cause or causes, then take corrective actions to minimize the additional cost. Perhaps the job requires more supervision or a change of supervision, a different composition of crew, more or less overtime, or better scheduling with other contractors working on the same project. The problem could also stem from architect or client lassitude. In any event, forewarned is forearmed and, with timely accounting and job-costing information, you can take action and run each and every job as profitably as possible.

With easy-to-use computerized accounting and job costing, you have the power to achieve instant and continuous evaluation of your business, as long as you perform your accounting functions through the program and maintain those efforts. You can pull up varied reports to evaluate many kinds of information, or the same information from different aspects.

Electronic accounting

Electronic accounting can help you track income sources and expenses, reconcile bank statements, collect owed monies, pay employees, track payments, and time them for optimizing credit terms and discounts. You can also use it to generate reports that summarize a company's financial situation. In a nutshell, computerized accounting can perform all the functions previously done (or attempted) by pencil and paper, but faster and with greater accuracy.

Basic terminology

Assets The total value of the money you have in hand, and the money others owe you.

Liabilities The total of the money you owe to others, whether they're suppliers, subcontractors, the government, the bank or other lender, or your employees.

Equity The total net worth of your construction business, which is equal to your total assets minus total liabilities.

Accounts payable The money you owe to others.

Accounts receivable The money others owe to you.

Chart of accounts Systematic breakdown of categories for where your company funds are coming from and where they're going.

General ledger All transactions listed by categories in a chart of accounts.

Cash basis Payment or income is recorded at the time money is received, not when it's invoiced; likewise, outflow is recorded when you pay the bill, not when you receive the bill.

Accrual basis Payment or income is recorded when payment is invoiced, not when you receive the money; likewise, expenses are entered when you receive an invoice or bill, not when you actually pay it.

The standard business accounting balancing equation is: assets = liabilities + equity.

General business vs. construction-specific accounting

As discussed in chapter 2 of this book, accounting software packages fall into one of two broad categories. The first encompasses general business programs, including many relatively inexpensive titles. The second type consists of software developed specifically for the construction industry. This type is much more expensive and—in many cases—harder to use, sometimes unnecessarily so.

All accounting software should provide, at minimum, the ability to write and print checks, maintain a register, reconcile monthly statements, process invoices and accounts receivable, track accounts payable, and maintain the general ledger. A program for contractors should generate up-to-date reports such as payroll, cash flow, balance sheets, budget, profit and loss statements, and project and job cost reports.

The easiest conversion from manual to electronic accounting is to a general Windows business accounting package. Suitable for businesses running work totaling up to a few million dollars yearly, many of these programs include a preformatted setup for contractors, from which you can modify your chart of accounts.

Most entry-level Windows-based software can memorize repetitive transactions, such as generating automatic invoices for monthly services rendered to regular customers, and the ability to pick up on the name or designation you're about to type from the first few letters, automatically filling in the rest of the name and address. This type of capability saves tedious transcribing and eliminates errors.

In most of these popular, broadly marketed programs, the screens look like the paper versions of traditional accounting forms. Basically, you follow instructions and fill in the blank spaces. The programs are relatively successful in shielding users not specifically trained in bookkeeping from accounting terminology or techniques. There's no need to know the intricacies of audit trails, debits and credits, and other accounting terminology. (Leave that for your accountant.) For example, with a checkbook interface, you simply enter the data on the screen check just as you would on a paper check. The software automatically places the entry into the appropriate ledgers.

Vertical market packages with construction-specific features

The second type of accounting software contractors can use, developed specifically for contractors and usually marketed through sales representatives and sold in modules, costs more and almost always calls for more training to use properly. Larger companies with commensurably larger, more complicated accounting needs will probably want to consider these.

Construction accounting software generally requires dedicated personnel, or at least personnel exposed to a considerable degree of employee training. If you make the investment in this type of package, you should train more than one employee, even for a one-person job, in case the key worker quits or goes on vacation. Keep in mind that most of these accounting packages are still DOS-based.

What's at the core?

Most contracting accounting systems start with either a general ledger or job costing at the core, and handle such industry-specific applications and reports as progress billing, retention, labor burden, bonding reports, and purchase-order tracking, in addition to the usual business accounting functions. Consider the relative importance to you of these types of specialty reports.

Other modules include accounts payable, payroll, purchase orders, time and billing, accounts receivable, and inventory control. Furthermore, some of the construction accounting programs tie in with the same developer's estimating software. If you use the estimating program to bid a job and then win it, you can transfer the bid data into the accounting program instantly and therefore be ready for accounting and possibly job-costing functions. This is an excellent tie-in feature if the estimating program is also suitable to your estimating style. Again, these are usually very costly programs that might not be worth the additional cost and training for remodelers and small contractors. Many small companies, in any event, work closely with their accountant, who can handle much of the complicated accounting procedures.

General programs

Look at the popular low-priced general business accounting programs sold in most computer retail outlets first. Generally, they're adept at what they set out to do, which is business accounting. If your particular construction business requirements are so demanding that you feel you need additional specific functions, make sure they're available in the construction-oriented packages you're considering.

Try before you buy

If you think you want to go with a construction-specific program, preview a few of what look to be the best of the bunch for you. Try to determine which works closest to your own bookkeeping style, but don't expect perfection. Sales literature alone can't tell the tale. If you have the opportunity, peruse software exhibits and demonstrations at trade shows and conventions.

Most construction-specific accounting packages are sold by regional direct sales representatives. It's customary to have a company representative come to your office and demonstrate the program. Supplement the salesperson's presentation/demonstration, which are designed to show program strengths, with a chance to work the program yourself.

As a rule, dedicated construction software isn't updated nearly as frequently as general business programs. Check the date of the most recent update. Look for assurances that the developer issues product refinements and upgrades periodically so you benefit from improvements and user feedback. Don't buy costly programs without careful evaluation.

In addition to on-site demonstrations or instead of them, some companies offer "test drives" with time-release working copies that either disable after a predetermined length of time, can't print, or have some other limitation that renders the program nonfunctional for real business applications. But at least you can view actual menus and activity screens and try the software, in much greater depth than in any other way. If you plan to buy a DOS-based program, look for a package that offers consistency of interface and commands among its modules. Is it easy to move around within the software and are the screens intuitive?

In general, it's best to purchase software from an established company with a track record for customer satisfaction, one that has been in existence for ten years or more. About half of all companies in the construction software field fold within three years, leaving purchasers out in the cold. With an accounting program, this can be a serious drawback because you need to keep your books for several years and you won't want to change systems midstream just because the company has dissolved. Look for longevity as a key factor in weighing your software decision.

If possible, take a look at the manuals to see if they're written clearly and have abundant screen shots and other illustrations, which are very helpful when learning a program.

As software sitting in the box won't go far in terms of payback, consider the training possibilities, as well. Larger, industry-specific modular programs might offer on-site training at your office, seminars for all interested staff, or periodic seminars at selected locations around the country.

Why Windows?

Going with a Windows accounting program allows you to use the financial data in other Windows applications, such as word processing and spreadsheets, through object linking and embedding (OLE). If the low-cost Windows program you're interested in doesn't offer, for example, job costing, you can buy an inexpensive job-costing program to perform that function. Make sure the electronic accounting program can handle the accounting system your accountant has set up for your company—either cash basis or accrual accounting.

A fully integrated modular system has simultaneous posting of all entries, which is called *real-time accounting*. Each entry in any module is reflected in an automatic adjustment that affects accounts everywhere within the system. Entries are always balanced in relation to one another. An alternative is *batch processing mode*, which relies on periodic updating from one part of the system to the others. Only after all updating, then, would all data be balanced.

When you buy an accounting package, you're also buying long-term support, so evaluate the choices of support services as well. It's common for a software vendor to offer free support for the initial break-in period and various types of fee-based customer support programs. Most companies offer unlimited free telephone support or fax-back customer support for an initial time period. After that, they provide service plans that allow customers to ask questions and receive answers to technical questions either for a specified number of minutes or hours, or without limit.

If you can, try the various phone numbers to which buyers have access and see who (or what!) answers, how fast they answer, and how quickly you can get an actual answer. (Factor in the aggravation in reaching a disinterested voice that says something to the effect of "Leave name and number and we'll get back to you within 24 hours" when your system is down.)

Regardless of the accounting package you select, always back up your accounting data from your hard drive frequently, using a back-up program that puts copies of your data either on back-up disks or tapes. And no matter what electronic accounting system you decide on, don't give up your old system immediately. Run parallel systems for a few months until you're completely fluid in the operation of the new software and can verify that the numbers match.

Four popular general Windows accounting programs

Below are four Windows accounting programs that have achieved a high level of popularity among general business users. They can all work well for a renovation or home building contractor.

QuickBooks Pro

QuickBooks Pro on CD-ROM for Windows 3.1 and Windows 95 (Intuit, 800-624-8742) is a double-entry accounting program specifically designed for small business owners with little or no accounting experience. For a relatively low sticker price, this could be a good match for small contractors who want to do their bookkeeping on a computer but don't want to get bogged down in accountantese. An extremely popular broad-scoped horizontal market program, each recent version of QuickBooks looks better and offers more time- and productivity-enhancing features than earlier releases.

Initial start-up proceeds with a series of questions that results in automatic configuration to suit your accounting style. Because there are so many customizing preferences available, you can arrange the overall operating of the program pretty much to suit your taste and company needs. Custom fields for items, customers, vendors, and employees expedite tracking and reporting information specific to the construction industry. You can access most tasks through customizable icon bars.

The user-friendly Windows interface for data entry mimics traditional forms; checks, invoices, purchase orders, credit memos, credit cards, and bills look pretty much as they do on paper.

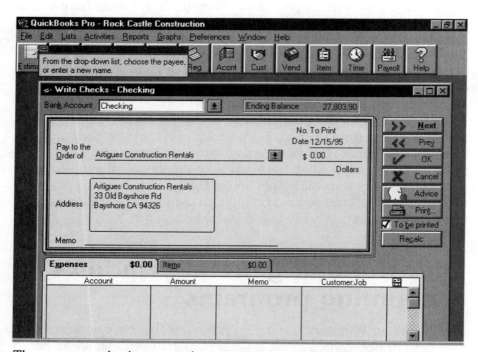

The on-screen check mimics the paper version in QuickBooks Pro.

Here's a small but nice feature: automatic calculation of vendor discounts tracks the payment terms of each vendor, which should help you not miss any opportunities to save a little on paying bills when earlier payment is an option. Once you set up the payment terms, the program tracks them and lets you know when a discount is available on any bill.

The Reports menu offers over 60 preset reports and graphs. A handy QuickZoom turns the mouse pointer into a kind of instant magnifying glass and lets you immediately see the details (or components) behind the numbers in your chart or graph.

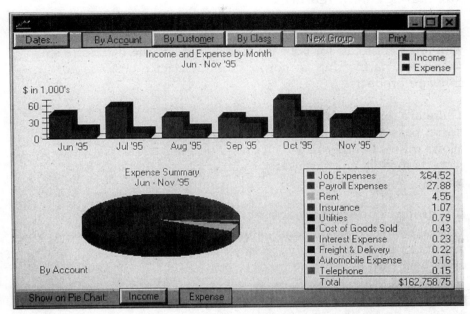

Income and expenses charts are easy to decipher in QuickBooks Pro. Intuit

Audit trails facilitate corrections

QuickBooks Pro also includes an audit trail that gives you a complete record of all changes made to the accounting records. You can find and fix mistakes almost instantly and have a complete record of what happened. The previous input—an account or an amount—appears directly below the new current transaction, under the heading *previous transaction*. Both note the exact time, to the second.

The point-and-click modification of invoice formats lets you easily customize the appearance of invoices by renaming various boxes and columns and opting whether or not to show them. You can also modify purchase orders and other business forms, and add a company logo.

Demo traces a construction company's records

The demo seems custom made for contractors. The QuickTour uses two years' worth of sample data from a fictional construction company (sole owner, two full-time year-round employees, five occasional employees). The mock company makes good use of the software. It invoices customers for labor hours and for items such as lumber, pipe, and windows, uses accounts payable for bills, and uses the integrated payroll records for payroll. The sample company also uses QuickBooks Pro for job tracking and reimbursable expenses. The software lets you classify projects by type, e.g., residential or commercial, to see which is more profitable.

Tax management features

The program also prints on 1099, 940, and 941 forms. The software will take the data you've been entering all year and generate a report with line item totals for your tax forms, and link the data for a sole proprietor, partnership, or corporation to selected business tax software products.

There are three kinds of passwords for different levels of access: owner password, for unlimited access; data entry password, which allows others to enter new data only; and transaction password, which restricts the editing of transactions in a prior (predefined) fiscal period.

Integrated contact management features

Several contact management features are built into the program. You can affix date-stamped notes on any conversation with clients and enter your own notes to an invoice, purchase order, or check.

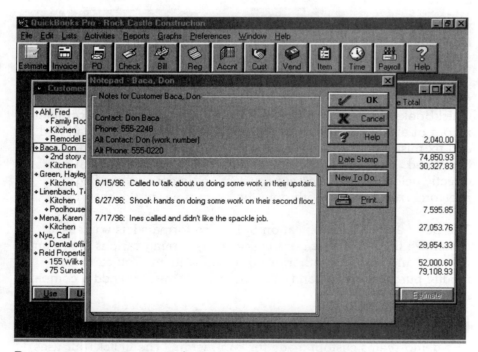

Basic contact management features are built into QuickBooks Pro. Intuit

Estimating and job-costing features

The estimating and job-costing aspects of QuickBooks Pro are discussed in chapter 5.

Audio advice

Extremely helpful audio advice is integrated throughout the program. On many of the screens, you need only click on a button to get a series of verbal instructions on how to use particular features on that screen.

DacEasy Accounting & Payroll 95

DacEasy Accounting & Payroll 95 (DacEasy, Inc., 800-DacEasy) is a strong, well-priced entry that integrates accounting software with (minimal) contact management and communications capabilities.

Part of the impetus behind the program is to bridge the gap between managing finances and managing contacts. Since most small business contacts (clients, subcontractors, vendors, and others) result in financial transactions of one kind or another, a program that keeps track of related information with those contacts is bound to save you time and effort in preparing mailings and reports.

DacEasy Accounting & Payroll 95 does an efficient job of tracking when and where you spend your money, writes checks, handles payroll, and prints numerous reports that give instant views of various aspects of business performance and status. The software handles the general ledger; cash management; inventory; the payroll (including 941s, and W-2s); overtime; sick and vacation hours; calculation of federal, state, and local taxes; tracking of federal and state withholdings; contributions to a 401K plan; invoicing and budgeting. It also provides contact management features like a phone dialer, fax integration, call tracker, to-do list, and reminder alarms. It's all integrated so information entered in one place is noted and used throughout the program, where appropriate.

The automatic dialer can select a range of names to fit a category, or you can select each name manually from the window. The program also keeps a running call log for any service phone calls, which is handy if you intend to bill for phone time. You can enter any notes in a designated note field. A special letter merge function allows you to send out collection or marketing letters for any range of clients or vendors meeting your customized criteria.

The software is very easy to set up. Among the choices of preset charts of accounts is one for construction and another for service. On-screen instructions tell you what to do each step of the way. Sample data is included for practice, and there's an interactive graphical tutorial.

Minding your money with M.Y.O.B.

M.Y.O.B. (Best!Ware, 800-322-6962) is a Windows-based CD-ROM that offers accounting on either a cash or an accrual basis, with or without payroll capability. This program comes with a good "getting started" manual, a CD-ROM visual and audio help guide, and a short videotape explaining the essentials of setting up your books.

The software has a very good graphical interface. The command center is the workhorse from which all activities start. It consists of a horizontal series of either six or seven (if you have the payroll version) graphical boxes. Each box represents a natural division of the program: general ledger, checkbook, sales, purchases, payroll, inventory, and card file. When you highlight any of the icons, a flowchart specific to the module appears below it. The chart diagrams how the flow of data ties together in the specified division. Furthermore, clicking on any of the flowchart boxes will take you to that part of the program for data entry or review.

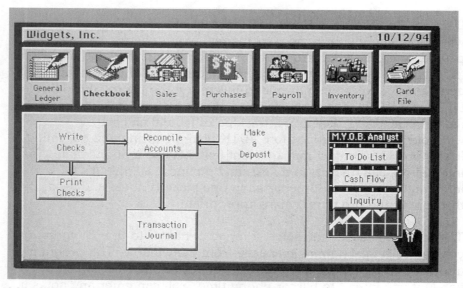

M.Y.O.B. sports an easy-to-manuever interface. Best!Ware

When entering various flowchart boxes such as journal entries, the software further defines where to place the information with a series of file folder tabs. Tabs are a great way to get around when there are multiple choices from which to pick.

Setting up a company is straightforward. There are many predefined charts of accounts, including ones for building contractor, developer, roofing contractor, electrical contractor, and landscape contractor. As they're not really industry-specific, count on modifying or adding items to the basic chart or creating your own from your account information.

M.Y.O.B. is strong on reports, with over 100 management reports, including two dozen general ledger reports, 26 sales and receivables reports, and several each of checkbook, purchases and payables, inventory, and card file reports. The payroll version also includes 12 payroll reports.

Feature-rich Peachtree Accounting for Windows

The robust Peachtree Accounting for Windows (Peachtree, 800-443-9361) is targeted at small to midsize companies, from one-man operations to companies with $10 million sales or more than 100 employees. Like QuickBooks, it's also a very popular program with a strong market share. It has bright, colorful screens, is well laid out, and benefits from user-friendly interfaces. The primary divisions of the program are general ledger, sales and receivables, purchase and payments, payroll, inventory, job tracking, and account reconciliation.

Peachtree offers two ways of moving around. If you elect to open a menu, which runs along the top of the screen, you can then select an option. All daily tasks are grouped on one linear menu, so it's easy to find what you want to do. Alternately, you can open windows in which you'll perform tasks or data entry through "navigation aids," a graphical representation of how information flows through the accounting system. File folder tabs of specific choices are set up on the bottom of the screen. You can use your mouse to select specific clearly marked icons to launch common functions. When you click on a tab, a folder pops up. On the folder is a schematic showing the flow of information within the selected general category. Clicking on a particular folder icon will bring up the appropriate screen.

Peachtree Accounting supports cash- or accrual-basis accounting with aging for either, and allows real-time or batch posting. You can keep two years of data open for easy access to information for review or editing, and no month-end closing procedures are required. By allowing two years to be open at the same time, you can process the next year's work before closing the current year.

The software allows you to pay invoices either one at a time or through a preprocessing routing that lets you enter the type of criteria desired (discount data, vendor ID, etc.) and then select from the invoices listed. The program has online tutorials, sample data, context-sensitive help, and tips on how to use various features more effectively.

One of the features is an event log, which is useful for scheduling and tracking custom events like phone calls or meetings, and automatic

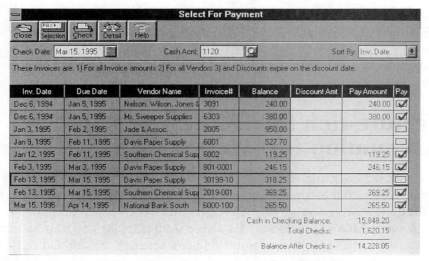

Invoice selection screen from Peachtree Accounting. Peachtree

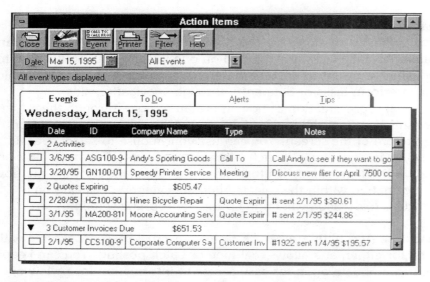

Event log screen from Peachtree Accounting. Peachtree

events like sending invoices. You can keep one event log for each of your clients, vendors, and employees.

Creating professional-looking reports is fairly straightforward. There are over 100 reports available, divided into nine categories of business forms, including accounts receivable, accounts payable, payroll, general ledger, financial statements, and job reports. You can print the form you want with default options or you can customize via filter options. For most reports, if you double-click on a row of the report, you can view the corresponding underlying transaction detail.

Advanced planning for retirement

Wherever you are in your business—in your prime, daydreaming about giving it all up, or only just starting out in your own—the saying "it's not where you start, it's where you finish" applies to just about everyone. If you haven't started planning for quieter days down the road, there's no time like now to start, and no easier place than at your computer, under the tutelage of a no-nonsense, to-the-point program devoted to that very purpose.

Analyzing goals and taking computer-based action

Quicken Financial Planner on CD-ROM for Windows (Intuit, 800-816-8025) offers contractors, remodelers, and others a step-by-step way to analyze current financial and retirement goals and to create a customized financial plan for saving and investing to achieve those goals. Whether you're using it to investigate strategies from scratch or to evaluate and refine strategies and plans already in place, there's lots of (inexpensive) professional guidance.

The software opens with a screen that replicates a spiral notebook with a dozen tabs on the side. The tabs make it easy to access the area—assets, loans, income, expenses, retirement benefits, etc.—from which you want information or to which you want to add or alter data.

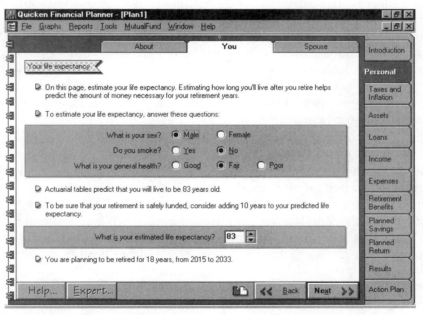

To get customized advice, you have to answer questions in Quicken Financial Planner.

What you own, how much you earn, what you owe, and how much you spend form the basis of your plan and both create and limit the financial possibilities open to you. Everything you need to enter is clearly delineated so the plan is customized precisely for your needs. Once you enter numbers (using reasonable estimates, not necessarily exact figures) and details, the program does the calculations.

Working with your latest bank statements, mortgage and loan papers, pension information, household budget, investment statements, paycheck stubs, tax-deferred savings information, and last year's income tax return, you enter data in an orderly fashion and make key decisions about retirement. (If you already use the checkbook program Quicken, also by Intuit, just a click of a button will transfer your Quicken data to Financial Planner.) If you can't decide on how to answer a particular question, you can call on screen-based help and expert multimedia advice.

Changing the variables

As your plan formulates on screen, you can make adjustments in one or more of the three variables: how much to save, how to invest, and when to retire. Financial Planner suggests one of ten investment mixes, depending upon the return you want to earn and how much risk you're comfortable assuming. (Expected returns range from a conservative 5½ percent to an aggressive 10 percent.) The software handles most major retirement plans, including 401K, IRA, 403B, employer-sponsored or self-employed SEP, Keogh, and tax-deferred annuities.

Fifteen different reports and graphs show how fast your planned nest egg (reflecting net worth, income, spending, savings, and investment variables) will grow with a specific plan over the years, taking into account social security benefits. The reports and graphs (available in both today's dollars or in inflated future dollars, at an inflation rate you enter) include net worth, investment portfolio, investment withdrawals, cash flow, income, expense, and savings. If after calculations your plan doesn't work on screen, consider saving more, retiring later, or taking more of a risk.

Perusing mutual funds

The program also includes Mutual Fund LookUp, a database of 4,400 mutual developed by Morningstar, Inc., a fund research firm, so Financial Planner users can instantly review performance and risk history, graphs, and statistics on those funds in order to hone in on the ones that meet proposed investment criteria. (Morningstar categorizes a particular fund's style as being either growth-oriented, value-oriented, or a blend of those two styles.) You can search by name, ticker symbol, fund family, or by criteria that match your investment preferences for risk, return, and fund-related expenses. For an extra annual fee, you can order quarterly database updates to keep investment information current.

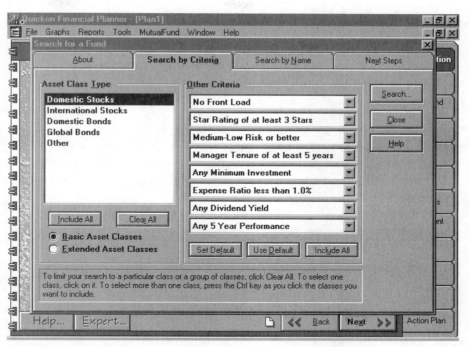

You can look up mutual funds in Quicken Financial Planner.

You can harvest details on any of the funds either graphically or in summary fashion. Graphically, the fund's performance is compared against domestic stocks and against Standard and Poor 500. The summary fashion shows total returns, rating and risk, fees and expenses, and general fund information.

The software developers don't assume you have any prior knowledge of technical terminology. Personal finance terms are explained both in online help and in a glossary in the succinct, clearly written, screen-shot-rich manual. This is a well-thought-out, user-friendly program.

Tracking time

Time is not literally money, of course, but for those who bill on time or on time and materials and for those who want bills paid fast, an efficient computerized billing program can save both time and money. This includes contractors and remodelers with multiple clients and/or projects at any one time.

Preparing job costs with Timeslips Deluxe!

Timeslips Deluxe! for Windows (Timeslips Corporation, 800-285-0999) is composed of several interconnected programs that work together to track activities accurately and help a company bill promptly for them. Not an accounting program, it automates tracking time and expenses, printing custom bills, recording client transactions, managing multiple projects, and maintaining an accurate audit trail. It prepares all this information for integration into an accounting program or for end use in preparing bills.

Conceptually, Timeslips works as two sets of interacting file cards. The first set holds clients' names and address information. The second set holds individual time and expense records. When you prepare billing worksheets, work-in-progress reports, or bills, the software matches the time and expense records with the client information and composes a form reflecting that match-up.

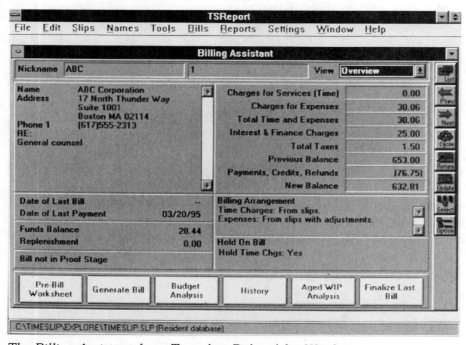

The Billing Assistant from Timeslips Deluxe! for Windows. Timeslips Corporation

The basic unit of information, within the software, is the *slip*, which is the record of performing an activity for the client. There are two types of slips: time slips, billed by time and rate, and expense slips, billed by quantity and cost. For time slips, you need only enter a beginning and an ending time and the program will calculate the actual time. For expense slips, you collect data using quantities and prices.

Not only can you accurately record time and expenses and create appropriate (generally internally circulated) reports and presentation-quality bills, you can also retrieve time, expense, and client data from other systems and use that in the program as well. You can define up to 250 combined time and expense activities.

If you have multiple projects for clients, you can track the budget, receivables, profitability, and other factors individually, and even establish different billing policies and bill formats for each project. You can learn the program by taking a guided tour or overview, by following the steps in the online tutorial, or by exploring individual program features through the tutorial database.

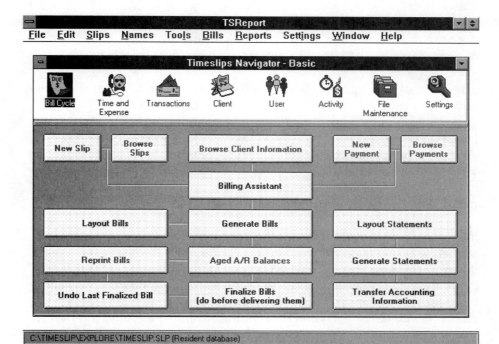

The Navigator makes for smooth sailing in Timeslips Deluxe! for Windows.
Timeslips Corporation

For contractors, the billing possibilities are a neat fit. You can use flat fees, hourly billing, or percentage complete billing. You can customize the appearance of bills with different fonts, graphics, and text and use up to 2,000 characters to describe each time and expense event.

Stand-alone job tracking for small projects

In the days of manual posting, if you wanted a job cost evaluation, your bookkeeper would first have to post all transactions to the general ledger, extrapolate the items pertaining to the given question, and hope that no item was overlooked in the process. With electronic job tracking and job costing, it takes only seconds to create a job cost evaluation. Job-tracking software is extremely useful for keeping tabs on costs so, at any point in a project, contractors know whether the job is running in the red or the black. You can also use this information to refine future estimates, minimize risk, and maximize profits.

DOS job tracking

JOB-TRAC (Soft Ideas, 716-798-4722) might be a good fit for a remodeling contractor specializing in home renovations, additions, and repairs who wants to keep track of job costs. The easy-to-learn, DOS-based software tracks all job costs entered under five categories: material, labor, subcontractors, travel, and miscellaneous. There are three kinds of printouts: customer billing, job information, and a job proposal form for short-form contract writing (with limited ability to change a number of lines of contract clauses).

The main work screen is divided in half. The upper half lists the billing address of the project and the five basic categories, with the designated percentage of overhead and the adjusted cost with the percentages added for each of the five. Also listed are the original estimated price, profit/loss to date, type of work, and job number. You see all vital summaries at a glance. The lower screen provides a listing divided into two columns of 10 items each of all functions performed by the program, each followed by a short description.

In the lower half of the screen, the 20 categories follow a logical sequence for your data entry and the highlighter automatically moves down to the next category when you close the current one. Or you can type any designating letter to enter a specific category. You set up the overhead rates for the five categories. If a project calls for a different rate base, you can override the settings by typing a different rate in the entry screen for any of the categories.

```
JOB TRAC  Proposal & Profit Tracking program by Soft Ideas(716) 798-5715
P&F                           12-28-1995            Job Tracking Program

BILLING ADDRESS ..                                    Est. $12000.00
      MATERIAL COST $ 4564.00  Rate  15%   ADJ. COST $ 5248.60 TAX $    0.00
        LABOR COST $ 1800.00  Rate  15%   ADJ. COST $ 2070.00
 SUB-CONTRACTOR COST $ 1500.00  Rate  10%   ADJ. COST $ 1650.00
       MILEAGE COST $    0.00  Rate   0%   ADJ. COST $    0.00
 MISCELLANEOUS COST $ 2245.00 Rate  15%   ADJ. COST $ 2581.75
DATE : 12-28-1995  Job No# : 001  TYPE :              PROFIT/LOSS $   449.65

 A - Enter Customer Information    K - SAVE DISPLAYED Job Information
 B - Enter Job Proposal            L - VIEW/CHANGE SAVED Job Info.
 C - Enter Material suppliers      M - CLEAR DISPLAYED Job Information
 D - Enter Labor costs            N - CHANGE/INPUT OVERHEAD RATES
 E - Enter Sub-Contractors         O - BACKUP/RECALL YEARS Jobs
 F - Enter Mileage Costs           P - VIEW/PRINT PROFIT/LOSS for YEAR
 G - Enter Miscellaneous Charges   Q - PRINT MAILING LABELS
 H - PRINT Job Information          R - EDIT STANDARD INFORMATION FILES
 I - PRINT Job Proposal            S - CLEAR JOBS START NEW YEAR
 J - PRINT Customer Billing        T - EDIT/VIEW LAST YEARS JOBS
        ———— PRESS < Esc > key to END ESTIMATION PROGRAM ————
 Enter option LETTER or USE the ARROWS to SELECT OPTION & PRESS Enter or Return
```

A split screen makes for easy data entry and viewing with JOB-TRAC.

The software provides predefined settings for 15 job types, which you can use to define an overall project type, and 15 aspects of a given trade. You can also enter up to 15 employees, 15 subcontractors, and 15 material suppliers. When in the appropriate category, you can pull down the list and type the number to automatically enter the entry into the form. If, for example, you select an employee, the program will automatically insert the predefined labor wage; you add the number of hours worked and the program will automatically calculate the total, with overhead included. Enter various employees at different wages and the program will calculate the average per-hour wage times the overhead rate, which is used to figure out work crew charges.

JOB-TRAC allows you to manually enter additional entries, up to 39 employees, trip entries, and miscellaneous charges, and 52 contractors and 52 suppliers per project. The program keeps the previous year's work in a separate file, thereby enabling you to view up to two years of work. Besides keeping a running total of your projects, you can use any of the five categories to run what-if calculations without setting up a project.

Though not designed as an estimating program, you can use JOB-TRAC to prepare quick estimates if you have all the prices and just want to figure totals, overhead, and what-ifs with different percentages.

The program is excellent for but essentially limited to projects of short duration, like roofing, siding, painting, and other small residential renovations or repairs. It doesn't perform cumulative weekly totals of your labor. For that matter, all entries are totals; the program doesn't provide for progress tracking or viewing your profit/loss by selected time frames. For those performing jobs of short duration and working in DOS, this could be an effective stand-alone tracking program.

Neat job costing with Trackit

Trackit (Berg Mechanical, 800-600-2374) has a single aim: to help builders track actual expenses against original projected budgeted costs on a project in order to avoid cost overruns. Actual expenditures appear in red while planned budget appears in blue. This facilitates almost instant line-by-line comparison of expenses. You can also import data from QuickBooks, Quicken, Microsoft Money, 3D Architect, FloorPlan Plus 3D, and numerous other programs.

You can easily build your own templates of actual cost vs. budgeted cost for the type of jobs you normally perform, and construct a simple time line taken from the dates the work was performed, showing how the job is progressing. As Trackit has a very powerful filtering system for fielding and evaluating queries, you can evaluate individual jobs, all jobs, or particular items. User-definable filters allow you to break out specific items and costs according to their specification. You can then view, print, export or e-mail the results.

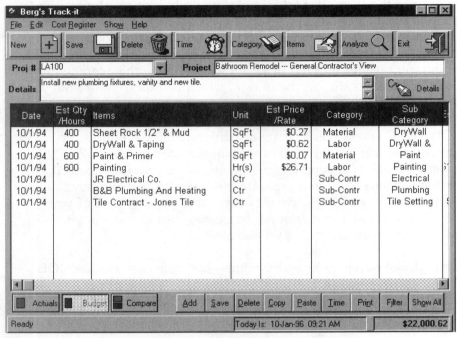

Date	Est Qty /Hours	Items	Unit	Est Price /Rate	Category	Sub Category
10/1/94	400	Sheet Rock 1/2" & Mud	SqFt	$0.27	Material	DryWall
10/1/94	400	DryWall & Taping	SqFt	$0.62	Labor	DryWall &
10/1/94	600	Paint & Primer	SqFt	$0.07	Material	Paint
10/1/94	600	Painting	Hr(s)	$26.71	Labor	Painting
10/1/94		JR Electrical Co.	Ctr		Sub-Contr	Electrical
10/1/94		B&B Plumbing And Heating	Ctr		Sub-Contr	Plumbing
10/1/94		Tile Contract - Jones Tile	Ctr		Sub-Contr	Tile Setting

You can easily view actuals, budgets, and comparisons of line items with Berg's Trackit.

Using templates and standard text to create documents and forms

MANY software packages use topic-specific preformatted text and questions that can save contractors time and effort in formulating words for signature-ready and other documents. Some, like contract-writing programs, are designed specifically for the construction industry. Others, like form-filling, form-creating, and data-filing programs, include broad-based text or forms that can be easily adapted to suit the construction business. This second category includes do-it-yourself legal programs and safety plan programs.

In the construction business, as much as or perhaps even more than in other businesses, it's important to get it all exactly right in print. A topic- or content-specific program can go a long way in helping you do a great deal of the document writing that can protect your business interests.

Typically, content-specific template software provides the basic, editable wording for a wide range of documents that fit within the title category. In most cases, you can customize the documents with company particulars.

Why contractors need to put it all in writing

The term "a gentleman's agreement" connotes an arrangement or understanding neither party cares or bothers to put in writing. In the real nitty-gritty world of contractors and remodelers, however, it's better to have the clearest possible understanding of each party's rights and responsibilities, as well as the scope and limitations of the work.

The construction business is fluid in the movement of money, and in a short time it's very easy to accrue labor expenses and large bills for material before you get paid by your client. This can lead to you hanging on a thin string hoping the client pays you. If you don't have a solid contract laying everything out in black and white, you're exposing yourself to a financial liability.

There are numerous excuses and reasons a client can give you for not paying for work done, such as: "I didn't understand what was involved," "I didn't really agree to that change," "I lost my job," "Your price is too high," We're getting a divorce and selling the house," and "I don't want to pay; you'll have to sue me." All are variations on a theme—disagreement over money—which most contractors unfortunately have experienced in their business dealings. The best protection against a wayward-thinking client is to have a well-written, signed contract and to get signatures on the bottom line for every change order as it comes into play, before you start the work.

No contract, no specification, and no set of plans will cover every conceivable disagreement. Therefore, the more bases you cover up front, the safer your money will be. Most contractors go into a deal with honest intentions and assume clients will act in good faith. While a strong contract can't guarantee payment, putting the details of the project in black and white can help your cause in informal arbitration or litigation.

Details are what makes a good contract

A contract-writing and specification program could certainly be a good investment for contractors and remodelers looking to formalize intent. Nothing serves a contractor better than a clearly written contract that's fair to all parties and—all things being equal—even more than fair to the contractor. The tighter you can write a contract, the better.

A contract-writing program not only gives form to the writing, but it should ensure that you include all necessary parts and produce a complete contract. Some contract-writing programs also include customizable construction forms that cover most daily contractor needs.

Many contractors, when awarded work through an architect, are given the A.I.A. contract to sign as binding between them and the owner. The A.I.A. contract is usually fine for architects because it self-servingly protects *them*. Period. And most architects aren't lawyers and are wary of deviating from the standard format. But standard contracts don't always cover all job-specific situations. For this reason, you should consider writing your own contract or using a contract-writing package that offers templated clauses that can be organized into a suitable contract or drafted, as an amendment, onto a standard A.I.A. contract.

Threshold Construction Computer Forms and Contracts

Threshold Construction Computer Forms and Contracts (Wilhelm Publishing, 800-842-2027) is a fairly comprehensive package that comes with almost six dozen forms covering many aspects of running a construction business. Not a stand-alone program, it's compatible with most word processing packages.

As is or as you like it

You can use the contracts as they are or alter the text by changing the wording or eliminating paragraphs. The forms and contracts are quite comprehensive and—highly appropriate but surprisingly not always the case in this type of program—are written from the contractor's perspective.

The builder/architect contract, for example, explicitly removes any item an architect would normally charge a general client but should not charge a builder. Some of the items excluded are: cost estimates or financial analysis, analysis of builder's needs, interior design, and as-built drawings. The contract also specifies that plans are the property of the builder.

BUILDER/ARCHITECT CONTRACT

THIS CONTRACT, made and entered into this * day of *, 19 *, by and between *, hereinafter referred to as "ARCHITECT"; and *, hereinafter referred to, jointly and severally, as "BUILDER";

WITNESSETH:

1. ARCHITECT hereby agrees to prepare plans and * specifications for BUILDER together with any changes BUILDER shall make from time to time.
2. BUILDER agrees to provide to ARCHITECT:
    (a) a budget;
    (b) information regarding requirements for the project;
    (c) a legal description and a copy of the land survey on which the project will be constructed, together with as applicable, property iron locations, zoning, deed restrictions, easements, utility services, street locations, information pertaining to existing buildings and trees, drainage, and grades;
    (d) data concerning soil, air, water and rock conditions (including test borings, percolation tests, air and water pollution tests, soil bearing values, ground corrosion and resistivity tests, together with recommendations) if needed;
    (e) other restrictions or conditions that might require a variance in the plans and * specifications.

3. BUILDER and ARCHITECT agree the following ARCHITECT'S services are not being provided as a part of this contract:
    (a) a cost estimate or other financial analysis;
    (b) analysis of BUILDER'S needs;
    (c) tests, studies or evaluations of any nature for soil, air, water, rock, waste, nor site grading or drainage evaluations;
    (d) submissions for governmental approval;
    (e) interior design;
    (f) consultation regarding any work damaged by fire, wind, water or other cause of loss during

Template for builder/architect contract in Threshold Construction Computer Forms and Contracts.

Other documents include builder/homeowner contracts; builder/subcontractor contracts; change order forms; subcontractor forms; numerous checklists such as move-in checklist, warranty, worksheet, payment, lien waver, and analysis; and 3 FHA forms, including the description of materials form. There are also several specification documents and cost-estimating documents.

Some of the documents are explicit and quite complete. The concrete flatwork agreement, for example, includes spaces for PSI, slump, finish, sealer, vapor barrier, and reinforcing rods, in addition to other requirements broken out for different locations in a residential dwelling.

There's an asterisk within the body of the text wherever you're to add names of the participating parties. With your word processor, you can use the Find command to locate each asterisk sequentially.

To verify appropriateness, you can print out the forms you're most likely to use, go over the wording carefully to verify it says what you want, and, if the documents are contract forms, pass them to your attorney.

Form-filling and form-creating software

Paper forms account for about 80 percent of all business documents. With a PC and a thorough software package, it's easy to make them look good. Some programs are dedicated to filling out commercially printed forms (loaded into the printer) or electronic versions of commercially printed forms. This type of software eliminates tedious typing, helps ensure against careless input and transposal errors, and assures a neatly turned out form. Other packages guide users in recreating paper forms currently in use in your office, customizing them as templates to meet your needs, and then filling them in. In either case, being able to generate the forms electronically eliminates stockpiling and assures availability of every form whenever needed, as long as you don't run out of paper and ink.

A solid electronic form-filling and/or form-creating program allows offices of any size to impart a consistent, professional look to everyday invoicing, contracts, work orders, proposals, and other correspondences vital to running a business. In addition—and herein lies the chief attraction for many users—you can fill the forms out on screen. A well-designed computerized form is generally more legible than a hand-written one and is easy to revise while filling in. Not only can most people type faster than they write, but an easy-to-use program will also automate transfer of information and fill in certain types of repetitive data, like the date and time, and sequential serial numbers automatically.

Even with computers, you can't entirely get away from paper forms. In most contractors' and remodelers' office, because of laws, rules, regulations, and custom, they still proliferate. With software dedicated to specific chores, however, you can speed up the filling-out process of preprinted forms or create your own templated forms and fill them out as well.

Filling out forms on a computer helps eliminate errors, speeds the often tedious process of filling out repetitive forms, and provides a database in which to store the records.

Form-Filling Software

Form-Filling Software (New England Business Forms, 800-225-9550), suppliers of traditional fill-in-the-blank business forms, is a dedicated software program designed specifically to fill in NEBS forms electronically. The inexpensive DOS-based program produces six different types of professionally filled-out laser or continuous paper forms, which you can customize with your company name, address, and even logo in minutes, speeding billing and routine business paperwork.

What you see is what you get: Unalterable forms

There are six templates: a job estimate, proposal, change order, letter of transmittal, agreement, and job invoice. It's an easy program to use because it's set up as WYSIWYG: what you see is what you get. The program works from simple commands in a menu format and offers fast type-and-print operation. As the software is dedicated form filling, not form printing, you can't change any of the fields or print to plain paper. You load the preprinted forms from NEBS into your printer and, when you've completed filling the on-screen form, you select the print command. The completed form is ready a few seconds later.

Easy operation

The general screen is divided into three areas: the pull-down menus across the top, the data entry fields, and a message line across the bottom listing hot keys for context-sensitive help for access to pop-up lists of entry choices. Once you learn the basics of operation, you can use any of the forms, as the keystrokes are the same for each form.

When you select Data Entry for a form, the screen shows all the data entry fields. As you enter the information, the cursor moves from field to field. For longer documents such as contracts, change orders, or proposals, you can use the forms as the formal first page, followed by either additional forms or the balance of the text produced with a word processing program and printed on plain paper.

Preprinted provisions as a starting point

On the back of the agreement form is a one-page printed Provisions of the Agreement, which provides limited contract clauses outlining both owner's and contractor's rights and responsibilities, conflict provisions, and general provisions. For contractors without a standard contract form, this could be a handy starting point and guide for developing additional contract clauses.

The invoice form allows for up to 100 tax codes. The codes represent assigned rates that are automatically calculated. Totals and subtotals are also automatically calculated.

Automating the basics on new forms by drawing from the old

There are two file-card databases: one for contacts, the other for products (material). Though you can fill out the "file cards" beforehand, the auto capture feature automatically saves the information into the appropriate file-card database as you type forms with new information on the fly.

The fields used with autocapture include customer and address, products, terms, shipping methods, and tax codes. The software is "smart," so if the information is already in the database for an existing client, when you fill out a new form you can retrieve the information from the file cards with the click of a hot key.

In fact, information in the file cards is accessible to all forms. For example, if you entered a client using the contract form, you can use the appropriate hot key in the job invoice form and have access to the client information there. This is a handy time-saving capability that cuts down on computer "paperwork."

Make your own macros for stock phrases

The software can also record up to ten macros (each having up to 240 keystrokes), which is useful for stock phrases like "Thank you for your prompt attention" or "Your payment is 30 days past due."

You can use the information stored on a file card to create a variety of reports. With each form, there are a number of reports available to summarize your work by customer, product, sales tax summary, and invoice total. You can view the reports on screen, print them out, or save them to disk for filing.

The program doesn't number the form until you send it to the printer. The timing of the numbering is designed to prevent printing duplication of forms.

Compatibility with other applications

Another plus if you start with the basic NEBS software and forms is that many companies writing software for the construction industry have written the code for various NEBS forms into their software. NEBS publishes a Directory of Software, which lists the vendors, type of software, price, and which forms are compatible with the program. The vendors under the contractor listing in the directory include accounting and management, job costing, integrated estimating, and payroll packages.

PerForm for Windows

If you prefer creating your own forms rather than buying premade forms, there's a package to help you automate the process. PerForm for Windows (Delrina, 800-268-6082) is a low-cost package with streamlined capabilities for both creating familiar-looking paper forms on a computer from templates and for starting from scratch and designing single- and multiple-page forms to exact specifications. For either type, it also serves as a fast, efficient form filler.

Lots of suitable, construction-related choices

You can use any of the almost four dozen forms as they are or customize them to suit your own purposes. The software lets you create multiple- as well as single-page forms. Though not developed particularly for the construction business, the program's templated offerings can work very nicely indeed for builders and contractors. Prepared forms include a work order, request for quote, quote, service report, time sheet, things to do, change order, payment, proposal, price list, invoice, and daily time report. Each choice has a one-line description at the bottom of the screen.

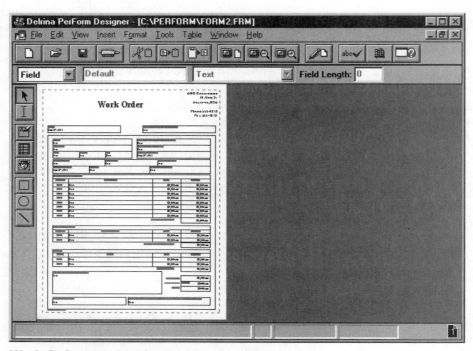

Work Order template for Perform for Windows.

Customizing the look

The software lets you sneak-preview four diverse set-up styles—standard, casual, modern, and professional-looking—so you can use the one that suits your business best. Once the style is established, the software proceeds through a dialog, asking refining questions. You pick one of ten supplied headers to arrange company logo, address, and form title, or you can either use your own predefined header or omit a header. If the program has already created a form for you, your previous choices are displayed as overrideable defaults.

Once you've set your form style and typed the company name and name of the form if different from the template, the program creates the form. After the form has been created, you can change size of any boxes to accommodate the amount of data for each area, if necessary. You can also resize and magnify the form on screen for easy filling and then click back to standard magnification for full viewing.

Adding a job photo as a personalizing feature

Here's a very nice feature, part of what makes PerForm such a refined program: you can use one of the provided images as a sort of identifying watermark for your forms or, even better, use one of your own images (perhaps a job photo) in the background. You can scan job photos into your computer, or take them with a digital camera and software that imports the images directly into your computer. With just a couple of clicks, you can create highly customized forms featuring a digital image taken of the actual job site for which the forms are being generated.

No more squinting at small print

You aren't locked into fitting your data into the preformatted form size; you can change box sizes to accommodate your needs—perhaps to more magnification for easy filling and then back to standard magnification for full viewing.

PerForm creates a database the first time you save information entered into a form, and the database is unique to that particular form. Every time you fill out the templated form, the information is entered into a record in that database. You can revise a record as often as you like.

Many of the tasks have a step-by-step "show me" demo that actually runs through the sequences like a movie. You can replay it or manually select one screen at a time, for slower or repeated viewing.

Making it perfectly, precisely clear

You can add text anywhere on the forms as explanatory notes when, for example, the text label isn't precise enough or it's next to a series of check boxes. You can also add text to a table's column titles and to individual cells. If you want to take forms to a job site or a job meeting, you can always print out the required number for filling in by hand. And you can program calculations such as taxes, variable discounts, and shipping charges into your design so the forms will automatically total invoices, statements, credit memos, and expense reports.

When creating forms, you can determine the field type for every field. It's then possible to set up a customized estimating form that includes fields for text, numbers, percentage, currency, and data. This takes some proficiency with the program, but if you haven't yet found an estimating program that works your way, this might be a customizable solution. The program allows you to add calculations to the fields and can calculate to compute subtotals, taxes, and percentage add-ons.

Essentially, the software saves the information, not the total form, for future use. And you can always pull up the information, slot it into the form and fax it directly, without creating any hard copy.

MyAdvanced Invoices & Estimates for Windows

MyAdvanced Invoices & Estimates for Windows (MySoftware Company, 800-325-3508), is an easy-to-use, double-duty package that produces professional-looking estimates and invoices along with a customizable products and services file into which you enter your products/services and price once. For contractors, this would be items along the lines of periodic maintenance jobs or other repetitive cost information. When the pricing is needed for estimates, quotes, or invoices, you select the service from the menu and the price and total automatically are entered.

MyAdvanced Invoices & Estimates for Windows allows you to choose how the forms are filled out by selecting the fields that appear on the form and in renaming of many of the fields. The overall configuration of the form, though, cannot be altered.

One click turns an estimate into an invoice

A particular program strength is that you can use the software to write a simple, short estimate or a quotation, giving a description of the work in outline form, and then change it to an invoice with a single click if and when you win the project. With generous record-keeping facilities (five kinds of sales reports and three cash-management features), the overall capabilities of this program make it more than a unidirected, dedicated form-filling program.

Though the service database—a listing of the type of work you perform—isn't contractor-specific, it can handle the needs of small contractors, such as those doing home repair, jobbing, running a fleet of trucks, or even performing annual service calls. You can set up invoice or estimate lines in the service database that describe individual or groups of items and descriptions with or without the pricing included. For example, if you do annual air conditioning maintenance, you can either bundle the elements of an annual checkup together or list them separately.

The program tracks customer information, service information, and estimates and keeps historical records. If a project becomes an estimate, all you have to do is pull up that estimate, update any pricing, and convert it to an invoice with the click of a button. Estimates are tracked as outstanding estimates, and as such are not tracked in sales reports or in any of the invoice balances.

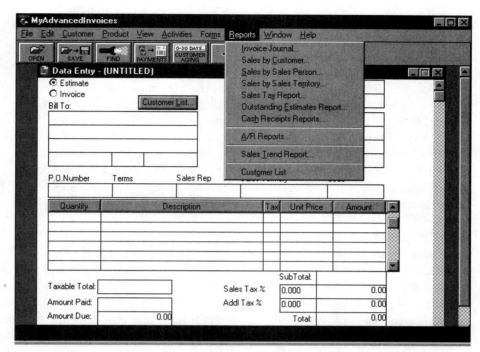

Estimate/Invoice screen in MyAdvanced Invoices & Estimates for Windows.

The customer list stores client names and addresses, billing terms, shipping information, credit limits, payment terms, tax rates, phone numbers, and contacts.

Creating assemblies speeds the billing

As you can use up to 99 characters for each item in the database, you can create small assemblies for billing purposes. You can add items to the service list by typing them directly into the invoice and then, by following the prompt, add them to the database. The descriptions can be flagged as taxable or not taxable and the program will calculate the total tax due.

You might want to set up several invoice files. The "files" are separate database accounts, useful for different companies you might own or for diverse projects. The reporting capabilities exclude information among files, but conveniently allow you to use the customer list among files. As you develop a database of customers, you can export the list to a mailing-list or brochure program.

Do it yourself, with electronic legal toolkits

Do-it-yourself business and personal productivity programs are among the best buys on computer outlet shelves. Numerous knowledge-intensive tasks formerly attended to primarily by professionals are now within the province of businesspeople and other individuals working on their own computers.

Covering all sorts of topics from wills and leases to retirement planning, many of the broad-based titles could be valuable time- and money-saving additions to any contractor's small office or home office software library. Even in general business packages, many of the templated letters lend themselves immediately to contractors' and remodelers' needs. Contractor-specific programs, on the other hand, have missives covering a myriad of topic-specific letters, including invitations to bid, unsolicited and solicited proposals, responses to bids, acceptances to proposals, requests for quotes, or notifications on bounced checks.

Both types of programs typically also have letters covering credit, collections, and disputes; orders and inquiries, notices and demands; and thanks and sorry, among others. Since the proverbial check that's always "in the mail" isn't unfortunately always in the mail, some packages thoughtfully include two ways to convey some of the collection messages, gently the first time, then more emphatically the next.

The letters are designed to read as if they were individually composed, but most developers realize that everything a software developer might think to say probably isn't everything you actually have to say, so they build in provisions for either overriding the template and editing in your own particulars. In most cases, you can use your own printed stationery and envelopes, or the program will print a letterhead (and return address on the envelope).

From taking on a partner to leasing more office space, running a construction business is rife with legalities. Protecting yourself from problems with verbal agreements, charges of breach of contract, or other snafus is important. And once again, do-it-yourself software enters the picture.

Typically, legal programs offer a great deal of technical information. Whether you use the program to create first-through-final drafts of necessary documents or to create working drafts to show your lawyer (saving the lawyer time and you money!), legal template software is a well-thought-out way to use the power of your computer.

Template legal programs can save you time and money in preparing all sorts of legal documents that cover a multitude of business-related matters. They're designed to let you take control—to greater and lesser degrees—of legal issues affecting your business and personal life, right from your desk.

This type of program is designed to let you learn about, create, and structure business, personal contracts, and documents in fairly short order before you speak to your attorney. In some cases, you can trust the templated form and use it as a direct document. Other cases might require live lawyer input, but at least you'll have a preliminary document in hand and can confer with your attorney without having to start from scratch.

Small Business Attorney Multimedia

Kiplinger's Small Business Attorney Multimedia (Block Financial Software, 800-813-7940) furnishes over 70 primarily business-oriented contracts and documents, along with context-sensitive guidance, examples, and options. A horizontal-market package targeted to small business/home office users, the software provides expert business guidance that should aid you in preparing for meeting with your lawyer and give you, in hand, a professional-looking, easy-to-revise product to present to a lawyer.

There are online guidelines and suggestions about when to use the documents. Context-sensitive, pop-up guidance windows explain, in everday English, the meaning and impact of just about every clause that could need decoding. Every blank "decision point" that requires individual filling is enclosed in brackets. If you aren't sure what to insert, a single click will bring up screen guidance to help clarify.

The eight easy-browsing categories of documents include financial, sales and marketing, personnel and employment, sale and purchase of goods, corporate, technology, and estate planning/personal asset

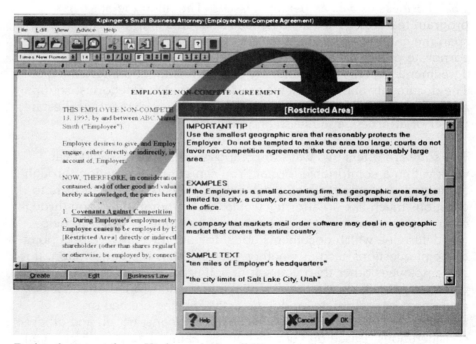

Boilerplate text from Kiplinger's Small Business Attorney Multimeda.
Block Financial Software

protection. The last category includes six distinct wills to cover almost every life situation, a living will, several different powers of attorney, and a prenuptial agreement.

Next to each document is a description that makes clear the purpose and intent of the document. There's also a video discussion on each topic. You can edit documents, though your alterations could affect the document's validity. If you prefer to work within you favorite word processing application, the documents can be exported into most popular word processing programs.

You can refer to the business law topics to further understand the legal aspects of running a company. Topics include arbitration; definitions of contract law, torts, and remedies; commercial documents; and the legal qualifications and ramifications of several types of businesses, including sole proprietorship, partnership, limited partnership, corporation, and limited liability company.

In addition to serving as a hardcopy how-to reference, the user's manual also provides advice on how to find an attorney and establish a good working relationship, and how to decipher various attorney billing options.

Quicken Family Lawyer

Quicken Family Lawyer CD-ROM for Windows (Intuit, 800-223-6925) is another legal software package that's useful for several kinds of small business as well as personal issues. The fill-in-the-answers program features 61 legally binding documents and worksheets that span the gamut from a simple will or bill of sale for a vehicle to corporate proxies, small claims worksheet, and employment agreements such as confidentiality and noncompetition agreements. The documents and worksheets are set up in nine categories, set up as file folders, including financial, corporate, employment, real estate, power of attorney, and health and medical.

The software offers two ways to compose a document, so you can work within a comfortable format. You can enter information through the interview method, which creates documents based on answers to questions much like an attorney would. The program talks you through each step in a nonthreatening conversational tone. In order to help you determine which documents apply to you, the software asks point-by-point questions such as whether your business is a corporation, if it has employees other than yourself, if you use consulting services, if your company deals with confidential information, whether you lease equipment or real estate, and if it's actively being created or restructured. It also queries you on licensing, loans, travel, and other considerations. Based on your responses, Family Lawyer will give you a list of documents that might apply to your current circumstances.

Alternately, you can, as is typical of template programs of this type, select a particular type of document and start there directly, using a fill-in-the-blank method. There are myriad spoken and text-based cross-checks and balances to ensure that you create and fill in the documents correctly. An extensive plain-language dictionary offers definitions for thousands of legal terms.

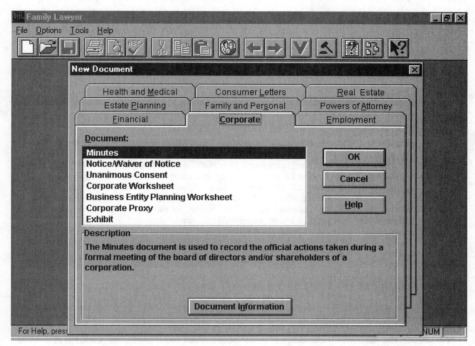

New document screen selection in Quicken Family Lawyer CD-ROM for Windows.

Two easy-to-use programs aimed at OSHA compliance

If you aim for full monitoring and compliance, below are two expeditious programs that can go a long way to helping you reach that goal.

FastRegs Compliance Libraries

FastRegs Compliance Libraries (Achieve Technology, 800-446-3427) is a straightforward, user-friendly, menu-driven, Windows-based, CD-ROM program designed to save you hours searching and documenting current OSHA safety regulations in order to comply with federal and state regulations. If you aim for full monitoring and compliance, this is an easy way to put you on the right track. You can purchase separate libraries for safety, hazmat, and environmental libraries, or a comprehensive library that includes all three.

Almost instantly, you can pull up any regulation—accessed by subject or by key words, phrases, or citation numbers—and browse through it, print it, or save it to a disk file for further editing in your word processing program. (As in the government's book-based version, black-and-white line drawings accompany some of the regulations.) You can also label specific sections with an electronic bookmark, for speedy recall, or instantly return to a regulation you were previously viewing.

```
  File     Help    Locate     Search              Updated Thru: 06/30/92

§ 1926.852  Chutes.

   (a) No material shall be dropped to any point lying outside the exterior walls
       of the structure unless the area is effectively protected.
   (b) All materials chutes, or sections thereof, at an angle of more than 45°
       from the horizontal, shall be entirely enclosed, except for openings
       equipped with closures at or about floor level for the insertion of
       materials. The openings shall not exceed 48 inches in height measured
       along the wall of the chute. At all stories below the top floor, such
       openings shall be kept closed when not in use.
   (c) A substantial gate shall be installed in each chute at or near the
       discharge end. A competent employee shall be assigned to control the
       operation of the gate, and the backing and loading of trucks.
   (d) When operations are not in progress, the area surrounding the discharge
       end of a chute shall be securely closed off.
   (e) Any chute opening, into which workmen dump debris, shall be protected by a
       substantial guardrail approximately 42 inches above the floor or other
       surface on which the men stand to dump the material. Any space between the
       chute and the edge of openings in the floors through which it passes shall
       be solidly covered over.
   (f) Where the material is dumped from mechanical equipment or wheelbarrows, a
       securely attached toeboard or bumper, not less than 4 inches thick and 6
 § 1926.852                         FastRegs 1.17 - (C) 1991, OSHA-Soft, Inc.
```

Sample text from FastRegs Compliance Libraries/Construction.

The program allows you to incorporate internal documents, such as standard operating procedures and policy manuals, so you can electronically search them as well. The FastRegs files are updatable on a monthly, quarterly, and annual basis. Regulations for individual states or for all 50 states are also available.

Putting an employee safety plan into place with SafetyPlanBuilder

In these days of sky-high insurance rates, it's good business practice to have an employee safety plan to protect employees and owners alike. Anything that can help contractors prevent or at least minimize the risk of on-the-job injuries or illnesses is a good investment all the way around. In many states and in many industries, not having an employee safety manual violates the law and opens an employer to punitive damages, which aren't usually covered by insurance. But writing a comprehensive safety plan looms as a huge research and development task for many builders and remodelers. As with so many time- and labor-intensive tasks these days, dedicated computer software rises to the occasion.

SafetyPlanBuilder (Jian Tools for Sales, 800-346-5426) is designed to both generate a written safety plan that's OSHA-compliant and help a company protect against lawsuits or noncompliance fines. This DOS-based program is an electronic alternative to both writing a comprehensive safety plan from scratch yourself or hiring an outside consultant to do the job.

The underlying theory in this, as in other programs of this type that contain boilerplate paragraphs, is that it's easier to edit preexisting text presented in an organized sequence than to start with a blank slate.

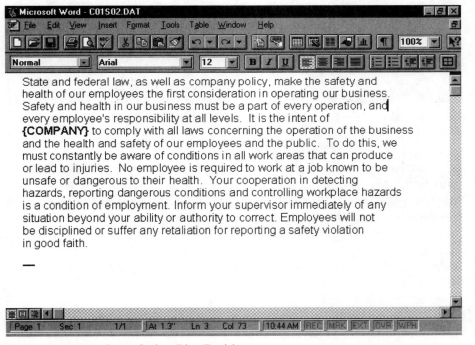

Boilerplate text from SafetyPlanBuilder.

The software is divided into 40 chapters, with each chapter divided into sections. The guts of safety program compliance are contained in the first chapter, Injury and Illness Prevention. The second chapter, like the first, is mandatory in any safety plan, and contains a General Code of Safe Work Practices, from which you select the paragraphs that apply to your own business. Once you select the construction-industry template (one of the 14 general industries listed) for your specific state, you'll get a default preselection of those paragraphs that are most applicable. (Twenty-two states and Puerto Rico have specific requirements; the other states are the same.) You then save the text you want in order to build the plan you want.

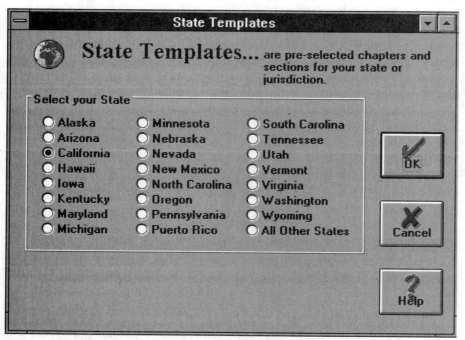

You can hone right in on the regulations specific to your home state in SafetyPlanBuilder.

The package includes copies of three required OSHA documents (Log and Summary, Supplementary Record, and Job Safety Poster). For further assistance in formatting and maintaining your injury and illness prevention program, 15 sample forms are included, in both hardcopy and as on-screen printable versions. They include: an injury and illness prevention program checklist, hazard checklists, new employee safety checklists, and employee safety record and notice of safety infraction.

You can select from over 250 pages of industry-specific safe work practices, including biohazards, explosives, fire safety, ladders and scaffolds, sanitation, ventilation, and ergonomics. A 300-page reference guide takes plan writers step by step through the actual preparation of a plan that accommodates individual company needs.

The program works by conducting on-screen interviews where you're asked for specific data in order to create customized plans. Basic elements such as safety training and a hazard identification program are also included, along with information on emergency response and employee health services.

The text of SafetyPlanBuilder is based on federal OSHA rules and regulations. In areas where there was no federal OSHA standard, the authors compensated by selecting the most stringent state standard available. You can reproduce all or part of plan in pocket size or in 8½ × 11 size, as many copies as you need, for dispersal to all your employees. The manual suggests you give all your employees a copy and have them sign that they received it.

Keeping an eye on equipment with PM Maintenance

The maxim "a stitch in time . . ." could be interpreted to be all about preventive maintenance. If you want to keep the equipment you use on the job well-oiled, figuratively and literally, you might appreciate PM Equipment Maintenance (KWN Coolware, 800-245-9399), a DOS program designed to keep track, internally, of all types of equipment, from electric drills to company vans. Properly updated with accurate data, it will keep tabs on the repair history, maintenance instructions, work orders, and location assignments of just about anything used by your company. It's also an excellent program for contractors who are in the business of maintaining and servicing equipment for clients on a regular schedule.

The main screen is a four-week calendar, by default flashing on the current day, but it will flash on any date you slot in. It can show what needs to be done on each day of the four week period.

PM Maintenance offers numerous equipment-relevant options. Under maintenance frequency, for example, you have ten choices, from number of hours, daily, weekly, etc. up to annually. Or, if you're dealing with vehicles, you can choose number of miles. The last maintenance date and all supplier information are available instantly.

The program creates a very complete dossier, ready for reference or action, on all equipment. Based on the data you supply, the software creates and prints reports on equipment by type, location, frequency of maintenance, and supplier of equipment. There's virtually no limit to the amount of information you can put in. There's an instant "pop-up and print" history of repairs, for when you need to know what came before (history sometimes repeats itself, even in breakdowns).

PM Maintenance has self-explanatory screens and numerous hot keys to get data into and out of the equipment history. All the reports are available on screen, in a text file, or printed out. (There's also a basic word processor for writing letters or notes relating to equipment maintenance.)

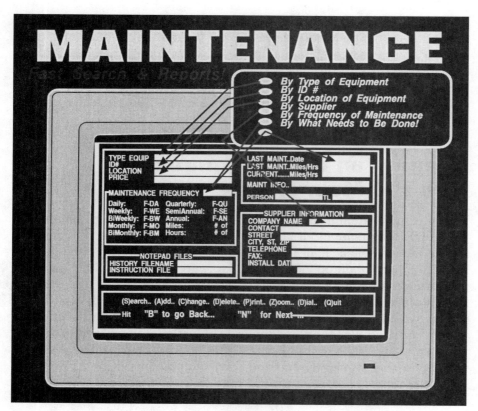

Data entry screen from Equipment Maintenance. KWN Coolware

The software comes with a simple-to-use financial calculator. It will give you costs based on daily, weekly, monthly, or annual interest charges. While intended to evaluate the cost of potential loans to buy business-related equipment and calculate mortgages, loans, and real estate annuities, it works independently of the maintenance aspect of the program as well.

Personal information managers and contact management programs

NO doubt about it, no matter how you look at it, contracting is a paper-intensive field loaded with details. Keeping accurate track of appointments, sales calls, activities, phone calls, and vital face-to-face conversations is often a helter-skelter, chaotic endeavor.

Daily activities for a busy contractor involve phone and personal contacts with so many people that, by the end of the day or week, it's often impossible to create and maintain the paperwork regarding who said what, what agreements were made, which change orders were requested and slow-downs encountered, and so on. Even with pockets bulging with scrap paper and truck visor clipped with notes, most information is often left—or worse, lost—to memory.

Personal information managers (PIMs) and contact management programs are increasingly popular software solutions. Potentially powerful tools that deliver the means for time and information tracking from a variety of perspectives, PIMs and contact management programs can help keep contractors and remodelers organized and informed of their schedules. Though the division between categories is fuzzy and there's some overlap, broadly speaking, contact management programs encompass more territory and a wider frame of reference than PIMs.

PIMs vs. contact-oriented contact management programs

PIMs are built around the address book and a personal calendar, while contact management programs are people- and company-oriented. Contact management is designed to track all sorts of contact information and automate routine scheduling, reporting, and communication not necessarily for just one person but for a company. Contact management programs are better for maintaining databases by categories of contacts, and for sending out reminders, occasional letters, and mass mailings. They can also contribute more functionality, increasing both personal and staff productivity.

Designed to optimize personal job productivity, PIMs allow you to quickly pull up a phone number, address, or morning job meeting. While contact management programs routinely provide those functions, they're typically more contact-oriented, with numerous detailed contact databases, integrated calendars, built-in word processors, and customizable searching and reporting capabilities.

A further distinction in a field that sometimes encompasses cross-over entries is that PIMs are generally focused more on scheduling individual time and activities, rather than keeping track of details about your contacts. With the frequent interaction that goes on throughout the day with clients, prospective clients, architects, subcontractors, and suppliers, contractors are usually a perfect match for either of these types of software products.

Another distinction between contact management programs and personal information managers is that contact management software typically uses integrating capabilities to improve productivity. Ideally, there's linkage between activities and contact records so you save time and have access to instant information without manual linking.

Another major difference is that contact management programs usually have fairly agile, user-friendly word processing capabilities. Some have templates that give you various types of predefined letter, note, or fax setups and, to speed correspondence, might even feature one-click mail merging to produce personalized letters, envelopes, and mailing labels on demand. This is a particularly nice aspect as it saves time when you have to send quick notes to subcontractors and suppliers. Many of the programs also have extensive spell checkers, so you can send out polished, word-perfect documents.

Portable printouts

Contractors used to carrying their lives around in pocket-sized or briefcase-sized books (or even Day-Runners, Day-Timers, or organizers of that type) will appreciate the ability to print out single-sheet schedules for the upcoming day, week, or month. With either a PIM or a contact management program, you should be able to print daily, weekly, or monthly calendar to go, with user-specified start and end dates and times. You should also be able to print it in the appropriate size to fit into a paper-based organizer, if you're still hedging your bets and carrying one around. (If you have your PIM or contact management program loaded into a laptop, you won't need the hardcopy at all.)

Whether a PIM or a contact management program is a better fit for contractors depends partially upon how much functionality you need and your natural working style.

PIMs: An electronic address book plus

A PIM is the electronic equivalent of a "little black book" that's usually filled to the margins and stuffed with inserts, and is an efficient way for a contractor to store and retrieve a variety of information about people, to-do items, expenses, commitments, and appointments. It brings paper-based organization to the computer desktop by providing several functions in easily navigated integrated modules.

Calendar view, with lots of notes

Most PIMs let you keep track of appointments, to-do-items, addresses, and phone numbers electronically, view it all on screen, and print out as little or as much of the data as you need. In effect, they serve as stand-alone notated calendars, electronic schedule keepers, and appointment books, with such categorized addenda as to-do lists and random notes to yourself.

Many PIMs also provide expense-tracking functions in integrated modules. This function is in no way intended to provide job costing, but rather is intended to track travel, meals, and other miscellaneous expenses that can be attached to a client or project. You should also be able to track time spent on meetings and phone calls.

Automatic conflict checking

Some of the more sophisticated PIMs that have networking capabilities offer automatic conflict checking and can locate the first available free time for all parties within your organization. Many offer cross-referencing, free-form note-taking capabilities, and key-word text searches.

Starting with a familiar look

The easiest PIMs to work with mimic the familiar paper-based organizers. The screen represents an open book, showing a day, a week, or a month at a glance. You can flip from screen to screen, scheduling, verifying, altering schedules, and saving all changes easily.

PIMs often follow a book-look format, but with electronic data entry, such as in this view of the Day-Timer Organizer.

In terms of filling in the screen, look for a program with drag-and-drop scheduling. This is the easiest to manipulate and should assure complete transfer of information without inadvertent changes.

The program reviewed in the following section is a typical strong PIM entry. It features the basic functions generally looked for in a PIM and offers many accessory enhancements that can boost productivity throughout a contractor's day.

The Day-Timer Organizer

The Day-Timer Organizer (Day-Timer Technologies, 800-225-5005) is the desktop version of the familiar paper-based Day-Timer organizational system. It prints to all popular (paper-based) Day-Timer formats. The individual and group scheduling features include drag-and-drop scheduling, automatic conflict checking, and pop-up alarm/snooze options. On planner views, it will also sort tasks by a priority designation familiar to you, in letter or numerical order, or by high/low/none delineation.

A built-in expense tracking capability lets you track travel, entertainment, and miscellaneous expenses by client or project, over any specified time period. Time spent on meetings and phone calls can also be tallied.

You can choose the amount of information to transfer to paper, and can opt for double-sided printing or use of overflow sheets to accommodate lengthy entries. You can also select a single module from the daily planner—a to-do list or a schedule, perhaps—to print independently.

Contact management programs

A contact management program offers the expanded ability not only to perform the usual PIM tasks but also to manage the day-to-day activities and correspondences associated with various lists of contacts. Some of the most popular contact management programs include Act 2 for Windows, Maximizer, Telemagic, and Sharkware.

Providing far more functionality than just an electronic calendar or Rolodex, a contact management program integrates contact and scheduling information with communications and reporting activities.

Groupings to suit your needs

Most contact management programs offer multiple ways of sorting contacts, so you can deal with information related to specific groups or projects quickly and easily in multiple ways. It's an excellent way to keep running notes on clients, subcontractors, suppliers, and others.

213

The contact management program also allows you to easily send letters to contacts either individually or via mass mailings.

You can set up several different databases within your contact management program in order to organize listings of (and relevant notes about) subcontractors, suppliers, architects, and others. You should also list projects, clients, and leads in user-defined categories that work for you.

If you use it frequently throughout the day, a feature-rich contact management program can serve as a potent high-tech business organizer almost worth a salary of its own. In a hectic office that either lacks a full-time secretary or has an already overworked one, it can, indeed, seem almost like an extra employee.

Limitless expansion possibilities

With a database preformatted to maintain and manipulate lists of contacts and information, this category of software is in effect an almost limitlessly expandable electronic "folder" full of the type of data you'd find on a business card, plus more detailed facts and impressions stemming from all your contacts over time.

Most contact management packages offer word processing to a greater or lesser degree, a full-featured calendar, and reporting capabilities, with easily editable scheduling, quick data lookups and retrieval, and contact specific note-taking. Other features generally include alarms, automatic phoning and faxing, mail merging (transmission of the same letter, addressed to suit, to any selected contacts), and import/export capabilities.

The point-and-shoot import/export capability saves a lot of time and effort as you eliminate the need to rekey information (possibly inadvertently changing letters or numbers in the process). This feature is a real plus, particularly if you're upgrading your database from a competitive product.

Typically, contact management programs are full of scheduling features. You can flag crucial phone calls, meetings, and other tasks with memory-resident beepers and pop-up reminders so you don't miss any conference calls, job meetings, or look-see appointments. There are usually simple ways to schedule recurring activities on daily, weekly, and monthly calendars. And there's often an optional automatic roll-over of uncompleted activities so, when you postpone what you should have done today, you can't forget about it entirely.

Keeping tabs and maintaining a job log

Contact management software paves the way for easy historical record-keeping on a daily basis. Take advantage of this capability. When working with a contact management program, you can set up a database for each new project you bid. If two projects are in the estimating stage and you're getting prices from the same subcontractor for both, enter the company into each database.

As each day unfolds, you can add to your previous notes of conversations and job meetings, prices from subcontractors and vendors, conversations with clients, architects, or others in the notes field for the appropriate estimate. By the time you're ready to quote a price, you will in essence have a complete dossier of who said what about various aspects of your projects.

Many ways to review notes

You can review notes by date, individual, or any grouping of your own devising. This gives you an added check and a different perspective than the one you get from reviewing an estimating sheet. If the estimate leads to a contract, the database is already set up and you can just continue to add daily notes.

Indisputable documentation

Though most contractors go into a project with honest expectations of doing a first-class job and making a fair profit, any documentation of time spent, change orders requested, and job meetings held can help supplement your memory of the way things were and therefore your side of the dispute. In essence, you're documenting a case history.

Contracting is rife with possible disputes and sometimes full of contentious clients. If somewhere down the line a project turns sour, if you have to go to arbitration or court, your daily notes in all probability will be the only job log for the judge to review.

If you're a home builder and have an active sales force, each member should ideally keep a record of every contact. Likewise, try to get the names of any visitors to your site who could be potential clients down the line. Keep their names and addresses or phone numbers in your database, and use the program to send out follow up letters or schedule follow-up calls.

Mail-merging capabilities

Contact managers that have mail-merging capabilities allow you to send customized letters to contacts clustered together by any categories of your choosing. You can create databases of contacts that are organized by the type of work in which they might be interested (decks, remodels, developments) or even by time periods in which they might be interested in having work done.

No need to lose a potential client who visits your job, likes your work, and mentions, "Perhaps in the fall." Come late summer, send that individual a note to rejuvenate his or her interest. If you've jotted some personal particulars into your PC, reiterate some detail of them in your note as an icebreaker. Likewise, when you make follow-up phone calls, a polite mention of some aspect of the original conversation, perhaps along the lines of "How was your vacation?" can makes prospective clients feel you actually remember and care about them. It takes just a moment to jot down little facts in the notes of a client.

Act! for Windows

One of the best-selling contact managers has long been the various versions of ACT!, an acronym for *automatic contact tracking*. Act! for Windows (Symantec, 800-441-7234) is the current version. With just about out-of-box usability, this is a good, solid program that has won many industry awards. It allows you to enter an unlimited number of contacts in 70 customizable fields, each with its own record of date-stamped notes entered into an unlimited notepad.

If you need a report of all client/contractor contact over the course of a project thus far, including letters, faxes, phone calls, and payments, or you want to review a report of all activity with everyone involved over a specific period of time (week, month, year), just select the desired contacts, call up the appropriate report form, and—within seconds—can view the data on screen, print it out, or save it on disk. You can also add custom look-ups as menu items, which is very handy if you want to send a pitch letter to hot prospects or a "time for a redo?" reminder to old clients. When you click on Write, the contact name and address is automatically placed on the letterhead, saving you the time of addressing the letter. You can also combine databases for creating mailing list groups for other types of call-to-action custom mailings or other means of contact, and save those groups for recall or modification at any time.

The instant lookup feature gives you immediate access to details about any name in the database. Transferring between databases is a very quick process. You can use the same subcontractors for different projects and keep the notes for them straight simply by listing the subcontractors separately in each job database. An icon toolbar offers 15 programmed "shortcut" macro buttons, plus up to five that you can designate yourself.

The software lets you pinpoint just the contact you're interested in by searching for key words or using Boolean logic for more sophisticated searches. You can save custom groups (drawn from other databases), like "hot prospects" or "clients to approach for seasonal work," who might take advantage of a new service you're offering through a special mailing.

The program has complete network support and integrated electronic mail (e-mail) support for easy communication with contacts via Act!Mail, which you can purchase separately.

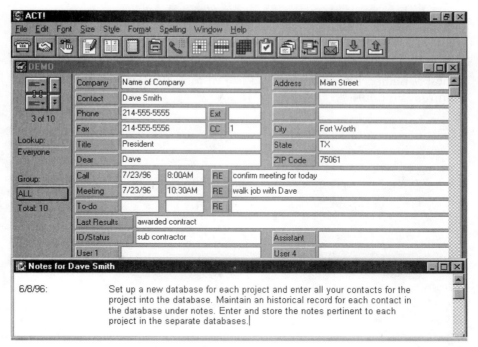

Sample contact screen, in ACT!, with the note window open.

You can also print calendars and address books in any of 20 organizer formats for several sizes of paper-based systems, including Day-Runner, Day-Timer, Franklin Day Planner, and Filofax.

Janna Contact 95

Janna Contact 95 (Janna Systems, 800-268-6107) is a Microsoft Office 95 contact manager that's designed specifically to take full advantage of Windows 95 and OLE 2 (object linking and embedding) system technology.

You can view your schedule not only by day, week, and month, but also by year. The action item lists remind you of one-time and recurring appointments, and activities or tasks with voice, text, and even video alarms. It's easy to create custom data fields for as few or as many contacts as you like.

The program is strong on handling correspondence. Because of the OLE 2 support, you can link every relevant letter, fax, spreadsheet, presentation, voice note, and even e-mail to a particular contact and/or appointment. If you keep the program open on screen when talking to a client or an architect, for instance, you'll have just about every correspondence you might need to refer to just a click or two away. Likewise, when preparing for a job meeting or an appointment, if you glance at what's in that database you won't overlook any details. And you can instantly print out anything in hardcopy.

Though the software isn't as easy as ACT! to become comfortable with, it offers many Windows 95 features that make it singularly attractive, including true 32-bit database performance, OLE 2 drag-and-drop (useful for customizing letters and other documents with contact-specific information), and use of long filenames. It also features Windows 95 help.

Marketing your business

WHEN marketing your company services, the size of your firm matters less than the level of sophistication and professionalism you bring to the effort. In many cases, the key to building a bigger business and increasing profits lies with selling prospective clients on the virtues of dealing with your company and ultimately getting the contract signed. You've got to stand out from the crowd—and not just for low prices.

The contractor who is always the low bidder is in danger of bidding the company into bankruptcy. Lots of low-margin jobs don't often add up to high profits. You want to win potentially higher-profit jobs, at least some of the time, on perceived quality of work and the reliability of your organization.

Creating a marketing plan

Once you've determined your marketing budget (for contractors, generally one to five percent of working capital), you can formulate a marketing plan that includes creating and distributing flyers, brochures, newsletters, and press releases, and conducting in-person presentations. If you work in a small town, perhaps you can include some coverage in the local media in your mix. Most of your efforts, however, should fall into the category of direct mail and be aimed at two targets: old contacts and cold contacts.

Old is sometimes as good as gold

Most contractors have found that satisfied clients are the best source of future work, as well as referrals to new clients. Property owners, architects, and designers for whom you've performed work fit into this category. For each subcategory, you can prepare and distribute narrowly targeted marketing materials that remind old clients that you're still out there, offering the same excellent services, quality of workmanship, and, perhaps, some new services.

You might want to focus a special mailing to past clients for whom you've done just a small renovation. Reminding them of your continued availability, via postcard or occasional newsletter, might be all the impetus they need to call you back for another job, often without having to go through the bidding process. Using a desktop publishing program and templates, you can even turn out different versions of the same documents to suit particular segments of your audience, even using one-shot personalizations. Here is where you can pepper your mailings with added phrases like "as before" or "once again," to reflect that earlier contact and contract. If you've kept notes on possible client interests for future renovations when you were dealing with them, you can bring them up as possibilities for which it might now be time.

Keep the effort going; keep that mail flowing

Even when you have a backlog of work, you should continue to market your firm with up-to-date promotional material. Use a contact management program to maintain a database of leads. Enter everyone, and note which marketing salvos you sent to whom.

When your marketing efforts lead to an appointment with a prospective client, be a good listener. Find out what the client wants, the motivations for the project, the projected budget, and the hoped-for start and completion dates. Most folks, given the chance, will tell all and probably take positive note of your interest. Enter your notes on the meeting in your PIM or contact management program. Use the built-in calendar to program in reminders for follow-up calls and mailings. When you send the client a follow-up letter, include a fair share of the details from the initial meeting.

Use emotional appeal

Marketing experts agree that honing in on what a client wants is key. Add emotional appeal to the pitch. Appealing to those wants is important. In remodeling, clients will generally go for an upgrading element, something that makes your price reflect the added value. If you're selling not by price but by the perceived value of your company's services, concentrate on projecting the concept that your price includes products or services that the client specifically wants—or that will benefit the client in the short or long run. In this way, you can appeal to a client's emotions and make your price, even if it's higher than the competition's, seem like a bargain. Try to weave in such benefits as energy savings and the added comfort and enjoyment that an upgraded installation will afford. Overall, try to create positive differences between your firm and the competition.

Use your literature—brochures, cards, flyers—to assure potential clients that you'll provide careful, premium-quality workmanship, coordination, and installation. You want the recipients of your mailings to believe that your firm offers more value for the buck and that it's in their best interest to go with your company.

When you make an in-person sales call, bring along your own in-house-produced sales literature, customized to address particular client needs. A strong targeted presentation can help persuade a client that your price is worth every penny and help reap a signature onto the dotted line in the next follow-up communication—the contract.

Even if those receiving your marketing efforts aren't themselves in a position to consider more work, your mailings might increase business leads by way of word of mouth from personally disinterested but impressed readers.

Breaking new ground

To attract new clients, you can blanket particular neighborhoods with introductory information about your company by using names and addresses from CD-ROM phone directories that list either residential or business names. Even though you're getting massive numbers of listings (sometimes tens of millions), the prices of the programs are so low, compared to buying commercial mailing lists, that it's extremely cost effective to winnow out potential clients for targeted mailings by zip code, street, area code, or even by business type. Unlike renting a traditional mailing list, where you're generally expected or contracted to use the names one time only, you can use CD-ROM names as often as you like.

New contacts include architects, designers, developers, homeowners, and commercial real estate owners as yet unfamiliar with your company. To this audience, you want to convey straightforward information about the services your firm offers, making it clear that you know your business and do it well, on time and within budget. You can achieve this, at least in part, with press releases, brochures, or newsletters that show off your company's accomplishments. In introducing your company, you should also directly encourage prospective clients to consider your company when they think about soliciting bids for renovations or new construction.

Be consistent in your efforts. In a variation on an old advertising adage, "when times are good, it pays to market; when times are bad, you *have* to market." Just like a homeowner who can never have too many closets, if you want your company to grow, you can never have too much work. When times are really busy, there's always the opportunity to bid a little higher and make a little more.

Flexible formulations

One thing is clear about marketing: the way to go is open to interpretation. The path to success might be strewn with detours, so if one set of mailings doesn't increase the percentage of responses, try either another form of mailing or the same type to a different audience. Vary your approaches—what you send out and to whom— until you find the right blend that works best for you.

Desktop publishing

Moses didn't have to worry about visual appeal when he delivered the message from the mount; the text was enough. In these competitive times, however, professional-looking materials definitely confer a competitive edge for most contractors and remodelers.

The happy news, in these high-tech times, is that you don't have to hire professionals to create professional-looking documents. You can do it yourself on your desktop PC. Desktop publishing (DTP)—using a PC and special software to turn out great-looking promotional materials and other presentations—can help a contractor with limited resources and experience in publicity and marketing produce, in-house, good-looking documents of all kinds. Direct from your desk, you can create business cards, letters, brochures, flyers, and postcards.

Promotional pieces

One of the easiest ways to start a marketing campaign is with a word processing program and an inexpensive template program that automatically creates press releases and other promotional materials. All that's necessary for you to do is customize the particulars in the text.

The dedicated program Publicity Builder (Jian Tools for Sales, 800-346-5426) is designed to work within most popular word processing programs. It's a step-by-step, hands-on, guided approach to producing professional, attention-grabbing publicity releases.

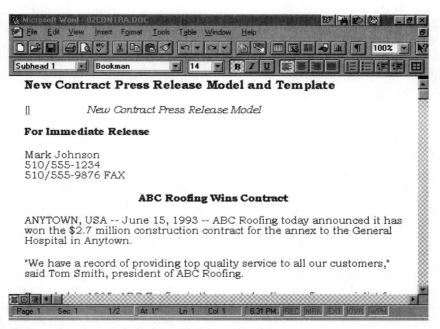

Press release template from Publicity Builder.

The software/book combination includes a more than 300-page manual and source book on proven publicity techniques, 17 press releases, and accompanying fill-in-the-blank templates, each customizable on screen to individual company needs. Once you've filled in the details, you can print on any paper that fit the template or on your company letterhead.

This program is particularly handy if your company is involved in the community, through sponsoring community service programs, local kids' sports leagues, or special holiday events, as the program includes several templates that focus on a company's participation in community events, sports leagues press releases, and various awards.

How to direct your efforts

By composing and printing with your computer, you save not only the expense of using professional designers, but also the time and effort of using an outside printer. In terms of quantity, you'll never be caught short or stuck with an oversupply. You control the print run either when you send the document to your laser or inkjet printer or when you make copies. Second printings can follow at any time.

You can also change the specifics of your message at a moment's notice, eliminating the possibility of having piles of out-of-date, paid-for, professionally printed materials. Instead, you always have personalized and up-to-date material on the spot.

For example, if you want to hand out flyers in the neighborhood in which you're doing a project, you can print up the appropriate number, customized with the location of your current project in that community. For your next job in a different neighborhood, just edit the details. You can even send out progress reports and invite neighbors or architects and designers in to see your work (client permitting).

If you're just thinking of donning a printer's cap now, you'll reap the benefits of the enormous surge in popularity of DTP programs among business users over the past few years. Prices have dropped greatly while the features in even low-end programs have risen dramatically. As high-end features winnow down to entry-level programs, it has become easier to create ever more complex designs with simpler-to-operate software.

There are several inexpensive entry-level programs with abundant features that offer excellent flexibility in page design, graphics import, and font (type) choices.

Four-step manipulation

Desktop publishing at any level involves manipulating four elements to turn out the finished product: layout and design of columns and pages on screen; text handling (essentially word processing functions that include writing and editing your message); graphics handling, including import capability; and printing (in black and white or color).

All DTP starts with the layout of the page. If you choose not to start with a preformatted template, you might want to use a pencil and paper to draw a thumbnail sketch of how you want your document to look. This includes deciding on such elements as number of columns per page (normally one, two, or three), whether the copy and graphics should be positioned symmetrically or asymmetrically, whether you want a formal or informal feel to the documents (depending on the message and the intended audience), and how much white space you want (clutter is never recommended; wide borders and ample spacing between lines generally makes for easier reading). Sketch an arrangement that—at both first and repeated glances—is pleasing to your eye. After all, your aim is to capture the audience's interest before they even start to read. In many instances, if you can't snag your reader's interest immediately, your message is as good as not sent. Once you've created a sketch of your layout, it's time to pull up your page layout program and find an arrangement that either matches your sketch or that you can customize to do so.

Alternately, many desktop publishing programs allow you to select a document type and then answer a series of questions to have the program automatically format and prepare a sample pamphlet, brochure, postcard, newsletter, or other document, properly laid out and ready for your text and graphics. When you've worked your way through the process, you have a formatted document ready for customizing with your company information.

Templates—which set up page layouts automatically—are another easy and fast way to get your feet wet in desktop publishing. Using a template, you can embark on any project using correct design principles (and often context-sensitive user assists) right from the start.

A template in desktop publishing programs is a ready-made page design. It contains all the design elements you need to create a particular kind of document. A letter template, for example, has the proper formatting for the heading, the salutation, and the closure, as well as the text frame and text styles, already set up. A newsletter template has a basic layout of columns and spacings, as well as font sizes for the headings, subheads, and body of the text. These elements are coordinated into style sheets that fit the broad spectrum of many different business applications.

Spreading the word through a newsletter

A newsletter is an excellent way of conveying the latest information on your company, either to clients or to an audience of readers themselves in the construction or architectural/design field. Use your own experiences in the business. Compose the text with the goal of presenting your firm as experts in the field. The newsletter can be as brief as a single-sheet self-mailer, or you can print on both sides and produce a two-page self-mailing trifold.

Traditional advice dictates that you "write about what you know." You can profile recent winning projects, possibly accompanied by before and after pictures (remember to get permission from the client), and talk about trends in kitchens, baths, lighting, windows, and other areas.

You might also incorporate news flashes about specials you're offering, tied to the upcoming season. For instance, consider running value-added packages for replacement windows and doors in a late summer or fall issue, where you upgrade the quality of the windows and doors or include a premium style for the same price, or for new decks (with a choice of woods) during a spring or summer issue.

You can also use your newsletter to let past and future clients know about new concepts you're offering, like CAD printouts for design-build services, or new materials, like new kinds of siding, a new line of shower towers that fit into corners, and other noteworthy developments like special discounts and extended credit.

Put together a glossary of common construction terms and definitions; explain the Americans with Disabilities Act (ADA) and other construction code updates, compliance with which could lead to a signed contract to perform the work; provide tips on selection, installation, and maintenance of certain types of products; and give experience-based, time-saving or safety tips.

Wherever you can, emphasize that you can do a better job for clients than competitors by saving them time or paying close attention to job details. Intersperse positive press about current projects, successful out-of-the-ordinary job case histories, and notable new contracts.

Straight facts presented with a little imagination will serve you well in any self-publishing venture. With the help of a computer, template software, and a printer, you too can be a bit of a modern-day Ben Franklin.

Feature-rich assurances

Many DTP programs come with various levels of spell checkers, grammar checkers, and a host of other features commonly found in word processing programs. You can either write your message right within the DTP program or import text written in your word processing program. (Though you can write text directly in desktop publishing programs, because they're graphically based, lengthy documents will probably take a lot longer to compose than they would using word processing software.) You can also add information from a spreadsheet or other type of program. In general, it's preferable to write a long document in a word processing program and then insert it into your DTP program. You can also insert symbols, pictures, and other graphics.

Unlike word processing programs, with desktop publishing programs your text or graphics go into a text or graphics box. The box, which you can resize on the page to suit, gives the form to the material. Text boxes from column to column or page to page are linked at your discretion. When text overflows the first box, it carries over into the next linked box. When you click on a box, highlighted handles appear on the box on the screen. By moving the handles, you can adjust the size on the page. Many of the programs include placement of borders, fancy first letters, text rotation, curved text, and other design attributes.

Once you're comfortable manipulating a program's design tools, including rulers, guides, objects, boundaries, and tool bars, you can deviate and create your own format to give your documents a bit of your own company's inimitable style. The fastest way to personalize or customize documents with flair is by inserting art.

Many DTP programs come with clip art you can set around text. If the included library doesn't offer enough choices, you can import electronic clip art from separately purchased software. You can also scan in your own art, use photos scanned into other programs on your computer, or use digital images taken with a digital camera. You might even want to use a flatbed or page scanner to import job photos (perhaps even with satisfied client testimonials as captions) into your presentation so you turn out "show and tells" that speak for themselves. Once you get into the swing of customizing mailings, the possibilities are almost limitless.

What's your type?

Most prepared templates use either Times Roman or Helvetica, which are basic types or fonts on every laser printer. Many programs also have numerous other typefaces available that vary in size, shape, and category (serif, with short line and curves that project from the ends of the letters; sans serif, without the finishing strokes; and script). Judiciously vary type styles to increase eye appeal and impact. Novices sometimes err, however, through overkill, using a confusing profusion of styles partly just because they're available. It's best to select a few clear-to-read styles and then vary them in size, for contrast and emphasis. Your goal is easy reading with maximum impact. The manuals that come with the programs usually reiterate standard rules and guidelines to supplant on-screen instructions so even beginners can put together a neat document.

Dress your press for success

It's important to establish a logo or slogan you want to see in print on all your printed materials. Keep your visual image consistent and coordinate the look of all your paper-based materials, from letterhead and business cards to promotional materials and business forms, with that logo. The logo should in some way reflect the construction business in general or the particular niche market in which you're involved.

Designing and printing a customized business card

Your business card is often the first image a potential client or business contact sees. It should be informative and eye-catching and include your name, address, phone number, fax number, certifications, association logos, and logo. Using a DTP template for cards would probably be the easiest way to get all that information arranged neatly. MyProfessional BusinessCards (MySoftware Company, 800-325-9095), for example, works with over 70 preprinted color business card stocks from several paper companies. Dozens of professionally designed layouts are available on screen or you can design your own from scratch. The package comes with a variety of more than 200 ready-to-print sample stock cards, in various designs, shades, and hues, any of which can be ordered in quantity. You can also use plain card stock, and request printing on the front only or on both sides of the cards. The package includes a logo library of 100 images for further personalizing.

Color improves impact

In small business communications of all sorts, standard-issue unadorned black and white doesn't cut it like it used to. Color is in. Color hitting the reader's eye increase the impact of and reaction to the document and improves the reader's memory of the contents. There are two ways to create colorful documents: by using color preprinted paper and a black-and-white laser or inkjet printer, or by using a color printer. With preprinted paper, a lot of the work is done for you by professional designers.

Preprinted papers and preformatted templates

With a black-and-white laser or inkjet printer, specialized desktop publishing preprinted color business and motivational/theme papers, readily available from numerous mail-order paper companies, and an inexpensive DTP program, you can produce a full array of colorful, impressive, professional-looking materials. You can look great on a low budget, giving the professional appearance, in print at least, of a flourishing enterprise while you convey your message.

Smart-looking papers

Styles for themed or strictly decorative papers run from conservative and sedate to upbeat and bold, with built-in pizzazz. Options also include a wide choice of paper frames (8.5-x-11-inch sheets with borders all around) suitable for creating smart-looking announcements, or unadorned granite, marbleized, or gradated shaded papers and a broad array of heavier-stock, decorative trifolds suitable for brochures. (Trifolds are 8.5-x-11-inch sheets prescored for folding into thirds to create six text-ready sides.)

Many of the layouts and styles are available with matching #10 size envelopes, postcards, labels, and business cards. Illustrated catalogs are available from mail-order houses like BeaverPrint (800-9-BEAVER); IDEA ART (800-433-2278), featuring 100 or 50 percent recycled papers; PaperDirect (800-A-PAPERS); NEBS (800-225-6380); QUEBLO (800-523-9080); and Image Street (800-IMAGE-ST).

Say it with headlines

Paper with snazzy to-the-point headlines like News, Attention, FYI, or Update (all from PaperDirect) can be used to pack a visual punch or act as lighthearted backdrops for one-shot communications or newsletters. Or perhaps office coordinates that add a sense of cohesiveness to your company identity by featuring a common background pattern and graphics but with a choice of headlines that announce such topics as Company News, Proposal, and Agenda (from Idea Art) might suit your needs. Queblo's contemporary, classic, rustic, or Victorian newsletter designs are printed on both sides with designated areas for newsletter name on the front and one, two, or three columns of text on each side.

If you want to imply savings in your mailings, you can use selections that make either subtle or not so subtle graphical references to watching your money, such as letterhead featuring reproduced photos of a $5 bill squeezed in a vise (from BeaverPrint) or a light bulb burning brightly against a black background, with the green lit filament doubling as a $ sign (from Idea Art). Preprinted photo brochure possibilities from BeaverPrint include a trifold with a $100 bill frozen inside a rectangular block of ice, or a fistful of dollars.

Say it with seasoning

There are also numerous seasonal choices, showing summer scenes or scenery, perhaps, or wintry landscapes. Such weather-related options might be good for sending out flyers or reminders that now is the time to think about decks, sunrooms, patios, thermal windows, skylights, or other types of renovations tied to changing seasons.

Say it with levity

You can also inform with humor. Try sending out a missive on motivational theme sheets of white laser paper headed with eye-catching graphics and clever tag lines such "a whale of an opportunity," "plan ahead," "on target," "look no further," and "win/win," all from Idea Art.

Before you don your metaphorical printer's cap, peruse all the paper catalogs. There's such a variety among the companies that you owe it to yourself to window shop a bit before you pick paper on which to promote your company image.

If you can't decide on which patterns will work best, each of the companies offers reasonably priced sample packs of their diverse offerings. Generally, companies will ship orders for as few as a hundred of a selection, so in any case you won't be locked into a major commitment to any one style.

Stand-alone Windows desktop publishing programs feature dozens of templates that work in concert with several hundred paper backgrounds for trifolds, four-folds, bifolds, business cards, mailing labels and envelopes, and other options, up through legal size paper. You can change the background on screen at the touch of a key, even after you've placed text and graphics. With just a few minor adjustments for each background, you can try on different looks for your project.

Some of the packages come with a library of clip art images and an easy-to-maneuver drawing palette with tools that let you create and edit simple graphics of your own devising. They might also include automatic mail merge so you can import names and addresses from other application programs to print envelopes. In many cases, the mail merge capability will print directly on self-mailing brochures, cards, or flyers.

Occasionally, stand-alone template programs come with a variety of on-screen sample papers from one or more direct mail paper companies already in the database, as well as with several hardcopy sample sheets packed right in the box with the program.

MyAdvancedBrochures, Mailers, & More

For those contractors who want a really quick and easy solution without getting involved in all the bells and whistles of desktop publishing, MyAdvancedBrochures, Mailers & More (MySoftware Company, 800-325-9095) is a dedicated CD-ROM program that provides on-screen templates in more than 20 paper formats (trifolds, business cards, flyers, postcards, letterhead) for over 600 preprinted paper designs from many of the popular direct mail paper companies. The margins of the individual templates are preset to each paper design. All you have to do is type in the text. You won't have any formatting worries.

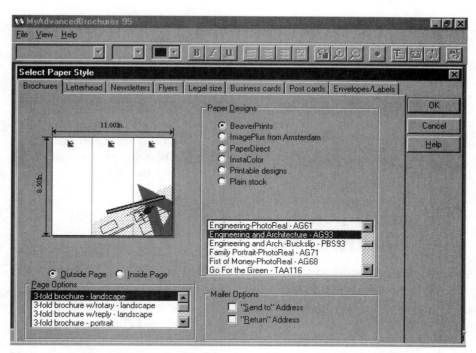

You can preview paper samples from several companies easily in MyAdvancedBrochures, Mailers & More.

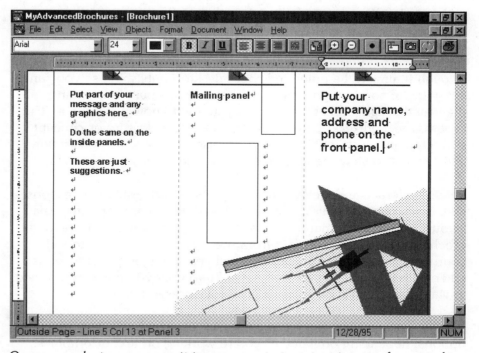

Once you select your paper, it is very easy to type text into preformatted text frames in MyAdvancedBrochures, Mailers & More.

User-friendly desktop publishing program possibilities

Fast to master, programs like Microsoft Publisher CD Deluxe for Windows 95, NEBS' Page Magic Gold Edition, and Serif PagePlus Home Office have a lot of tricks of the trade loaded in. If you don't muck around too much with changes in style and format, you're practically assured use of correct design principles in turning out a single- or multiple-page promotion or other document.

Microsoft Publisher CD Deluxe for Windows 95

Microsoft Publisher CD Deluxe for Windows 95 (Microsoft, 800-563-9048) packs a lot of professionalism into its easy-to-use package. Optimized to run under Windows 95, not only can you use long filenames, but you can also drag and drop text and charts from other applications and exchange information quickly with Microsoft Office applications.

You get over 100 publication styles, more than 150 all-purpose and theme borders for spicing up your documents, 60 TrueType fonts, and over 1,000 choices of clip art, including 25 different buildings, and several choices within the business and household categories that lend themselves to contractors' intents.

Though it aims to be point-and-shoot desktop publishing so you can get going almost straight out of the box, there's built-in assistance all the way through, sometimes even if you don't know you need it. The program recognizes if you're new to a particular feature or concept and offers you instructions. There are also 15 online demonstrations you can opt to view the first time you try the features covered.

Twenty interactive PageWizards (design assistants) ask you questions, take assessment of your answers, and lead you to appropriate basic layouts for common marketing materials like newsletters, flyers, and brochures. It's easy to deviate from the layout or embellish to suit your needs and taste. You can also add your own job pictures, either taken with a digital camera and loaded into your computer or scanned in via a flatbed or page scanner, into your presentation.

The context-sensitive toolbar changes the selectable choices of options, depending on whether you're working on text or graphics. Everything is lined up, formatted, and screen-ready for your custom text and graphics, or even for precise positioning of text and picture elements for numerous choices of preprinted paper. You can even scroll through the choices for previews.

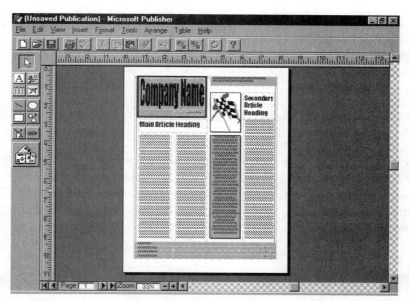

Text- and graphic-ready newsletter layout, created with wizards in Microsoft Publisher.

There are a lot of text-handling options that make experimenting fun. Special design effects include predesigned Fancy First Letters and WordArt, which offers dozens of ways to create singular effects for headlines by stretching, slanting, rotating, shadowing, or curving text. There are more than 100 plain and fancy border designs: starbursts, arrows, 3-D boxes, and other shapes that can be rotated up to 90 degrees. You also get automatic bulleting and numbering for lists, right from the toolbar. This is a real assist when you have to insert entries within existing listings.

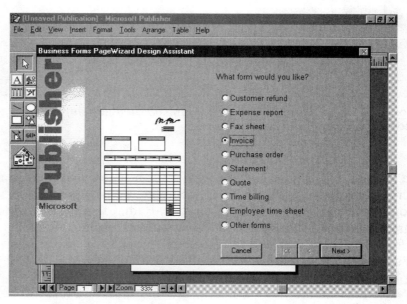

It is a quick process to produce any of several forms templated in Microsoft Publisher.

Special graphics and design features include a logo creator to help you design an identifying emblem for your letter and forms, and banner and poster printing, either of which might be handy for placement at a job site to increase name visibility.

Page Magic Gold Edition CD-ROM

Page Magic Gold Edition CD-ROM (NEBS, 800-882-5254) is a Windows desktop marketing software suite for small businesses. The package combines Page Magic, which is the desktop publishing component of the suite, Design Magic, a drawing and illustration program, and NEBS Business Image Collection, a selection of small business clip art, photo images, and business logos.

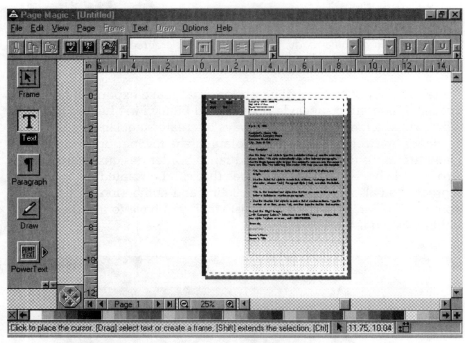

You can use NEBS designer stationery with coordinated templates in Page Magic Gold Edition CD-ROM.

Page Magic's 170 predesigned templates for business and marketing materials coordinate with the NEBS Company Colors preprinted stationery line, as well as with plain paper. Rather than wizards, the program has PagePilots, which lead you step by step through the design process. The forms include boilerplate text so you can see precisely how a document will look when written. Just replace the sample text with your own. Alternately, you can start with bare templates that feature just a frame, preset margins, and text format. You type in what you want to say in the allotted spaces. The program supports OLE 2 (object linking and embedding) support, so it's easy to integrate data from other applications into desktop publishing material.

A clip-art browser features over 200 exclusive business logos, including 20 for the contractor. You can also import your own clip art and scan images into any document you create. An 80,000-word spell checker eliminates typos and misspellings, while a built-in thesaurus offers word choices to enliven your text. You can also automatically fit text around a graphic image and stamp an element, such as Confidential or another blurb, on top of the page.

Serif PagePlus for Home Office

Serif PagePlus for Home Office (Serif, Inc., 800-697-3743) is a 32-bit Windows 95 program. The program offers three levels of operation, from an introductory level that features maximum on-screen help to a professional level for experienced users who want the flexibility of powerful features without much help.

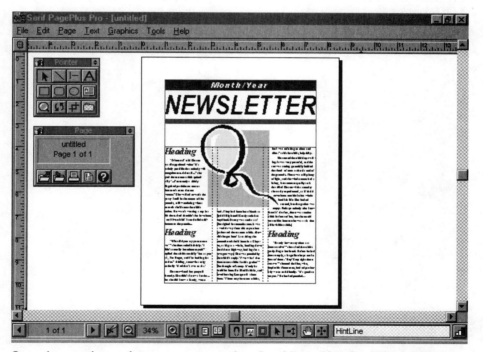

Sample newsletter front page created in Serif PagePlus for Home Office.

You can either write your documents in the built-in word processor, complete with multilingual thesaurus, spelling checker, keyboarding cursor controls, and find/replace, or you can import fully formatted text files complete with styles from just about any free-standing word processing program. The files will flow automatically into your layout.

The software also comes with a variety of clip-art images, a wide choice of fonts, OLE 2 support, and a nifty screen capture utility, enabling you to take a picture of any on-screen image and paste it into a document. If you already have a color inkjet printer, you can include color job photos and catalog cuts in any of your marketing documents, adding even more impact.

For overall speediest delivery of your marketing missives, be sure to barcode all mailings with a nine-digit zip code. The first five digits signify the delivery office. The first two of the last four digits of the expanded code stand for a particular geographic position, a precise section of a rural route, a box section in a post office, or an official designation. The two final digits indicate a particular office building or apartment building, or even the floor of a building, a row of P.O. boxes, or other exact site.

If you mail in any sort of large numbers, try to implement a software solution. Windows 95 has built-in mail merging capabilities, as do many DTP programs. Alternately, you could use a free-standing package, like MyProfessional MailManager or MyAdvancedMailList (MySoftware 415-473-3642), both of which are Windows programs dedicated to maintaining customer and mailing lists and streamlining mail merge procedures.

Digital imaging for
business on the go

SEVERAL innovations in the hardware arena and software to help the hardware do the job have made it possible for contractors to manage more and more business while a key player is out of the office.

A digital-imaging solution for problems in the field

The scenario is all too familiar; your crew has been on the job since 8:00 A.M., but the foreman has just phoned you to tell you about a major snag that's holding up the work. Without seeing the job condition first-hand, it's too risky to agree on a resolution that will satisfy all interested parties, so you or someone in your office has to cut short a previously scheduled meeting, alter other plans, and hurry down to the job for a personal inspection. The clock ticks, and (down) time is, no question about it, money.

On all kinds of construction projects, this type of scene repeats itself in various permutations. Something has gone wrong and someone in authority has to take a look.

Even with all of today's cutting-edge technology, you can't be in two places at once—at least not yet. But by implementing compact point-and-shoot digital cameras and digital imaging on your computer, along with electronic transmission of instant digital photos to and from on-site and other remote locations, you can run your business almost as if you are.

Stand-alone and direct-connection digital cameras offer immediate information through photographic quality electronic visual communication. The photos are instant in the truest sense because they require no film and no developing.

As software developers understand that business users might not have a high understanding of photography, cameras are typically designed to be intuitive and therefore easy to use, while producing high-resolution images for small-size reproduction. Though grayscale (black and white) digital cameras preceded color models onto the market, the color cameras are fast becoming the norm for the entry-level, stand-alone digital cameras that contractors are likely to buy.

This new type of eminently portable tool, potentially affording owners more than a thousand words worth of value for each photo, has great applicability for contractors and remodelers. It's one of those easily operated products that can yield wide-reaching advantages, both in terms of your bottom line and your crew's productivity, and could become a valuable staple in an arsenal of high-tech peripheral tools of the trade.

The potential applications and implications of digital imaging for the construction business are tremendous, particularly in such areas as implementing change orders, resolving on-site crises, verifying conditions, settling disputes (with indisputable documentation), and justifying billing.

By using a digital camera to take photos and software that allows you to download the images to your computer for later manipulation and electronic transfer, you gain several immediate benefits. First, the person who needs to assess the situation doesn't have to make the trip in order to get a clear picture of the problem. The camera, in someone else's hands, does the job. Second, you save the time and money it would take to capture the same images on conventional film, have the film developed, and deliver the pictures to whoever needs to see them.

Documenting design problems

If, for instance, design problems on the job are passed on immediately to the architect or designer, you'll likely get speedier clarification of the resolution or faster implementation of field changes. (And you've shifted the weight of responsibility for decisions to the proper people.)

You use a digital camera in conjunction with either a job site computer, a portable notebook, or a computer back in the office. The digital cameras—typically weighing between 10 and 20 ounces and looking like flattened 35-mm cameras—are easy to use. They can be held in one hand and feature one-button operation. The cameras come with serial cables and software packages that make it easy to transfer and download the images.

With a job site computer equipped with a fax-modem board, you can instantly transfer images to the home office or to any other computer or fax machine for immediate evaluation or for incorporation into relevant documentation. Alternately, field workers can return the small camera to the office so whoever is responsible for the project or top management can evaluate the pictures.

The cameras can hold several dozen pictures before requiring downloading. This allows the on-site photographer to shoot photos from every angle. Management, clients, and others involved will be able to see the subject of discussion almost as if they were at the site themselves.

The software transfers small previews of the photographs to the screen. You then select those you want to view in an enlarged form. You can delete photos you don't want and save the others.

Historical documentation

Beyond immediate viewing, the saved images can be used repeatedly in many types of applications. Contractors can take photos for numerous reasons, including site pictures, project documentation, blueprint change documentation, inspection reports, damage reports, equipment inventory, property ID, and even personnel photo IDs. You can also use the camera to provide verifying photos to help evaluate and handle safety considerations if a job site has any hazardous conditions.

Furthermore, on-site photographers who are present when material is delivered can take photos of defective material or equipment if it arrives on the job that way, and send a vendor a visual representation of the defect. In essence, by using a digital camera you're getting a direct form of visual note-taking.

Image-editing software makes a core variety of instant dark-room adjustments available. You can zoom in and out, crop the background, adjust size, and modify the contrast, all without losing any image quality.

Keeping digital photo records of delays caused by other trades or by subcontractors adds to your protection and gives you an easy, valid way to show where and how they are impeding your work.

You can even use the camera before the job starts, when you're still in the estimating phase. Images taken on a walk-through can be loaded into your computer and pulled up or printed out to refresh the estimator's memory or to check the actual conditions against those shown on the plans. You might also want to incorporate the photos in your bidding documents to clarify your bid.

Manufacturers of affordable digital stand-alone cameras include Logitech (a leading supplier of small computer peripherals such as mice and scanners), Kodak, Dycam (the company that introduced the first mass-produced digital camera back in 1990), Canon, and Casio.

Programs
FotoMan Pixtura and Kodak's Digital Camera 40

Logitech's FotoMan Pixtura (Logitech, 800-231-7717 outside California, 800-552-8885 in California) is typical of the lightweight models that are designed for easy one-hand operation. The sturdy little camera has an automatic flash, a self-timer, and a hand-strap for support or carrying. There's also a liquid crystal panel display next to the viewfinder that shows the picture number, exposure, and level of battery charger, among other data.

You can easily adjust the F stops up or down by half stops up to a full stop. If you want, you can delete either the last picture taken or all photos without having to connect to the computer.

FotoMan Pixtura. Logitech

The camera works on four AA lithium batteries and can take more than 800 pictures on one set. Even if the batteries are completely discharged or removed, the pictures remain intact in the camera for up to a year. It stores up to 150 pictures without downloading in standard resolution, but only 48 in high resolution. You can snap a shot as frequently as every five seconds without a flash.

The similar sized and shaped Kodak Digital Camera 40 (Kodak, 800-235-6325) operates in basically the same way, saving up to 99 pictures without downloading in standard resolution, and 48 in high resolution. Both cameras accept a variety of lenses for close-up, wide-angle, and telephoto shots.

While manufacturers don't foresee immediate displacement of conventional camera and film for the home and personal market, the opportunities for business applications—integrating images into instant business communications and into desktop published documents—is quite an enticement for software developers. Contractors are among the earliest beneficiaries.

QuickCam for Windows

QuickCam for Windows and Windows 95 (Connectix, 800-950-5880) is a plug-and-play, black-and-white digital camera that connects directly to your computer. Selling for less than $100 with accompanying disk driver, this product represents another, less expensive approach to digital imaging. Smaller and lighter than a baseball, the innovative eyeball-shaped camera plugs into a standard parallel port. The wire acts like the optic nerve of the eye and carries the signal from the external device to the computer.

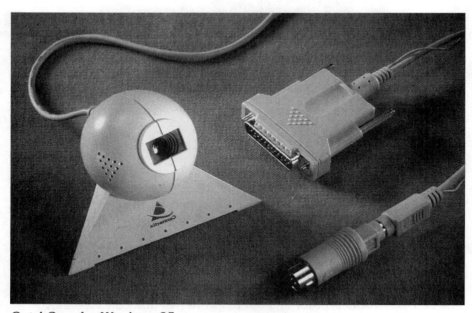

QuickCam for Windows 95. Connectix

Contractors can use the camera to take full 64-shade grayscale images of objects, places, or people in the vicinity of the computer. The images will appear on your computer screen instantly. You can also use the device to digitize photos you already have on hand. The camera takes pictures in bitmap or TIFF forms for use with just about any word processing, desktop publishing, presentation, or graphics program. This means you can easily and inexpensively add product photos to any estimate, proposal, or contract or take a photo on site if the camera is attached to a laptop computer.

Unlike stand-alone digital cameras, which have all the electronic mechanisms self-contained and download after the photos are all taken, QuickCam transfers the photos one at a time as they're taken.

You can also make video clips with sound if a microphone is added to the mix. If you carry a laptop to job sites on a regular basis, you can even document progress of any project from kitchen renovation to an entire house construction, from ground breaking on up. By compiling the photos in a file as you take them, by the end of the project the time-lapse video clip is just about complete. The camera works along the lines of a conventional video camera. You don't need a supplementary flash, as the camera adjusts automatically to differing lighting conditions.

When you plug the camera in and turn it to snapshot, you'll see on screen whatever the camera is pointing toward. Turn the "eye" and you'll get a different view. Clicking the on-screen shutter button saves the picture to the Window clipboard for pasting into any application. The resolution of the pictures isn't as fine as that produced by palm-sized color digital cameras.

The Lynx Digital Photo Management System

An innovative company, TRF Systems, Inc., developers of estimating and accounting software, have linked several cutting-edge computer technologies, including the digital camera, and their own applicable software into a potent package made specifically for field personnel to assist management in making quick, informed decisions.

The Lynx Digital Photo Management System (TRF Systems Inc., 800-TRF-0700) is designed to allow field personnel to take, annotate, and transfer job site color photos electronically. It offers excellent capabilities for tracking and documenting job site conditions, and passing along that visual and graphic information to all interested parties almost instantly, as well as amassing day-to-day documentation for an archival image database. It's the kind of innovation that can change the overall look and expectation of job documentation and becoming a veritable staple in any complement of electronic tools.

Field personnel equipped with the camera and a job site computer loaded with Lynx software can snap photos of any part of a project, indoors or out, and immediately transfer those photos, along with keyboarded or hand-written annotations (via Microsoft Pen Extensions for Windows, discussed later in this chapter), to any other computer furnished with a modem and the Lynx software.

From camera to computer to recipient

If the intended recipients—subcontractors, architects, designers, clients, loan officers at banks, or anyone for whom a picture might be worth 1,000 words—don't have the Lynx software, you can transfer pictures via fax or diskette. You can also transfer them to another location over the Internet. In addition, you can insert any of the color photos into documents in other programs for printing or presentations.

When you're ready to transmit the pictures, just connect the camera to the serial port of your computer. Cables are included with the package. The accompanying software makes it very easy to transfer the photos. Three clicks and the full complement is downloaded.

Tuesday, December 20, 1994 9:55 AM   Building E - Pouring 3rd Floor Slab

Digital photo taken on a job site displayed through the LYNX Digital Photo Management System. TRF Systems Inc.

Alternatively, when a camera is kept at a remote field location furnished with a computer and modem, every night when the camera is connected to the computer and modem before field personnel leaves the job, the home office can automatically retrieve the pictures without any further involvement of field staff. You can, therefore, take advantage of lower telephone rates by bringing the pictures in at night.

Inexpensive storage

The Lynx software is capable of a very high compression ratio, storing 35 to 38 pictures in one megabyte of hard disk space. That comes to a couple of pennies or less a picture at current street prices for a hard disk. As disputes over building or renovation projects almost invariably arise, it's very important to document jobs, with photos and notes, as they progress.

There are two ways to annotate photos directly. In the primary mode, initial notes, including who took the snapshot, the date taken, and a short description, are unalterable. The program developers specifically wrote the software with that capability so the notes could hold up legally in court if there were litigation regarding the project. (What better litigation-avoidance tool than indisputable photos!) Secondary notes linked to the photos can be added later. Users can add or modify the secondary notes, including key words for later look-up.

Interconnected modules

The software operates as a series of several interconnected modules. They include Job Manager, a primary contact management program that allows filing and retrieval of contract-related information and job

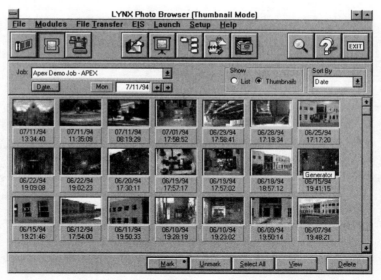

Lynx Browser showing thumbnail views. TRF Systems Inc.

photos by project; Daily Job Log, for detailing job delays, inspections, number of workers on the job, weather conditions, visitors, etc.; and Executive Information System, for using the transmitted information, whether filed under photos, daily diary, or notes, once it gets to the home office. There's also a Rolodex for storing names and addresses of daily or occasional contacts.

You can create dual historical documentation for every job by either electronically attaching specific pictures to particular job notes or to a specific issue setup for a designated purpose, or saving all photos in historical files for later call-up.

Lynx-generated documentation offers a significant advance over using traditional instant or conventional photos. Photos from instant cameras are expensive and take considerable time and effort to reproduce beyond a photocopy. Regular photos take several hours or even days to process the first time and then even more time if you want to make duplicates. Hardcopy photos have only a limited amount of room on the back for notes, which isn't even accessible if the picture is affixed to a document.

Generally, construction personnel working on a job site aren't trained to maintain a historical log on a daily basis of all facets of a job. Even if copious hand-written notes were taken, they might not cover an item or field condition that might become contentious down the road.

If a picture is worth a thousand words, in one load of a camera field personnel could potentially have enough data to fill a small book. When taking snapshots of a job, you take all views of site conditions so whatever might crop up later as a problem or delay is likely covered.

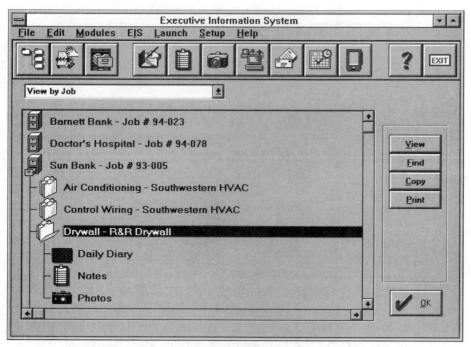

You can store job photos in folders maintained for several companies connected to the job. TRF Systems Inc.

The Microsoft Pen Extensions for Windows

To further ensure ease of use in the field, TRF has tied in Microsoft pen-based computing technology, which allow you to use a digitizing tablet and electronic pen to input hand-printed data. Personnel working or visiting on site can use a small digitizing tablet and a cordless pressure-sensitive electronic pen to literally jot down job notes either related to the pictures or to put into the notes database created for the job. The pen technology, Microsoft Pen Extensions for Windows (Microsoft, 800-563-9048), includes handwriting recognition software (really printing) that converts the message into typed text in a word processing program.

The character recognition software works by comparing letters and shapes on the digitized surface with characters and symbols in the database. The software recognizer will also accept examples of users' letter shapes and can hold the character style of several different inputs. Thus the program can learn individual printing styles, minimizing transcription errors. While it's no substitute for a keyboard for extensive typing, it's great for notes on the fly.

Also, by using an electronic notepad, anyone can draw a field sketch with handwritten notes and send it as a graphic. This is handy, as well, for recording instant authorization to proceed with a field change order, on the spot, because you can get a transmittable sign-off signature by the authorizing party. The note and any accompanying drawing becomes part of the change order.

Field photos and annotations for periodic progress reports

Contractors can use the camera and software capabilities as a selling tool in presentations to prospective clients, explaining all the information, i.e., documentation, the system can generate. Management personnel who use Lynx can send daily updates and job photos along to any owner who has a computer and modem, thereby keeping the owner totally appraised of progress, problems, and field conditions throughout the life of the job. This type of arrangement works nicely for both sides by taking care of progress payments, change orders, and disputes.

Operating from a similar premise, the system can also help you control uncooperative or sloppy general contractors, subcontractors, or suppliers, shifting the burden for delay claims onto them.

Built-in reporting capabilities

To help access job-related problems, Lynx provides a feature-rich Executive Information System that facilitates optimum use of all the inputted information back in the home office. It starts off with one "file cabinet" for each job. The software takes full advantage of the Windows metaphor; you click on an icon of a file cabinet to open it. Files, in categories, then drop down. Select one and it opens to offer choices, such as a daily diary, notes, and photos. You can have separate notepads for different people on the same job.

When you pull up the photos for a particular project or date, you initially get 12 pictures at a time on screen. Position the cursor over a picture and the short descriptive title you originally gave the picture appears on screen adjacent to the picture. That's a nice memory-jogging aid. Alternatively, you can pull up a list of photos by filename or locate photos by key words put in notes at an earlier time.

You can either electronically attach specific pictures to particular job notes or to a specific issue set up for a designated purpose, and you can save all photos in historical files, as on-call paper-free historical documentation.

Noncrisis applications

Contractors using Lynx can periodically send job photos and updates to clients who have a modem or a fax, thereby supplying graphical progress reports on a regular basis, justifying those all-important progress payments, or to subcontractors, justifying delay claims. They can also use photos to document blueprint changes, for inspection reports, for equipment inventory, for safety considerations and conformity to OSHA requirements and for creating personnel photo IDs.

You can also send a photo via modem as a JPEG file to anyone who has a graphics program that can capture and open that file. But then you can't annotate the photos or receive any annotations. Thus the system can reach out to subcontractors, architects, designers, engineers, owners, and others as long as they have a computer with either a modem or a fax.

Lynx also allows you to draw field sketches and affix handwritten notes via an optional digitizing tablet and electronic pen, and send them on as graphics. This capability is terrific for transmitting instant authorization to proceed with a field change order.

Offering even more interactivity, the Lynx Connection allows you to sit on the Primavera P3 scheduling program of Primavera's SureTrak scheduling screen, click on an activity, and instantly view all photos pertaining to that activity. If you want, you can limit the photos to a specified date range within the activity.

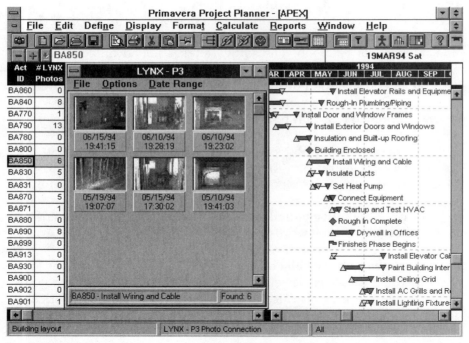

The Lynx photos can be annotated into Primavera SureTrak Project Manager. TRF Systems Inc.

There's also a tie-in feature that allows you to import images from faxes, scanners, and video capture boards into Lynx and store them for instant availability. This means you don't lose the utility of your old job photos; just scan them in. (They won't have the same authoritative impact because they weren't date-stamped at the time they were taken, but they're better off in Lynx than in your filing cabinet.)

Two portable computers for strategic assets on the go

Disseminating information and being able to quickly access data from numerous sources is important to all contractors some of the time and some contractors all of the time. Any computer solution that dramatically improves information processing and communications should be considered a strategic asset that can reduce costs, increase revenues, improve productivity, and heighten customer satisfaction.

Two new computer hardware products, the X-C 6000 Cross Country ruggedized notebook computer and the really lightweight Pentax PocketJet printer, fit very nicely indeed into the increasingly potent concept of a contractor's portable electronic toolbox.

Notebook computer for a hard-knock life

The X-C 6000 Cross Country (Itronix Corporation, 800-555-4104), made by long-time developers and manufacturers of vertical market ruggedized computers for mobile use, is specially designed to meet the needs of the mobile workforce who use notebooks in the field. It was engineered specifically to withstand street life and a daily share of hard knocks. (On some types of jobs, an off-the-shelf notebook or laptop computer might be considered frequently endangered, like a working lightbulb mounted without a shade.)

The weather-sealed Itronix notebook with heavy-duty, built-in protection to the hard drive, display panel, and other components, provides environment-immune access to client/server applications and can survive all types of bumps, vibrations, and tumbles. On a construction site, this is a real advantage. Product specifications require that the units survive intact 42 falls (at 42 different angles) onto a concrete surface from over three feet.

An innovative adaptation of a great product for contractors to begin with (a notebook computer), it's the first fully integrated ruggedized notebook with both wide area wireless communications and data applications capabilities.

The 6.5-pound, 486, full-function notebook features a black-and-white backlit monitor with 64 gray tones and has both a full Windows interface and support for (network) communications over ARDIS, RAM, and switched circuit cellular (voice and data) CDPD.

Contractors or foremen in the field could use the units in numerous daily applications, including call dispatching, material ordering, billing,

249

The X-C Cross Country ruggedized notebook computer. Itronix Corporation

and even change order and contract writing. Field personnel would also be able to pull up customer records, service histories, and other data from the home office in real time.

The overall design of the X-C 6000 is streamlined for efficiency on the go. A built-in RJ-11 jack provides on-site connection to telephone lines for internal fax modem. The microphone is built into the keyboard and the speaker is integrated into the underside of the unit, so it's a hands-off process to use the phone. (For an additional cost, you can purchase a wireless adapter that gives the computer the functionality of a wireless phone.) The easily accessible parallel port connects to external floppy and CD-ROM drives, printers, and other peripherals.

The computer case is constructed from lightweight magnesium that eliminates radio frequency interference, and is covered with thick Santoprene elastomer bumpers. The tight design of the computer and its fully-sealed keyboard protects the components from humidity, dust, dirt, grime, water, beverage spills, and other elements. A sturdy shoulder strap, durable handle, and textured handling points provide a variety of carrying options, even when the unit is wet. The wireless phone configuration is an optional add-on.

Ultralight portable printer

The Ultralight Pentax PocketJet printer (Pentax Technologies, 800-543-6144) is the quintessence of portability and turns out very nice photos and text documents at 300 × 300 dpi on single sheets of special thermal paper. At just 1.1 pounds with the battery, and 1.98 pounds with the ac adapter, it's so light it can easily be transported with a portable computer to most any job site. Though it feeds one sheet of thermal paper at a time and doesn't do envelopes, for low-volume printing as you go (printing out a job condition photo to pass around or for a change order, proposal, or even a short contract form) it's great for no-delay printing. The old saying "a bird in the hand is worth two in the bush" translates—for contractors—into, with respect to getting a client's signature on the dotted line, "the sooner the better."

Made of 20-pound cut sheet stock specially formulated to work with the printer, the thermal paper is much less shiny or slick than old-style thermal fax paper. You can even write directly on it. Judging from the sample printouts we've held in our hands, the printing quality and the feel and look of the thermal paper are all excellent. One drawback: the paper has a minimum life expectancy of five years, so you might want to photocopy or scan into your computer any documents you foresee keeping for more than a few years.

Pentax PocketJet printer. Pentax Technologies

Powered by a rechargeable nickel cadmium battery, the PocketJet can produce three letter- or legal-size pages per minute and a total of up to 35 pages per charge. (It takes about 70 minutes to recharge the battery.) There's also an ac adapter included, which in effect grants you limitless printing. Based on current paper prices, printing costs about 8 cents a page, about one third of the average of the heavier-weight inkjet portable printers.

The package comes complete with battery, adapter/recharger, power cord, a parallel interface cable, carrying case, and a 100-sheet box of paper, so you're ready to go right out of the box.

Index